Co

CONTRIBUTORS

Editor
Kate Sleight

Consultant
Una McGovern

Contributors
Lorna Gilmour
David Hambling
Simon Hill
Una McGovern
Steve Moore
Michael Munro
Alan Murdie
Jenny Randles
Bob Rickard
Gordon Rutter
Dr Karl P N Shuker

Editorial Assistance
Katie Brooks
Stuart Fortey

Picture Research
Kate Sleight

Prepress
Becky Pickard

Publishing Manager
Hazel Norris

INTRODUCTION

Throughout the ages people have attempted to make sense of the mysterious and the unknown, finding rational explanations for inexplicable occurrences as well as extraordinary meanings behind seemingly ordinary events. From the Bermuda Triangle to eclipses and earthquakes, *Myths and Mysteries* examines the superstitions, bizarre stories and intriguing legends that have sprung up as a result.

The book covers a broad range of topics. These include superstitions associated with naturally-occurring phenomena, long-forgotten beliefs behind the building of ancient monuments such as the Easter Island statues, and legendary characters from Robin Hood to King Arthur. Also featured are mythical creatures, traditional and modern folklore from Herne the Hunter to Elvis Presley, secret societies, unexplained disappearances, lost cities and the classic tales of the Holy Grail and the Knights Templar.

Cross-references to other relevant entries in the book are signified in the text by the use of small capitals. A glossary is provided to supply further explanation of some of the terms used, while a thematic index enables particular areas of interest to be found quickly and easily.

It is impossible to be comprehensive when investigating such a vast subject, but we hope we have provided an informative and unbiased guide. And, as well as proving an entertaining and absorbing read, the book will hopefully whet readers' appetites to find out more.

A

ABCs *see* ALIEN BIG CATS

Aberfan premonitions

Various claims exist that the Aberfan tragedy, when coal waste engulfed the school in the Welsh village of Aberfan, had been foretold in premonitions.

On 21 October 1966, 144 people, including 116 children, were killed when coal waste slid down the mountain above the village of Aberfan, engulfing the Pantglas Junior School, a farm and several houses. Abnormally heavy rain had made the slag heap unstable, resulting in the tragedy. Soon after the terrible event, a number of people made claims that the tragedy had been foretold in premonitions. Most famously, Eryl Mai Jones, a nine-year-old schoolgirl killed in the incident, is said to have had a strange dream, which she told her mother about on the day before the accident. Eryl is said to have told her mother that in the dream 'I went to school and there was no school there. Something black had come down all over it'.

In the weeks following the disaster numerous people claimed that they had had premonitions about it. Many of these had come in the form of dreams – one woman reported that she had had a nightmare in which she saw a child and a black billowing mass. Other premonitions took the form of visions; for example, shortly before the events occurred one woman claimed that she had had a vision of a moving black mountain burying children. The London psychiatrist Dr J C Barker made an appeal for premonitions relating to Aberfan, and collected and studied those that were reported. He discarded those he felt were not genuine, but became convinced that a number of them were – he took note, for example, as to whether the premonition had been reported to at least one other person prior to the tragedy. Barker was so convinced that premonitions might be of use in preventing future disasters that he helped set up the British Premonitions Bureau, to collect and monitor premonitions, in the following year.

Sceptics point out that the majority of premonitions are only revealed after the event they relate to has occurred, and as such their veracity should be doubted. Also, many premonitions are made about events that never come to pass. Others are convinced that some premonitions are genuine. See also CINCINNATI PREMONITION.

abominable snowman *see* YETI

acoustic archaeology *see* ARCHAEOACOUSTICS

alien big cats

Mysterious feline cryptids, variously likened to black panthers, pumas, lynxes and other large non-native cats. Sightings of alien big cats are reported regularly from the UK and elsewhere.

There were spasmodic reports of alien big cats, or ABCs for short, in the UK long before the 1960s, but this was the decade when they first attracted headline media coverage, courtesy of the Surrey Puma. That was the name given in newspaper stories to a very large tawny feline cryptid, most often likened to a puma, that was frequently observed in several regions in and around Surrey but never caught. A photo alleged to be of this creature was taken at Worplesdon in August 1966, but the felid depicted looked more like a large domestic cat than a puma. By the 1970s, however, puma sightings were being claimed throughout the UK, with numbers having risen dramatically by the late 1970s. There

were also reports of powerful, ebony-furred, pantheresque ABCs.

It has been noted that in 1976 the Dangerous Wild Animals Act came into being, which required anyone keeping a big cat in captivity to purchase a licence and provide suitable caging facilities. This not inconsiderable added expense is nowadays thought by many cryptozoologists to have led private owners of such animals to deliberately release their exotic pets into the wild, and this perhaps explains why sightings of sizeable feline creatures escalated in the following years.

The next major ABC case in Britain began in April 1983 on Exmoor, in south-west England. Several sheep were found killed at Drewstone Farm, and numerous people reported seeing a large, all-black, panther-like creature in the area. The animal soon became known as the Beast of Exmoor. In addition, there were reports of a brown puma-like beast in the area, and some people claimed to have seen a lynx-like cat with tufted ears and a short tail – leading investigators to consider the prospect that more than one species of big non-native cat was stalking the moorlands, and not only on Exmoor but also on Devon's Dartmoor (where a Dartmoor Beast had been reported). In May 1983, the army was brought in to seek out the Exmoor Beast – or Beasts – but failed to do so, even though sheep-killings continued. Yet although decidedly feline cryptids were often spied here, they were never seen actually killing sheep, or even eating the flesh from sheep carcases.

It has been suggested that the mysterious animal in this photograph, taken in 1987, may be the Beast of Exmoor. (© 2006 TopFoto/Fortean)

Consequently, some ABC seekers, including Devon-based naturalist Trevor Beer, suggested it was possible that stray dogs were the real sheep killers, and not the ABCs after all.

Also during the 1980s some strange, gracile black cats, much smaller than a panther but with very prominent fangs, were captured in the Scottish Highlands, especially in the vicinity of the village of Kellas. This mysterious feline form was dubbed the Kellas cat by the cryptozoologist Dr Karl Shuker, who correctly predicted that it would prove merely to be an unusual crossbreed of a domestic cat and a Scottish wildcat.

The principal ABC of the 1990s was the Beast of Bodmin, a panther-like creature seen and even videoed stalking this famous Cornish moor, and blamed for a number of livestock kills. However, when government officials from the Ministry of Agriculture, Fisheries and Food were sent to investigate, and succeeded in measuring the background features visible in one video of the alleged beast, they were able to confirm that the cat in that video was much smaller than it had seemed, and was far more likely to have been a hefty black domestic moggie than any panther.

Nevertheless, sightings and photos of ABCs recorded all over the UK continue unabatedly to the present day, and to add substance to investigators' claims of their reality, some actual ABC bodies have turned up from time to time. Most of these have been shot or found dead, but a few have been captured alive – including a bona fide puma caught and caged at Cannich, Scotland. This became known as the Cannich Puma, and was captured in October 1980 by a farmer whose reports of a puma stalking his livestock had gone unheeded by the authorities. Other non-native cats procured in Britain during the last few decades include a black panther cub, an escape, clouded leopard, at least three Asian jungle cats, several Asian leopard cats and a lioness found dead in a Lancashire lake during 1980. More recently, an adult lynx that had been shot just outside Norwich by a game-keeper back in 1991, but whose exist-ence had remained unpublicized since then, belatedly made the headlines in March 2006 after a police report of the case was released following a freedom of information request made by a local newspaper.

What is particularly interesting about the ABC phenomenon, but is not widely realized, is that it is not confined to the UK. Corresponding reports of panther-like and puma-like cats in particular, and even the occasional maned leonine version, are frequently reported in many countries on the European mainland, from all over the USA and Canada, and also in Australia and New Zealand. True, the puma is native to North America, but many puma sightings have emerged from the eastern USA, where this species has been extinct for many decades. It would seem that wherever exotic big cats are being maintained in captivity, especially as pets by private individuals, escapes and/or deliberate releases are occurring, and the creatures are surviving in the wild.

Indeed, for most cryptozoologists nowadays, the mystery of ABCs is no longer whether or not they are there but whether they are actually breeding. Quite a few reports in recent years from the UK, for instance, speak of sightings of a big cat with one or more smaller cub-like cats, or the discovery of tracks in the snow which show a set of large tracks accompanied by a set of smaller ones. If it is ever established that ABCs are mating and rearing young, the whole issue of ABCs in the UK will take on a more serious aspect.

alignments *see* LEYS

alignments, stone *see* STONE ROWS

alligators in sewers

A well-known urban legend (attaching particularly to the city of New York) which may actually have some basis in fact.

One of the more popular URBAN LEGENDS revolves around the assertion that there are alligators living in the sewers under the streets of New York. The source of these alligators is usually supposed to be New York residents bringing back baby alligators from holidays in Florida and then flushing them down the toilet when they become too unwieldy. These discarded pets then continue to live and breed in the sewer system and are sometimes even said to have lost their eyesight and colouring through living in constant darkness. This version of the story may stem from a fanciful tale told by a retired sewer worker which appeared in a book called *The World Beneath the City* (1959), written by Robert Daley. However, it is generally accepted that (among the many other practical difficulties) it is extremely unlikely that an alligator would be able to survive the winter temperatures in New York.

Despite this, there is a suggestion that the story may have at least some earlier basis in fact. A claim that an alligator had been captured in a manhole near the Harlem River appeared in the *New York Times* on 10 February 1935, although there was no implication that the animal had been living in the sewer system – it was decided that it was probably there because 'a steamer from the mysterious Everglades, or thereabouts, had been passing 123rd Street, and the alligator had fallen overboard'. Over the years there have been numerous other reports of sightings, usually in lakes or rivers rather than sewers.

Perhaps more interestingly, the long-standing legend appeared to have become fact (see OSTENTION) when in June 2001 there were a number of sightings of a small alligator in the Harlem Meer in Central Park. This time the animal was eventually captured – a spectacled caiman that was 60 centimetres (2 feet) long, and was, indeed, believed to have been an abandoned pet.

Anastasia (1901–?1918)

Russian duchess reputed to have survived the execution of her family.

The Grand Duchess Anastasia Nikolay-evna Romanov was the youngest daughter of Nicholas II (1868–1918), the last Tsar of Russia. When, in July 1918, the Russian Imperial family were executed by their Bolshevik captors at Yekaterinburg, it was rumoured that Anastasia had somehow survived.

In subsequent years, several women claimed to be Anastasia, the most persistent and successful being 'Anna Anderson'. She had tried to drown herself in Berlin in 1920, only to be rescued and committed to a mental asylum. It was there that she first identified herself as Anastasia.

Her cause was taken up by various Russian exiles, who worked over a period of decades to have her formally accepted as the heir to the Imperial throne. These supporters had various motives, ranging from a romantic desire for a Romanov restoration to a simple greed for the riches believed to have been smuggled out of Russia by the Tsar before his death.

Romanov relatives were divided by the case, some believing in its legitimacy and others maintaining that Anderson had been carefully coached in her apparent knowledge of life in the Imperial family.

Anna Anderson, who maintained to the end that she was the Grand Duchess Anastasia. (© TopFoto/AP)

Although Anna Anderson died in America in 1984, interest in her claims was revived when the Russian government revealed in 1992 that the bodies of the executed Romanovs had been discovered. Two bodies were missing, one of them apparently being that of Anastasia.

DNA testing carried out on samples of Anderson's body tissue seemed to rule out any relationship with the Romanovs. However, the methods and results have been attacked as inaccurate and many continue to believe that Anastasia did indeed end her life as an American housewife.

ancient astronauts

A name given to hypothetical beings from outer space who it is suggested visited the earth and interacted with ancient peoples.

The theory that ancient astronauts visited the earth in our distant past is widely attributed to Swiss writer ERICH VON DÄNIKEN. He has certainly popularized the idea, but he was not the first writer to develop the concept.

Several UFO writers during the 1950s recognized that there were stories in ancient texts that could potentially be interpreted as UFO sightings. Examples included the fiery cloud seen in the sky by Ezekiel and a number of other dramatic visions in the Old Testament.

From 1960 onwards the British scholar Raymond Drake wrote several books known as the *Gods and Spacemen* series. The books contained analyses of the records of a number of ancient civilizations, including the Greeks and Romans. Many reports of what could be described as UFOs were uncovered, using words that were relevant to the time and place in question. These reports were of 'UFOs' in the strict sense, but may often describe phenomena (such as meteors, comets and atmospheric mirages) that have since become well understood.

Ancient astronaut researchers have been intrigued by the occasional discovery of artefacts that can be reliably dated back to civilizations believed not to possess such advanced technology. Examples include the

PHAISTOS DISC, the unusually accurate Piri Re'is map (featuring a perspective suggesting an aerial viewpoint long before the discovery of flight) and the extraordinary NAZCA LINES in Peru. However, other scholars point out that it is easy to underestimate the capabilities of our ancestors – suggesting, for example, that balloons may have been used for mapping many centuries before the technique was rediscovered in Europe.

Details of one of the most intriguing cases which seemed to support the ancient astronauts thesis were published in 1976 by Robert Temple. He discovered that the Dogon tribe

This stone is one of many carved with ancient petroglyphs in the desert of Toro Muerte near Arequipa, Peru. The figure with the halo was identified as an 'astronaut' by Erich von Däniken. (© 2005 TopFoto/Fortean)

in Africa appeared to have possessed detailed knowledge relating to the bright star Sirius, including the existence and orbits of its companion stars, long before modern astronomers. The Dogon had a set of myths linked to Sirius that included the appearance of beings from the sky who had taught them knowledge of the heavens. Sceptics have countered that the first contact with the tribe by European missionaries was made after scientists had gathered some knowledge about Sirius. It was, therefore, possible that influence from Western culture had caused the folk stories to be partly adapted.

ancient structures

Structures erected by ancient cultures, the exact purpose of which is often obscure.

In various sites around the world ancient structures are still visible today which were built by the people of cultures that are now long dead, often for reasons that remain largely unexplained.

Among the oldest man-made constructions in the world are the great STONE CIRCLES found in the British Isles and Europe, especially that of STONEHENGE, the building of which is thought to have begun around 3100 BC. The complex of STANDING STONES and DOLMENS at CARNAC in Brittany is believed to mark the oldest continuously inhabited site in Europe. Various theories are advanced as to the reasons behind the erection of these structures, which must have entailed colossal effort on the part of the technology-poor peoples responsible. Dolmens have been explained as ceremonial tombs, with many grave sites having been excavated beneath them. Stone circles are often interpreted as giant astronomical observatories or calendars to chronicle the changing seasons or mark important days in the year. However, the fact that the surviving remains of these structures often represent only a small part of the original means that their true purposes can only be guessed at.

The PYRAMIDS of Egypt were, of course, built as royal tombs, beginning with that of Zoser at Saqqara (c.2700 BC), but mysteries remain as to the exact methods of their construction and the significance of their alignment with points of the compass or celestial bodies. Similar questions apply to the pyramid-shaped stone temples built in Central America (beginning c.1500 BC).

On the island of Crete, the Minoan culture which dominated Bronze Age Greece has left behind ruins of many extensive and once-magnificent palaces, notably those of Phaestos and Knossos. These contain many courtyards and rooms which seem to have been designed for use in religious observances about which little is known. It is believed that the complexity of the ruins of Knossos gave rise to the traditional stories of the labyrinth of King Minos, the Minotaur imprisoned within it and the escape from it of the legendary Greek hero Theseus.

In North America, in the south-west of what is now the USA, the Native American culture known as the Basket Weavers built large round underground chambers known as kivas (beginning c.700), which were entered through a hole in the roof. Excavation of the remains of these structures leads archaeologists to assume that they were for communal use, probably for religious or ceremonial purposes. The same peoples later built the impressive cliffside Anasazi dwellings.

apparitions, Marian *see* MARIAN APPARITIONS

appearances

An appearance is the sudden arrival of someone or something at a place where they were not present (or had not been seen) before.

As used in discussions of forteana, the term 'appearances' applies not to the way something looks but to the phenomenon of sudden arrival (or the noticing) of a person, animal or object that is 'out of place' or which was not present (or not noticed) a few moments before. It is the opposite of the phenomenon of DISAPPEARANCES, and both might indicate the beginning and ending of a teleportation transaction. This hypothetical process may manifest differently in different sub-categories of phenomena.

Charles Fort, a US philosopher who collected and studied reports of anomalies, wondered whether teleportation might play a part in

explaining some of the peculiar characteristics of FALLS – ie objects or creatures falling under unusual circumstances. He suggested that if teleportation existed, it could show up in data of fishes, frogs or stones, etc, disappearing from wherever they were plentiful to materialize at an 'appearing point' in the air from which they are seen to fall. Almost any object or substance may be teleported in this way, so the hypothesis can be extended to account for the appearance of, for example, persistent stains or the flow of blood-like liquids on bleeding images (see IMAGES, BLEEDING).

Such a theory would certainly account for reports of stones falling from beneath the ceilings inside rooms or the way falling frogs seem to fall in defined areas instead of being scattered by the whirlwinds as envisaged in the standard explanation. There are several cases in the poltergeist literature of investigators, having been pelted with stones, picking up one or two, marking them and throwing them back in the direction of their trajectory, only to be surprised by the reappearance of the marked stones in another volley. When objects appear during poltergeist disturbances or during the séances of physical mediums they are usually termed apports.

Perhaps the largest category of appearances concerns the origin of out-of-place animals – especially those like ALIEN BIG CATS – which are 'alien' to the local ecology and landscape. Usually, the first we hear of them is a local news report of their sudden appearance, ie they are sighted where they have not been seen before. Very few cryptozoologists believe teleportation is involved, but they don't discount it either, even though experience shows that more ordinary explanations for the animals' presence are probable.

Appearances of humans under mysterious circumstances are very rare and the few accounts very subjective. KASPAR HAUSER, the enigmatic boy found near Nuremberg in 1828, is often described as a mysteriously appearing person but there is no suggestion here of teleportation, only of abandonment. In his case, all authorities agree he was probably raised locally, but no one knows where or by whom.

The most unusual class of appearances consists of objects or creatures that are sometimes found inside seemingly solid material. Examples would include a toad found entombed in a cavity in a rock or anachronistic artefacts found in geological strata laid down millennia earlier (see ENTOMBMENT). In the absence of any convincing explanation for these anomalies, some forteans have suggested, half in jest, that they might result from a hypothetical malfunction of the hypothetical teleporting force.

archaeoacoustics

The study of the acoustic qualities of prehistoric constructions.

Among the theories developed to explain the siting and layout of prehistoric buildings is the idea that they may have been designed to have particular acoustic qualities. In the United Kingdom, research into the great megalithic STONE CIRCLES of STONEHENGE and AVEBURY has shown that sound is reflected from the standing stones in patterns that some would argue are probably no more accidental than their alignment with astronomical phenomena. Similarly, the passage tomb at NEWGRANGE in Ireland has been the subject of experiments into the reverberation of sound within its domed chamber, leading some to suggest that its distinctive decoration of concentric rings may even be an attempt to depict the patterns made in smoke by the reflected sound waves during periods of chanting.

In the Americas, it is claimed that the sound of a handclap made in front of the Mayan temple at Chichen Itzá will be reflected from the building to sound like the chirp of the holy quetzal bird. The ritual chambers of the Anasazi cliffside dwellings of New Mexico are also believed to have been constructed to reflect and amplify sound.

One area of research into this phenomenon involves experiments, at various locations, to establish whether the sound reflections and reverberations would have been likely to have had a mental, or even physical, effect on people if the initial sounds were produced by human voices – whether speaking, chanting or singing. This would support the theory that the effects were deliberately engineered to serve some social or spiritual purpose.

Arthur, King *see* KING ARTHUR

Arthurian legend *see* KING ARTHUR

Atlantis

A legendary vanished island in the Atlantic Ocean.

The legendary lost island of Atlantis is mentioned by the Greek philosopher Plato (c.428–c.348 BC) in two short pieces: the *Timaeus* and the *Critias*. In these works Plato describes a civilization that was already ancient at the time of his writing, a powerful and almost ideal kingdom ruling an empire that extended into the Mediterranean from its island home in the Atlantic Ocean. According to Plato, Atlantis was at war with Athens when it was rocked by earthquakes and floods before being entirely swallowed up by the sea.

Plato discusses the structure and layout, as well as the political and social organization of Atlantis in some detail but is more vague about its precise location. This has led many scholars to believe that it was imaginary and that the philosopher was merely using a convenient fiction, based perhaps on myths brought to Greece from Egypt, to make points about the ideal form of government. However, many believe in the reality of Atlantis and have suggested various possible locations for the vanished civilization. Candidates include the Greek city of Helike (known to have been destroyed by earthquake and tidal wave in 373 BC), the Caribbean and Polynesia.

One of the more popular theories connects the story with the Bronze Age civilization of Minoan Crete which was largely destroyed by ash and tidal waves generated by the massive volcanic explosion of the island of Thera in c.1500 BC.

There are those who believe that the concept of Atlantis really concerns an extraterrestrial race who colonized the earth thousands of years ago but established their civilization in the deepest parts of the sea. According to this theory, Atlanteans still operate from undersea bases and this explains the numerous reports over the years of unidentified metallic craft that can move at great speed both beneath the water and in the air. The existence in many parts of the world of structures that have been identified as UNDERWATER RUINS has fuelled speculation that these may be remnants of Atlantis. The Bimini Road, a linear stone formation in the Caribbean off the island of Bimini, has been particularly identified with the story ever since the American psychic Edgar Cayce prophesied that Atlantis would be discovered in that very location.

Madame Blavatsky, founder of the Theosophical Society, believed that Atlantis was peopled by the inhabitants of the (similarly lost) continent of LEMURIA, and, at around the same time, the US politician and writer Ignatius Donnelly did much to revive interest in Atlantis with the publication of his *Atlantis, The Antediluvian World* (1882). He believed that Atlantis had disappeared below the Atlantic 12,000 years earlier. The Scottish poet, anthropologist and occultist Lewis

Spence also wrote on the subject in a series of books beginning with *The Problem of Atlantis* (1924), claiming to find evidence for its existence and cataclysmic destruction in the myths of Native American cultures. In any case, the idea of Atlantis exercises an enduring grip on popular imagination and continues to turn up in many places, from the novels of Jules Verne to the animated children's films of Disney.

Aurora Borealis

Dramatic light effects seen in the sky at high latitudes in the northern hemisphere.

Also known as the Northern Lights, the Aurora Borealis is an atmospheric phenomenon characterized by vast trembling streamers or curtains of light. In simple terms, the aurora is an electromagnetic effect generated by electrons colliding with atoms in the upper atmosphere, driven by the combined effect of solar radiation and the earth's magnetic field. However, the scientific model is incomplete and has had to be developed greatly in recent years to accommodate new observations. Various colours are seen in the display; mainly red, blue, green and violet, with red being dominant. Sometimes the colours combine to give white light. The effect grows stronger the closer the observer is to the North Pole and the further away they are from the light pollution of large cities.

A spectacular display of the Aurora Borealis, as seen in the sky above the Canadian town of Churchill, Manitoba. (© Topfoto/Imageworks)

The rhythmic movement of the light effects led observers in the distant past to attribute the phenomenon to the dancing of spirits in the sky, and this is reflected in the traditional Scottish name, 'the merry dancers'. In other societies the aurora was thought variously to be caused by the actions of gods or the reflections from heavenly shoals of herring, or (inspired by the predominance of red) to presage bloodshed and war.

In some folklore traditions it is believed that the lights are accompanied by sound, which takes the form of a continuous crackling or hissing. Even now there are many anecdotal reports of this phenomenon. However, it has not been successfully recorded and there is no widely accepted scientific theory for the mechanism by which such sounds might be produced.

There is an equivalent phenomenon in the southern hemisphere, called the Aurora Australis.

Avebury

A large Neolithic stone circle in Wiltshire.

The village of Avebury in Wiltshire is the site of a Neolithic stone circle even larger than STONEHENGE. A huge circular ditch encloses the main ring of individual standing stones, which measures almost 1.6 kilometres (1 mile) in circumference, with some of the stones almost 5 metres (16 feet) high. Two smaller rings, which are much less complete than the main ring,

are enclosed within this. Two curving lines of stones, known as avenues, lead away from the circle, but so many stones are now missing that their exact significance remains unclear. It is thought that one of them connected the site with another nearby hilltop stone circle known as the Sanctuary. It is believed that building began in c.2800 BC, using stones quarried from the nearby Avebury Hills, and continued over the next 500 years.

Various theories have been put forward as to the purposes of this ancient complex of stones. Some believe that the two inner circles were used as temples. Both of them had a central standing stone. The larger of these, which was known as the Obelisk until its destruction in the 18th century, is believed to have been erected to cast a shadow (in much the same way as the gnomon of a sundial) which could be interpreted as marking the changing seasons. Similarly, the 'Cove', a group of three stones (two of which remain) at the centre of the other inner circle, is thought to have been aligned with the position of sunrise at midsummer.

The relatively close proximity of other significant Neolithic remains, such as those at SILBURY HILL and the Sanctuary, suggests that Avebury may have been part of a large area of interconnected sites with particular religious significance. It has been discovered relatively recently that some of the stones have faces carved into them but it is not known whether the builders or subsequent inhabitants are responsible for these.

In modern times, the stones were 'discovered' by John Aubrey (1626–97), the English antiquary, biographer and folklorist, who assumed that the structures must be connected with ancient druidic worship. He was supported in this theory by the antiquary William Stukeley (1687–1765), whose accounts of his researches at Avebury also record his dismay at the removal of stones by local farmers. Stukeley also suggested that the two avenues of stones represented a great serpent passing through the circles.

Several of the largest stones have been given names in local folklore, including the Swindon Stone and the Devil's Chair, which has a hollow in which one can sit.

B

ball lightning

A moving ball of light seen during thunderstorms.

There have been many accounts throughout the ages of the mysterious phenomenon known as ball lightning. In general terms this is taken to mean the appearance, during a storm of thunder and lightning, of a roughly spherical glowing body of light. There are various descriptions, with quite a range of colours, durations, behaviour and eventual disappearance ascribed to the phenomenon, but what they have in common is that the light is ball-like and it moves, sometimes in the air, sometimes near the ground. The ball of light is said to be visible in daylight and photographs have been taken which, it is claimed, show ball lightning.

Ball lightning has been described as entering buildings, often appearing to be attracted to metal objects, and there is even a report from the 1960s of ball lightning appearing inside a passenger jet and rolling down the aisle. Some argue that sightings of ball lightning are responsible for many reports of UFOs. It has even been claimed that the movement of ball lightning on the ground is the true explanation of CROP CIRCLES. Could being struck by ball lightning be the true cause of the phenomenon known as SPONTANEOUS HUMAN COMBUSTION? Some theorists think so.

Scientific opinion is divided as to whether ball lightning really exists, although some claim to have created similar, if smaller-scale, effects in laboratory conditions. Various explanations of ball lightning have been suggested. One theory is that it is a form of plasma; another that it is electrically charged (or superheated) gas or air. Others believe that ball lightning is a form of radiation or microwave energy. Some scientists say that it results from silica in the soil being vaporized by a conventional lightning strike, with the resultant gas condensing into floating dust which continues to oxidize.

Some witnesses maintain that ball lightning is hot and destructive and can kill whatever it comes into contact with, but others report no sensation of heat and no damage to anything at all, whether living or inanimate. The fact that descriptions vary so widely would seem to suggest that ball lightning may be merely a 'catch-all' category for several very different types of phenomenon. See also BLACK DOG OF BUNGAY.

banshee

In Irish and Scottish folklore, a female spirit who wails and shrieks before a death in the family to which she is attached.

The word banshee comes from the Irish *bean sidhe*, meaning 'woman of the fairies' or 'woman of the mounds'. The banshee is a ghostly white lady whose cry foretells death. According to tradition, a banshee only wails for members of certain old Irish and Scottish families, and once a banshee has attached herself to a family, she is even said to follow them abroad if they emigrate. When several banshees wail together, it foretells the death of someone very great or holy.

The banshee is sometimes thought to be the spirit of a woman who has died in childbirth, although in some places she is said to be the ghost of a dead friend or family member. She may appear in one of three guises – as a young woman, a stately matron, or an old hag; these forms represent the triple aspects of the Morrigan, the Celtic goddess of war and death with whom the banshee is associated. To see the banshee portends the death of the one who sees her. In the Scottish Highlands, the banshee is known as the Bean-Nighe, and it is said that she can be seen washing the winding sheet or bloodstained clothes of the doomed person; in some stories, the Scottish banshee is described as having only one nostril, one long front tooth and pendulous breasts.

The banshee's cry is variously described as being so piercing that it can shatter glass; as a thin sound somewhere between the wail of a woman and the screech of an owl; and as a cross between the shriek of a wild goose, the howl of a wolf and the cry of an abandoned child. However, when she loves those whom she calls to death, it is said that her song may be a low, soft chant which reassures the dying person and comforts the survivors.

Barghest *see* BLACK DOGS

Bealings bells

The unsolved mystery of ringing bells at Great Bealings House, Suffolk in 1834.

In 1834, Major Edward Moor was greatly intrigued by the mysterious ringing of bells in his home in Suffolk. The bells, which were used to summon servants, seemed to be ringing for no reason. Later that same year, Moor wrote a book about his experiences called *Bealings Bells*. The mystery was also recounted in William Howitt's *The History of the Supernatural* (1863):

> On Tuesday, February 2, 1834, the bells in Major Moor's house, at

Great Bealings, near Woodbridge, commenced an unaccountable ringing without any visible agency, which they continued almost every day, more or less, till March 27, in all fifty-three days. On returning from church on Sunday afternoon, on the aforesaid February 2, he was told by the two only servants left in the house, a man and a woman, that the bell of the dining-room, in which nobody was, had rung several times. The next day the bell rang several times ... though no one was in reach of the bell-pull. In the afternoon, all the bells in the kitchen, a row of nine, rang violently. Whilst the Major was watching the bells, five of them rang again so violently that he says he should not have wondered to see them broken from their fastenings. To make a short story, these ringings continued, all the time mentioned, at intervals, though every means were used to discover the cause.

Moor wrote a letter to a local newspaper describing the mysterious bell ringing, and in response received numerous accounts from people who claimed they had suffered from the same phenomenon. While many believe that Moor was the unwitting subject of a hoax perpetrated by a member of his household, others think a more supernatural power was behind it, possibly a poltergeist. The mystery of Bealings bells remains.

Beast of Bodmin *see* ALIEN BIG CATS

Belmez faces

Mysterious images of faces which appeared in the fabric of a Spanish house in the 1970s.

In early 1971, mysterious marks resembling human faces appeared on the cement floor of the house of a lady named Maria Gomez Pereira in Belmez, Spain. The case received international publicity and many people, including a number of parapsychologists, visited the house. To some the faces were evidence of spirit manifestations on the part of deceased

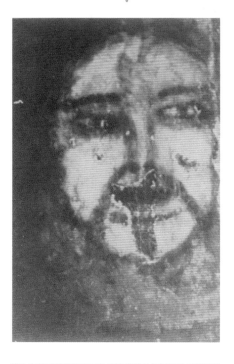

One of the famous facial images from the cement floor of a house in Belmez, Spain. (© Mary Evans Picture Library)

~ 17 ~

occupiers of the house or persons buried on the site. Consideration was also given to the possibility that they were created by the mind of Maria Pereira through psychokinesis, the expressions on the faces being an external pictorial expression of her inner moods.

The case stimulated much debate, with some people claiming that the faces constituted a 'permanent paranormal object' – a physical item which could be used to refute the arguments of sceptics. To others the faces were simply faked. Separate studies conducted by Spanish researchers J J Alonso and Manuel Martin Serrano reached diametrically opposed conclusions. Alonso considered that there was potentially a paranormal origin for some of the faces, while Serrano concluded they must all be forgeries. Both studies have been criticized and, regrettably, laboratory tests performed on some of the faces in 1975 and 1976 also proved less than satisfactory, failing even to determine the chemical composition of the markings with complete certainty.

The story of the faces of Belmez resurfaced sporadically over the next 25 years but gradually faded from public attention. In October 2004 the house was reported to be empty and up for sale, the mystery still unsolved. See also IMAGES, SPONTANEOUS.

Bermuda Triangle

An area in the Atlantic where ships and aircraft are alleged to have disappeared.

In the 20th century a belief arose that the roughly triangular area of the Atlantic bounded by Bermuda, Florida and Puerto Rico was a region in which ships and aircraft mysteriously vanished. Central to this legend was the unexplained disappearance of Flight 19 in this area on 5 December 1945. Later known as the 'Lost Patrol', Flight 19 consisted of five US Navy bombers and their 14 crew, who set off on a training flight from the airbase at Fort Lauderdale but failed to return. The name Bermuda Triangle was first applied to the area in *Argosy*, a magazine specializing in fiction, in a 1964 article by Vincent Gaddis ('The Deadly Bermuda Triangle'). However, it was not until the publication in 1974 of *The Bermuda Triangle* by Charles Berlitz (1914–2003) that the term became very widely known. In his book, Berlitz recounted not only the Flight 19 case but many other strange disappearances of ships and aircraft.

In 1975 a sceptical reply to Berlitz was published by Lawrence Kusche, *The Bermuda Triangle Mystery: Solved*, in which the author claimed that many of the cases cited by Berlitz were inaccurately reported. Some described incidents that had taken place in areas other than the Bermuda Triangle; some turned out to have explanations and outcomes that Berlitz chose to ignore; some 'incidents' had simply not happened at all. However, the idea was too deeply rooted in the popular imagination to be so easily discounted and various explanations were suggested, including alien abduction, freak waves and giant bubbles of methane gas rising from the ocean floor to sink ships and disable aircraft instruments. Several Hollywood movies were made, notably *The Bermuda Triangle* (1979), either recounting the story of the missing aviators or simply using the triangle as a handy plot device.

The Flight 19 case is not considered a mystery by the US Navy, which cites radio messages from the flight commander reporting that his compasses were malfunctioning and that he was, in fact, lost. The Navy believes that the aircraft ran out of fuel and were forced to ditch in the open ocean at a location that it was impossible to pinpoint. Believers in the mystery point to the fact that an aircraft sent to search for the missing flight was also lost, but the official explanation blames an exploding fuel tank for the plane's loss. The failure of the aircraft compasses might also possibly be due to this being an area of natural MAGNETIC ANOMALIES, where compasses point to true north rather than magnetic north. Unless a pilot was aware of this and could compensate for it, extreme navigational errors would inevitably result.

However, while the Bermuda Triangle is an area of the Atlantic that is subject to heavy nautical and aerial traffic, the US Coast Guard maintains that the rate of accidents within it is no higher than in any other comparably busy region. Similarly, the nautical insurance specialists Lloyd's of London do not consider the area to be so hazardous as to warrant special consideration.

bigfoot

A very large bipedal man-beast, North America's most famous cryptid.

Today, the bigfoot or sasquatch is the most famous North American cryptid, yet until as recently as 1967 this man-beast had attracted minimal attention outside that continent. It came to prominence through the claims of ranchers Roger Patterson and Bob Gimlin. According to their reports, they were riding through Bluff Creek, California, on 20 October 1967, to look for a bigfoot that had allegedly been seen in the area, when Patterson saw a very large ape-like creature squatting by the river. He said that as he rode towards it the creature stood upright on its hind legs. He described it as covered in dark fur, with a conical head, and apparently female as it had breasts. Patterson said that the sight of the creature caused his horse to shy, and he was thrown to the ground. Nevertheless, holding the cine camera that he had brought with him, Patterson says he stumbled after the creature, filming it as it strode away on its hind legs across the clearing towards some trees. Momentarily, however, it paused and looked round at him before disappearing into the forest.

Other snippets of film and numerous still photographs purportedly depicting bigfoots have subsequently been publicized, but Patterson's film remains the most famous – and controversial

The most convincing evidence for the existence of
bigfoot, or an elaborate hoax? A frame from the
cine film taken by Roger Patterson at Bluff Creek,
California, in 1967. (© TopFoto/Fortean)

– piece of evidence. Numerous experts
have analysed it, but remain divided as
to whether it depicts a genuine bigfoot.
Those in favour have included the late
Professor Grover Krantz (the leading
scientific believer in the reality of the
bigfoot), veteran bigfoot investigator
John Green and Russian anthropologist
Dr Dmitri Bayanov. They consider the
manner in which the filmed creature
(nicknamed Patty, after Patterson)
walked was fundamentally unlike the
gait of a human, and that its muscle
movements could not be successfully

mimicked by a human. They estimated
its height to have been around 2
metres (6.5 feet), and reasoned that it
was far heavier than a human from the
depth of the footprints it left behind.
The opposing school of thought,
championed by, among others, the
late Mark Chorvinsky, an expert in
special effects as well as a long-
standing cryptozoological investigator,
remains convinced that Patty was a
man in a skilfully designed ape-man
suit. Moreover, veteran Hollywood
'monster-maker' John Chambers was

frequently named as a likely candidate to have produced such a suit, though he always strenuously denied this charge. Intriguingly, when John Green contacted the special effects department at Walt Disney Studios in 1969, they stated that they could not have created such an authentic-looking man-beast at that time.

Although it took the Patterson–Gimlin film to introduce the bigfoot to the world at large, reports and sightings of such creatures had long been documented within North America. The bigfoot has allegedly been seen throughout mainland Canada (where it is most commonly referred to as the sasquatch) and every mainland state of the USA, but most frequently in the continent's Pacific Northwest region. As with other commonly reported cryptids, eyewitness descriptions of the bigfoot vary greatly. However, the 'classic' bigfoot stands 1.8–3 metres (around 6–10 feet) tall, is almost invariably bipedal, is ape-like in overall appearance, has no tail, is covered in shaggy black or auburn-brown hair and, like certain other man-beasts on record from around the world, is often claimed to emit a foul stench. The bigfoot's head is said to be conical, and its face is ape-like, with a sloping brow, prominent eyebrow ridges, light-reflecting eyes, a broad flattened nose and a slit-like lipless mouth. Its neck is short and thick, its shoulders are huge, its chest is muscular and powerful, and its arms are very long, with paw-like hands that have hairless palms and thick fingers. Its legs are

muscular and sturdy, and its feet are very large, leaving footprints that are 30–55 centimetres (1–1.8 feet) long and that reveal two pads beneath the first toe on each foot. Many sceptics dismiss all bigfoot tracks as fake, and there have certainly been a number of crude attempts to produce hoax tracks. However, there are also some bigfoot tracks on record which are so detailed that the presence of dermatoglyphs (fingerprints) can be discerned, which Krantz claimed would be impossible to reproduce convincingly as a hoax.

A particularly enigmatic piece of bigfoot evidence is the Skookum cast. In September 1999, a team of investigators from the Bigfoot Field Researchers Organization travelled to Skookum Meadow in south-western Washington, where bigfoot reports had previously emerged. They set food baits of fruit in mud wallows, daubed trees with gorilla scent, and played the cry of an alleged bigfoot (which was apparently answered, but the caller was not spied). On 22 September, they discovered that some of the food had gone, but although no footprints had been left behind, they did discover that in one of the mud wallows there appeared to be a deep impression left behind by some animal having rested there. After photographing it, the team made what is now referred to as the 'Skookum cast' of the impression, which shows the outline of a large humanoid creature's left arm, hip, thigh, testicles, buttocks, ankles and heels. As with the Patterson–Gimlin film, opinions as to the impression's authenticity are deeply split, though anthropologists such as Dr Jeffrey Meldrum and Professor Krantz were particularly impressed with the details of heel, sole and dermatoglyph presence that were visible.

Other physical evidence obtained in recent years includes hair samples that, when analysed via detailed trichological and DNA studies, have proven to be of primate origin yet recognizably different from the hair of any known primate species; and recordings of alleged bigfoot cries whose acoustics, though primate-like, could not have been produced by a human larynx. Faecal droppings said to be from bigfoots have occasionally been obtained too, but none has been submitted so far for a detailed DNA analysis which might well determine the zoological nature of their originator.

Assuming that the bigfoot does exist, and is not something as mundane as a bear that has been misinterpreted by witnesses, the most popular crypto-zoological identity for it is a surviving species of *Gigantopithecus*. This was a giant ape that was 3 metres (c. 10 feet) tall and officially died out around 100,000 years ago. It is also popularly said to be the true identity of the Tibetan dzu-teh or giant yeti (see YETI), to which the bigfoot bears a strong resemblance according to eyewitness testimonies. However, *Gigantopithecus* fossils are known only from Asia – none has ever been obtained anywhere in the New World. Nevertheless, while this ape was known to be still alive in Asia, a land bridge across what is now the Bering Strait connected far eastern Asia to northern North America. Many mammalian species entered North America across this land bridge, explaining why the mammalian faunas of Eurasia and North America contain so many shared species. Consequently, it is possible that *Gigantopithecus* also made the journey via this land link into the New World. An alternative identity that has been proposed is *Paranthropus* – an early species of hominid – but as this is currently known exclusively from African fossils, its existence in modern-day North America would be even more difficult to explain.

Black Dog of Bungay
A famous black-dog legend.

On 4 August 1577 the townsfolk of Bungay in Suffolk reportedly witnessed a terrifying attack by a spectral BLACK DOG. The story has since become one of the best-known black-dog incidents, achieving the status of a local legend.

According to a pamphlet apparently written soon after the event by Abraham Fleming, the attack occurred some time after 9am. While the parishioners cowered in the church praying for salvation, a violent thunderstorm raged outside. Suddenly, a fearsome-looking black dog burst into the church, lit by flashes of fire. It ran among the congregation, causing fear and panic, and as it passed between two people kneeling at prayer, it:

> ... wrung the necks of them bothe at one instant clene backward, in so much that even at a moment where

they kneeled, they strangely died ...

And a third man whom it touched was so severely burned that:

... therewith all he was presently drawen togither and shrunk up, as it were a peece of lether scorched in a hot fire; or as the mouth of a purse or bag, drawen togither with string. The man albeit hee was in so strange a taking, dyed not, but as it is thought is yet alive: whiche thing is mervelous in the eyes of men, and offereth much matter of amasing the minde ...

Fleming says that the church tower was struck by lightning and the church clock was broken, although no physical traces of such damage remain. Also, a further attack is said to have occurred later the same day at the church in Blythburgh, just a few miles away. This time two men and a boy were killed and a number of others blasted by the hound. Again, the church tower was struck by lightning (collapsing through the roof). Scorch marks were reputedly left on the church door which can still be seen to this day.

There is no official record of the Bungay attack by a black dog. However, the storm appears in the parish records (and in other accounts of the period) and the churchwarden's account book mentions that two people were killed. The fact that both of these attacks were said to have taken place amid severe thunderstorms has led to the suggestion that a manifestation of BALL LIGHTNING is at the root of the tale – a theory supported by the fact that one

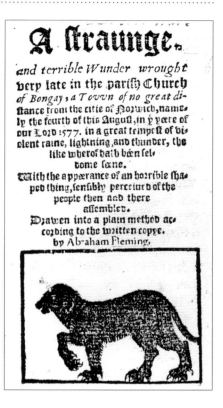

The title page of Abraham Fleming's pamphlet on the Black Dog of Bungay, the 'horrible shaped thing' that reportedly terrorized the congregations of two Suffolk churches in 1577. (© TopFoto/Fortean)

person was burned and scorch marks were left on the second church's door. The remainder of the story could be put down to the overactive imagination of a superstitious congregation.

It may also be relevant that Abraham Fleming is known to have been a Puritan propagandist. He is believed to have lived in London and may never have even visited Bungay. Fleming (or his source) may simply have been exploiting the story of the damage caused by the storm, along with a long-standing local belief in a spectral black dog known as Black Shuck, to produce a terrifying image to reinforce the message of repentance. Indeed, in some versions of the legend it is stated that the visit was from the Devil himself.

The story of the Black Dog of Bungay is now regarded with some affection in the town, and a black dog appears on its coat of arms. The legend is also kept alive in names such as the Black Dog Marathon and the Black Dog Running Club, and by the local football team, who are known as the Black Dogs.

Black Dogs

Legends of large black spectral dogs are common all over the British Isles.

Many places in the British Isles have traditions of spectral Black Dogs, known by a variety of local names. For example, in East Anglia, the Black Dog is known as Black Shuck or Old Shuck, in Yorkshire it is called the Barghest or Padfoot and in Wales black dogs are referred to as the Gwyllgi ('dogs of the dusk'). Black Dogs have a number of characteristics that set them apart from the phantoms of domestic dogs and from normal domestic animals. These include their great size (they are frequently described as being as big as a calf), and their eyes, which are large and luminous, often described as blazing red saucers.

The Black Dog is often described as walking through solid objects, and its appearance is frequently said to be accompanied by lightning, or a fire or explosion; it may vanish or fade gradually from view, or disappear with a bang or flash, if the person who sees it lets their gaze wander, or tries to touch it. It is usually seen at night. It leaves no tracks, and makes no sound as it walks. Occasionally it is described as having the head or limbs of another animal or a human being, or being headless, and although it is generally reported to be black and shaggy, there have been a few reported sightings in which it is white or (particularly in Scotland) green. In some stories Black Dogs have supposedly left physical traces in the form of burns or scratches on places or people, most famously at the churches of Blythburgh and Bungay in Suffolk during a thunderstorm in August 1577 (see BLACK DOG OF BUNGAY).

The appearance of a Black Dog is often interpreted as an omen of impending death or disaster for the person witnessing it – although in some areas, such as Essex, they traditionally have a protective function. Stories of such creatures have been told in one form or another for centuries, both in ballad and pamphlet form and in oral tradition. While in some legends the Black Dog is a manifestation of the Devil (leading to another popular name for the phenomenon, 'Devil

Dog') or the transmogrified spirit of a wicked human being, the majority of Black Dog apparitions have no such accompanying legend to 'explain' their appearance. It is possible that the name of Shuck by which the Black Dog is generally known in East Anglia is derived from *scucca*, the Anglo-Saxon word for demon.

Perhaps surprisingly, there is a considerable amount of 20th-century testimony for the appearance of Black Dogs at different locations, although these more recent appearances have been somewhat less dramatic then those in earlier stories. Country roads, churchyards, ancient monuments and parish and county boundaries have historically been the favourite haunts of Black Dogs, with their appearance being celebrated in some local place names (eg Black Dog Lane, Uplyme on the Devon/Dorset border; Dogland and Shuckmoor in Coventry, Warwickshire). Black Dogs are rarely reported inside or close to buildings and a study conducted in the 1970s by a Lowestoft-based researcher called Ivan Bunn suggested that Black Dogs have an affinity for bodies of water such as rivers, streams and the sea. It has been suggested that Black Dogs are gradually being superseded by sightings of ALIEN BIG CATS.

Black Shuck *see* BLACK DOGS

Booth, David *see* CINCINNATI PREMONITION

Brahan Seer

Kenneth Mackenzie, also called Coinneach Odhar, a legendary seer said to have lived in the Scottish Highlands in the 17th century.

Most of what we know about Kenneth Mackenzie, also called Coinneach Odhar, but better known as the Brahan Seer, comes from the Gaelic oral tradition; in a generally well-documented century, there is very little direct evidence of his existence. He is reputed to have been born some time around the beginning of the 17th century at Baile-na-Cille on the Isle of Lewis. Nothing is recorded of his early life, but as a teenager he is said to have obtained the gift of second sight through a mysterious touchstone. In one version of the story, he was given this stone by his mother, who was guided to it by the ghost of a Norwegian princess, and in another version he found the stone after falling asleep on a heath. All the accounts agree that after gaining possession of the stone Coinneach's reputation as a seer began to spread far and wide. He moved to the Brahan estate of the third Earl of Seaforth in Ross-shire, where he worked as a labourer, but he was much sought after by the local gentry for his psychic abilities.

His prophecies deal mostly with Scotland; his believers claim that some have come true already, while the fulfilment of others is still awaited. He is said to have foreseen events such as the coming of mechanization and industrialization, and his mention of 'black bridleless horses' is often interpreted as being a reference to the advent of railways. Some say that he also predicted the Highland Clearances, the building of the Caledonian Canal and, a hundred years before it took place, the Battle of Culloden. He made several prophecies regarding the River Ness, including one that when a ninth bridge crossed the river, there would be fire, flood and calamity; the ninth bridge over the river was built in 1987, and within a few years of its completion the Piper Alpha oil rig in the North Sea exploded, a passenger plane crashed in flames on Lockerbie and the rail bridge across the River Ness was washed away when the river flooded. Another prophecy he made concerns the Eagle Stone at Strathpeffer, which was allegedly put up by the Munro clan after a battle with the Mackenzies. He said that if this stone fell over three times, Loch Ussie would flood the valley below. It has already fallen twice, and is now firmly concreted in place to ensure its stability!

The Brahan Seer's most famous prediction is the one which was said to have cost him his life. Isabella, the wife of the third Earl of Seaforth, was anxious because her husband had not yet returned from a trip to France, and consulted Coinneach. He assured her that her husband was safe and well, but she pressed him for more details, and he eventually informed her that the Earl was enjoying the company of another woman over in France. Isabella furiously accused Coinneach of lying to destroy her husband's

reputation, and had him arrested, convicted of witchcraft and sentenced to death. Before his execution, he was said to have thrown his seer's stone into Loch Ussie, declaring that it would one day be found in the belly of a fish, whereupon his prophetic gift would pass to its finder. He then made one final prediction – the downfall of the Seaforth clan. He prophesied death and destruction for the family, the loss of property and the end of the clan's line. It was said that all of his predictions for the clan came true, and the last Lord Seaforth died in 1815, after which the title became extinct. A small memorial stone at Chanonry Point marks the site where Coinneach was said to have been put to death.

Brodgar, Ring of
A megalithic stone circle in Orkney

The Ring of Brodgar is a circle of standing stones in the parish of Stenness in Orkney. Situated on a narrow strip of flat land between two lochs, it dates from the late Neolithic or early Bronze Age, between 2500 and 2000 BC. Of the original 60 stones, 27 remain standing and the circle is surrounded by a ditch. It is the third-largest STONE CIRCLE in the British Isles, being approximately the same size as the inner ring at AVEBURY.

It has been suggested that this construction, like many such stone circles, is a kind of giant astronomical observatory, built so as to align with movements of the sun or moon. In fact, the supposed traditional name for the circle is the 'Temple of the Sun', but this

The Ring of Brodgar, Orkney. (© Richard Harding/TopFoto/UPP)

was probably invented by antiquarians guessing at its purpose. Brodgar itself is a Norse name, deriving according to some sources from words meaning 'earth-bridge'. About a mile away is a smaller stone circle, the Stones of Stenness, and it is possible that the two sites were connected in some kind of ritual use.

Some of the stones have carvings on them, but these are Norse runes dating from a much later era than that of the original builders. According to local legend, the megaliths are the figures of giants who came out to dance one night and, too caught up in their dancing to notice the break of day, were turned to stone by the rising sun.

Bungay, Black Dog of *see* BLACK DOG OF BUNGAY

C

Cagliostro, Alessandro di *see*

EGYPTIAN RITE FREEMASONRY

cairns

Stone mounds covering prehistoric burial sites.

A cairn (derived from a Gaelic word) is a man-made pile of stones built up to mark something, such as the site of an important event, a pathway or a boundary. In archaeology the term is specifically applied to the large mounds of stones covering various types of prehistoric tombs. They were probably first used to protect recently buried bodies from being dug up by wolves or other scavengers, but the more elaborate and extensive cairns covering some ancient graves suggest that they came to acquire ceremonial or symbolic value and were associated with the power and status of the person interred beneath.

An unexcavated cairn simply looks like a low grassy mound, but what lies beneath is often a fairly sophisticated tomb. The dating of bones found in these burial places has shown that many cairns were in use over periods of hundreds of years and it may be that they were often revisited rather than being simply closed up and abandoned after an interment. Auchenlaich Cairn, near Callander in Scotland, is a fine example of a chambered cairn, that is, one containing separate burial 'rooms' or chambers. It is the longest megalithic cairn in Britain.

calculating horses

Horses that have apparently been trained to answer questions on maths and other subjects.

Over the years, several animal trainers have claimed that they are in possession of a horse that has developed an unusual degree of intelligence. Among the best known of the equine intelligentsia are 'Clever Hans' and 'Lady Wonder'.

Clever Hans was acquired by German teacher and amateur animal trainer Wilhelm von Osten in the late 1800s or early 1900s. Von Osten believed that through training, or education, animals could develop an intelligence similar to that of humans. First, von Osten taught Clever Hans to recognize numbers, by word and by figure. He did this by lining up a certain number of skittles, then repeating that number to the horse. He then wrote numbers on a blackboard, again repeating the number out loud so that the horse would recognize it, and use his hoof to tap out the number on the floor. From this beginning, Clever Hans was apparently taught to do simple sums as well as more complicated mathematical problems. Von Osten toured Germany with Clever Hans – giving displays of the horse's ingenuity to rapt audiences, and sparking interest in the case from academic circles.

Professor Claparède was one of the first people to investigate von Osten and Clever Hans, writing in the *Archives de psychologie de Genève* that as well as doing maths:

> [Hans] knew how to read, and in music he could distinguish harmonious sounds from discords. He also had an extraordinary memory. He could tell the date of each day of the week. In short, his performance was up to the level of an intelligent 14-year-old schoolboy.

A formal commission was soon organized to investigate Clever Hans and his trainer. Among the members of the 'Hans Commission' was German psychologist and sceptic Oskar Pfungst. After a series of tests, Pfungst concluded that the horse had no special powers, and while deliberate fraud was not actually involved, Clever Hans was able

to apparently get questions correct simply by watching subtle changes in the body language of the questioner. As Clever Hans reached the hoof tap that was correct, the facial expression or posture of the questioner would change very slightly (presumably in relief that the horse had got it right) and so Hans would stop tapping. Von Osten's reputation was in tatters.

Lady Wonder is a more recent example of an allegedly intelligent horse, whose powers were not limited to mathematics. Lady Wonder lived on a farm between Richmond and Petersburg in Virginia, USA, the property of Mrs C D Fonda. Fonda had apparently taught the horse the alphabet from an early age, and then constructed a set of wooden letters, somewhat like a typewriter, so that the horse could press the letters with its nose (causing the letters to stand up) and spell out the answers to questions.

The most curious thing about Lady Wonder was that its owner claimed the horse had psychic abilities, and people flocked to the farm to ask the horse questions. As well as answering questions to which no one but the questioner knew the answer, it could also apparently predict the weather and sporting results, and even locate missing people. Lady Wonder was studied by parapsychologist J B Rhine of Duke University, who concluded that the horse could read people's minds. Sceptics believe that the horse, unknown to Mrs Fonda, was able to pick up on subtle signals from the owner in the same way that Clever

The remarkable standing stones at Callanish on the Isle of Lewis, a location from which a periodic 'lunar standstill' can be observed. (© TopFoto)

Hans is thought to have done, and that no special abilities were involved.

Callanish standing stones

A megalithic stone circle on the Isle of Lewis.

At Callanish (in Gaelic, Calanais) on the Isle of Lewis there is a remarkable complex of prehistoric MEGALITHS. There are several STONE CIRCLES as well as individual MENHIRS, but the most important is the great circle popularly known as the 'Stonehenge of the North'. Unlike many such constructions, the layout is not a simple circle but rather a cruciform shape with a circle at the centre, almost like a Celtic cross. Around 50 stones are to be seen, in four avenues, meeting at the central circle of 13 stones, in the middle of which is a single, taller monolith. A CAIRN tomb has been excavated at the centre but this is of later date than the standing stones themselves, which are thought to have been erected before 2000 BC.

The stones are made of Lewisian gneiss and were covered by peat until they were excavated in the mid 19th century.

Like many stone circles, Callanish is believed to have been built along astronomical lines, and its western row points towards sunset at the equinoxes. More importantly, it is suggested that Callanish is the site mentioned by the ancient Greek historian Diodorus Siculus, who described an island of hyperboreans where, every 19 years, the moon came very close to the earth. Modern research shows that, at Callanish, the moon can be observed rising briefly before immediately setting (a phenomenon called a 'lunar standstill') at certain times of the year every 18.5 years.

Local folklore has it that the stones are the petrified forms of giants who plotted to resist the encroachment of Christianity.

Cannich Puma see ALIEN BIG CATS

Carnac

A huge complex of megalithic structures near Carnac in Brittany, France.

The area near to the town of Carnac in southern Brittany is home to one of the most important megalithic sites in Europe. Thousands of individual standing stones have been used to create an extraordinary complex of STONE ROWS, cromlechs (stone circles attached to dolmens) and DOLMENS.

The site also contains tumuli (see TUMULUS) under which passage graves have been discovered and excavated.

The stone alignments occur in three major groupings: the Alignments of Kerlescan, with 555 stones in thirteen rows, the Alignments of Kermario, with 1,029 stones in ten rows and, largest of all, the Alignments of Menec, with 1,169 stones in eleven rows. The Kercado dolmen is a particularly fine example and is rare in that it still stands under its original CAIRN. The Tumulus of Saint Michel is a huge mound constructed of earth heaped above a dolmen and at least two further burial chambers. There are also several large MENHIRS, notably the Manio Giant which is around 5.5 metres (over 18 feet) high.

It is believed to be the oldest continuously inhabited site in the Europe, dating back to at least 5700 BC, which means it is older than STONEHENGE, Knossos or the Egyptian PYRAMIDS. Nothing much is known about the people who created and inhabited the site. Findings from graves suggest that they were short, in both stature and lifespan. Whoever they were, their culture was an enduring one – it has been shown that some of the monuments at Carnac differ in age by as much as 5,000 years.

While the dolmens and tumuli had obvious purposes as burial sites, opinions differ on the intentions behind the construction of the stone circles and alignments. Some argue that these constructions had astronomical uses, whether as calendars of the seasons or for observing and marking the passage of celestial bodies across the heavens. Others maintain that their purposes were more likely to be symbolic, marking the territory of the local people or demonstrating their power and sophistication. Perhaps adding another monolith to an existing alignment was a regular event, helping to strengthen the bonds of the community by the immense co-operative labour that would be needed. Many stones have been moved or taken away completely over the generations, and it is probable that the remains of prehistoric Carnac, impressive as they are, bear little resemblance to the appearance of the site at its zenith. For this reason, much of the thinking about the meaning and purpose of the megaliths can only be speculative.

Carnarvon, 5th Earl of *see*
TUTANKHAMEN, CURSE OF

Carter, Howard *see* TUTANKHAMEN, CURSE OF

cats

Cats have historically been associated with superstitious beliefs.

In world folklore a vast range of (often contradictory) beliefs and superstitions have attached to cats. Although, along with dogs, they have long since been domesticated and have lived alongside humans, their independent behaviour, nocturnal habits and often apparently cruel behaviour when hunting have attracted suspicion.

The cat has long been associated with good and bad luck in equal measure, black cats especially so. To have a black cat cross your path was said by some to be bad luck, but to others seeing a black cat, or owning a black cat charm, was said to be good luck. Cats were also sometimes credited with the power of affecting the weather, perhaps leading to the somewhat ambivalent relationship between cats and sailors. In some areas a stray black cat on board ship was considered unlucky, but in others, a black cat would be taken on board as a good luck charm. Throwing a cat overboard to drown was believed to bring on a storm – in 1590 the North Berwick witches were accused of raising a storm in an attempt to drown James VI (James I of England) by baptizing a cat and then throwing it into the sea.

Cats are also as important a part of the popular image of witches and witchcraft as pointed hats, cauldrons and broomsticks, although their position as the primary animal companion of witches only really dates back to the 19th century. Cats were originally only one of the many animals associated with witches and in earlier folklore a witch was as likely to keep a hare, crow, owl or toad. However, cats did appear regularly in the anti-witchcraft propaganda of the Middle Ages. It was often claimed that a cat belonging to an accused witch was her familiar, assisting her in carrying out her evil work, and some witches were even accused of being able to assume the shape of a cat themselves.

Although the majority of the superstitions relating to cats have almost died out, there is still a belief among some people that they are particularly sensitive to the presence of ghosts and other paranormal phenomena.

Cerne Abbas Giant

The giant figure of a man cut into a chalk hillside in Dorset.

Near Cerne Abbas in Dorset a figure of a man appears on a hillside, marked out by cutting through the grass and soil to expose the white chalk beneath. The man is of gigantic proportions, around 55 metres (180 feet) tall, brandishes a huge club 36.5 metres (120 feet) long, and is shown in a state of sexual arousal.

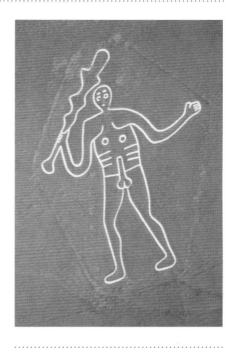

An aerial view of the 55-metre-tall Cerne Abbas Giant, cut into a chalk hillside in Dorset. (© TopFoto/Fortean)

Different theories exist as to who created this image and why. The fact that such a striking and obvious landmark is not mentioned in any documents before the 17th century leads many to believe that it cannot have existed before then. They explain its creation as either a caricature lampooning Oliver Cromwell, put there by the anti-Parliamentarian landowner, or as a kind of joke perpetrated by monks from a local religious house.

However, many landmarks and monuments that are known to be ancient go unmentioned in written records and those who argue for the figure's antiquity point out that an Iron Age earthwork has been found very close to the figure's head. A popular explanation is that the giant represents Hercules, who is often depicted in classical art as carrying a club, and that worship of the demigod came to the area along with the Romans, perhaps linking neatly with that of a local Celtic deity.

The giant's obvious virility led local people to ascribe fertility powers to it and local women hoping to conceive would spend the night there. It is a commonly believed myth that the scandalized Victorians covered up the offending member, and study has shown that the phallus has been cut to different lengths at different times, but the giant is now maintained in its full glory by the National Trust.

chalk figures

Giant figures created on hillsides by cutting away turf to reveal the chalk beneath.

In the south of England several hillsides are adorned by giant figures, mostly those of horses, 'drawn' by cutting lines through the turf to expose the chalk underneath. Famous examples include the CERNE ABBAS GIANT in Dorset and the UFFINGTON WHITE HORSE in Oxfordshire. Various claims are made as to the age of many of these chalk or hill figures. While the Uffington White Horse is now generally accepted as belonging to the Bronze Age (although it was traditionally believed to have been executed to commemorate Alfred the Great's victory over the Danes at nearby Edington), some argue that the Cerne Abbas Giant is only a few hundred years old.

Certainly, the cutting of chalk figures as some form of commemoration is a long-established activity, perhaps because it is relatively easy to perform and the contrast of the white figures against the green turf is a striking one, although one which requires maintenance. In the 19th century particularly there seems to have been something of a craze among southern English landowners, especially in Wiltshire, for the cutting of white horses, such as those at Alton Barnes

and Broad Town. During World War I soldiers exercising on Salisbury Plain often carved their regimental badges into the turf and as recently as 1999 a white horse was created at Devizes to mark the millennium.

Some of the figures that we see now have been radically changed in the years since they were first documented: at the Westbury White Horse in Wiltshire, the realistic 'modern' horse was cut in 1778, replacing an earlier design; it was reshaped again in 1873, and in the 20th century the horse was concreted and painted white to reduce the maintenance required.

As far as genuinely ancient chalk figures are concerned, there are various theories about their meaning. Some suggest that they represent local gods, the horse in particular being sacred to Celtic peoples, and played some part in religious observances. The fact that they are often best observed from the air lends credence to the idea that they were intended to be seen by heavenly eyes. Another explanation is that they are symbols of the tribes that created them and are a means of asserting ownership of areas of land.

In later times, many chalk figures were maintained by local people ('scouring' the chalk areas to keep them white and trimming back encroaching grass) long after their origins were forgotten. Some, particularly the Cerne Abbas Giant, became associated with fertility rites and traditional folk beliefs. On the other hand, some chalk figures whose existence was recorded in documents were allowed to become overgrown and lost.

changeling

In folklore, a fairy baby substituted for a kidnapped human child.

One of the oldest traditions of European fairy lore is the tendency for fairies to steal human babies and leave a substitute in their place. Various tales suggest that many fairy children die before they are born, and that those which do survive are often feeble, stunted or deformed. A healthy human baby may be stolen to reinforce the fairy stock and revive their dwindling race, and the sickly fairy baby, called a changeling, is left in its place. Babies most at risk are those who have not yet been christened, and whose parents have not taken adequate precautions, such as leaving something made of iron, for example a set of tongs or a knife, in the cradle – an infallible protection against fairies, who cannot bear iron. The changeling is usually identifiable by its ill temper, ugliness and voracious appetite; no matter how much it is fed, it always wants more, but remains scrawny and weak. It may have some physical deformity, such as a crooked back, and will grow a full set of teeth long before a human child would, by its first birthday or even earlier. Alternatively, the fairies may leave a piece of wood called a 'stock', shaped roughly like a child and endowed with the appearance of life, or an ancient and wizened fairy of no further use to its tribe, who prefers a cosseted life being fed by its human 'mother'.

If the changeling can be made to reveal its true nature in time, the fairies must return the human child unharmed. In some tales, a baby that was suspected of being a changeling would be deliberately tortured so that its fairy parents would take it back; one popular method was to place it on a shovel and hold it over a fire. If the changeling was an old fairy, it might be tricked into revealing its true age by various ploys, the favourite being to boil water in eggshells so that it would say something like, 'I have lived many hundreds of years, but I have never seen brewing in an eggshell before!' When a changeling has been forced to reveal its fairy nature, it will disappear up the chimney, cursing, and the real baby will be restored, being found at the door, in its cradle or at the nearest fairy mound. See also FAIRIES.

Chariots of the Gods *see* DÄNIKEN, ERICH VON

Cincinnati premonition

A classic case which is cited as an example of a premonition, in this instance in the form of a precognitive dream.

In 1979 David Booth, an office worker in Cincinnati, had the same dream ten nights in a row. In his dream Booth would see an American Airlines jet take off from an airport, then crash and burst into flames. On 22 May, spurred by the apparent reality of his dreams,

Booth contacted the Federal Aviation Authority (FAA). The FAA apparently took his dreams seriously and attempted to identify the type of plane (possibly a 727 or DC-10 from Booth's descriptions) and which flight it was. Booth awoke from his last dream on 25 May. Later that day American Airlines Flight 191, a DC-10 leaving from Chicago's O'Hare International Airport, lost one of its engines on take-off. The plane flipped over on its back and burst into flames, exactly as predicted by Booth. A total of 273 people were killed in the disaster.

Those who doubt whether this was a 'real' premonition point to the fact that airlines and related organizations must receive calls of this type regularly, and that at some point a 'premonition' will come true.

In 2003 David Booth had what he believed to be a second premonition, in which a large object from space descends towards the South Pole and an enormous explosion takes place in western USA.

cities, lost *see* LOST CITIES

comets

A comet is a type of heavenly body to which many interpretations and theories have attached throughout history.

A comet is a body of rock and ice moving through space that periodically passes close to the earth on its eccentric orbit around the sun. In earlier times the appearance of a comet in the night sky was often taken as an evil OMEN. This was perhaps because, unlike the familiar charted stars and planets, a comet's appearance was unpredictable and its movements erratic, leading to its being interpreted as a frightening disturbance in the natural course of events. It was an obvious step to conclude that a comet was a kind of heavenly message that mankind dare not ignore.

This association between comets and disaster is seen in many cultures. The ancient Romans, for example, believed that a fiery comet appeared after the assassination of Julius Caesar. A comet was said to have appeared to the Jews before their unsuccessful revolt against Rome that led to the destruction of Jerusalem in AD 70. In South America, the Incas observed a comet before the arrival of their conqueror Pizarro in 1531. One of the most famous comets, Halley's Comet, was believed to presage the Norman Conquest in 1066 and is thought to be depicted in the Bayeux Tapestry. It was also associated with the outbreak of the Black Death in the 14th century. Legend has it that Pope Calixtus III later identified the comet as an instrument of the Devil and formally excommunicated it in 1456.

However, the association of comets with disasters is not just a phenomenon of the distant past. When the earth passed through the tail of Halley's Comet in 1910, newspaper reports spread a fear that poisonous substances contained within it would kill millions of people. An example of a more extreme reaction to the approach of a comet occurred in 1997, when one photograph of Hale-Bopp appeared to show a small dot near to it. This prompted a claim that a spaceship containing aliens was hiding behind the comet – an occurrence that was supposedly taken as a sign by members of the ill-fated Heaven's Gate movement that the time was right for their mass suicide.

In the early 1980s, the British astronomer Fred Hoyle offered the theory that evolution on earth was driven by the periodic arrival of viruses transported by comets. This formed part of his overall criticism of the mainstream explanation of the origins of life and the process of evolution. Although this was the subject of much derision within the scientific community at the time, the idea that there could be extraterrestrial life in the form of micro-organisms existing in comets and other bodies in space has not been universally dismissed.

contemporary legends *see* URBAN LEGENDS

continents, lost *see* LOST CONTINENTS

corpse candle *see* WILL-O'-THE-WISP

corpse light *see* WILL-O'-THE-WISP

crop circles
Mysterious flattened circular areas in growing cereal crops.

In southern England in the late 1970s and early 1980s farmers were baffled by the overnight appearance of strange circular patterns in their fields of standing cereal crops. The patterns were created by flattening stalks, but the force or forces that produced this effect were a mystery.

Initially the patterns were generally simple and based upon circles; however, as the phenomenon developed, the patterns became more complex and advanced, with interlinked circles of varying sizes, swirling patterns, and symmetrical designs of geometric precision. Various explanations have been suggested.

One theory is that the circles are entirely natural, having been caused by the effect of fungi or infection on the growing crops, causing the stalks to weaken and bend. The patterns are, therefore, produced completely by chance. Another explanation is that localized meteorological effects are to blame, such as freak tornado-like winds, BALL LIGHTNING or the hypothetical plasma vortex. However, the complexity and precision of many of the patterns tend to count against these explanations – certainly for all occurrences of the phenomenon.

Others have suggested that the circular patterns are caused by extraterrestrial action, whether accidentally, marking the places where the aliens' spacecraft have landed

An incredibly complex crop circle which appeared in a field of wheat near Alton Barnes, Wiltshire, on 8 August 1997. It measured 71 metres (234 feet) across, and included 192 small circles around the edges of its snowflake design.
(© English Heritage/HIP/TopFoto)

and taken off, or deliberately, as some kind of as yet unexplained messages to humankind. Satellites originating on earth have also been blamed, with conspiracy theorists suggesting that the military is secretly testing a microwave beam weapon on empty fields.

Many people now believe that crop circles are nothing more than elaborate hoaxes, which have fooled a public all too ready to believe in aliens and conspiracies. Indeed, in 1991 two Englishmen, Doug Bower and Dave Chorley, famously confessed to having created crop circles since 1978, and various methods of producing patterns have been demonstrated. There is no doubt that hoaxers have been shown to have been involved in some circles, but many people hold that this does not adequately explain all of the recorded occurrences. The fact that crop circles have appeared in many parts of the world, including some relatively remote areas, is cited as evidence against the hoax theory. There is also at least one historical precedent for the phenomenon – a case known as the MOWING DEVIL, dating from the 17th century.

Some crop circle researchers, know as cereologists, claim to have detected strange electromagnetic fields within certain circles, causing radio interference and the malfunction of mobile phones (see ELECTROMAGNETIC PHENOMENA). This leads them to conclude that some electromagnetic force is responsible for the circles. However, this is not necessarily extraterrestrial in origin, but could be a product of unexplained anomalies in the earth's magnetic field. They also claim that seeds taken from affected crops are seen to have undergone mutation and that their subsequent growth is faster and stronger than unaffected seeds from the same field.

While films have been made of people setting out to create crop circles, and do-it-yourself instructions are available on the Internet, it remains true that many circles have not been 'claimed' by hoaxers or anyone else and, in the absence of reliable witnesses to their appearance, their origins remain unexplained. There are also occasionally examples which are so large, complex and accurately produced that the suggestion that they could have been produced in a single night, unobserved, seems unbelievable. For example, a formation that appeared at Milk Hill, near Alton Barnes, Wiltshire, in 2001, was nearly 300 metres (980 feet) across and contained 409 separate circles in a precise pattern of arms spiralling outwards from a central point.

Crying Boy

The name given to a painting, popular as a print in the 1980s, that was linked with stories of a curse or jinx.

In the autumn of 1985, the British tabloid newspaper *The Sun* printed a story about a chip pan fire at a house in Yorkshire. Apparently, the house and its contents were badly damaged, but a somewhat mawkish print of a child crying, dubbed the 'Crying Boy', had escaped the fire unscathed. *The Sun* went on to print a series of articles about the Crying Boy, saying that it was bad luck and was causing fires in the homes of those who owned it. According to the newspaper, firemen were well aware of the cursed and dangerous nature of the picture, having seen it in the ruins of many burnt-out homes. They said that after the initial article many readers contacted them, relating stories of the fires that had occurred in their homes after they had hung a copy of the print on their walls.

The Sun offered to destroy any now unwanted copies of the print, and claimed that they flooded in. Somewhat distastefully perhaps, they burned the prints on large bonfires. For a time, the story was very popular, and the legend of the curse of the Crying Boy became widely known. However, by early 1986 the story died out, and while there are some who claim that the curse of the Crying Boy still causes fires, most have forgotten all about it.

D

Däniken, Erich von (1935–)

A hugely successful author who popularized the idea that aliens visited the earth in the distant past, leaving behind archaeological evidence of their interaction with ancient human cultures.

Erich von Däniken was born in Switzerland and, after working in the hotel trade for a number of years, he began writing in 1959, developing an interest in the frequent references to contact with sky gods and similar intelligent beings that appear in the texts of some ancient civilizations. The contemporary academic position was that these textual and pictorial portrayals were either allegorical or represented wise men dressed in ceremonial costume. Von Däniken suggested that they might be literal descriptions of alien beings with whom there had been contact.

Although von Däniken was not the originator of this ANCIENT ASTRONAUTS hypothesis he became its most prolific spokesperson. In 1968 he published his first book, *Chariots of the Gods?*, which became a worldwide bestseller. In the next decade he sold 40 million copies of this book, and a string of sequels, in which he discussed evidence gathered from around the world. He included details of various anomalous artefacts that had been found by archaeologists – for example, an item found in Persia which appeared to be a battery, dating from centuries before its modern invention. Sceptics point out that throughout history there have been instances where technology has arisen out of accidental discoveries, long before human science was able to explain the processes involved. Even if we accept von Däniken's interpretation of the purpose of the items, they could simply be examples of technology that was accidentally discovered and then later abandoned or forgotten until reproduced in the modern era.

Von Däniken's worldwide public profile diminished during the 1980s. However, he remained a popular lecturer and media figure in German-speaking countries, and published further books in the late 1990s. See also NAZCA LINES.

Dartmoor Beast *see* ALIEN BIG CATS

Da Vinci Code, The

Controversial bestselling novel which has helped to promote interest in theories concerning the Holy Grail legend and the role of Mary Magdalene in the history of Christianity.

In 2003, the US author Dan Brown published *The Da Vinci Code*, a sequel to his 2000 novel *Angels and Demons*. The story combines the popular literary genres of detective fiction, thriller and conspiracy theory, and was an instant worldwide bestseller. It has now been translated into around 44 languages, and a film adaptation was released in 2006. Part of the advertising campaign for the novel was a competition – the book itself included four codes, and the reader who solved all four would win a trip to Paris. In fact, several thousand people solved the codes, so the winner was drawn from a list of these at random.

The novel begins with the murder of the curator of the Louvre Museum in Paris, on whose naked body have been left several cryptic messages. The solving of the mystery requires the interpretation of these messages, together with others supposedly hidden inside Leonardo da Vinci's paintings *Mona Lisa* and *The Last Supper*, and a number of other anagrams and puzzles. The solution is found to be

connected with the possible location of the HOLY GRAIL, a secret which has been preserved for 2,000 years by a mysterious society called the Priory of Sion, along with the KNIGHTS TEMPLAR and the Catholic organization Opus Dei. A key element of the story is the premise that the figure seated at the right hand of Jesus in *The Last Supper* is not John the Apostle, but Mary Magdalene, who, according to the novel, was Jesus' wife, and was pregnant with his child at the time of the Crucifixion. The absence of a chalice in the painting is seen as proof that Leonardo was a member of the Priory of Sion, and that by deliberately leaving it out, he was indicating that the 'Holy Grail' was not, as the Church has led us to believe, an actual chalice used by Jesus at the Last Supper, but was instead a symbolic reference to Mary Magdalene, the bearer of Christ's bloodline. The Grail relics, traced in the novel to a possible location in a secret crypt beneath ROSLYN CHAPEL, near Edinburgh, are in fact Mary Magdalene's bones and documents testifying to this bloodline. The Grail-keepers have been guarding the secret of Christ's descendants to this day.

The novel's popularity helped to spur a widespread interest in theories concerning the Holy Grail and the role of Mary Magdalene in the history of Christianity, but many Christians hold these theories to be heretical, since they question the entire legitimacy of Christian history. *The Da Vinci Code* is influenced by several other works, in particular the 1982 book *The Holy*

Blood and the Holy Grail, by Michael Baigent, Richard Leigh and Henry Lincoln, which is actually mentioned in the novel. Because it claims to contain elements of historical truth within its fictional narrative, many of its readers have mistakenly accepted it as being factually correct throughout (a mistake which has had positive benefits for the tourist industries of Paris and Edinburgh). These historical claims, together with the author's tendency to treat what are just (often controversial) opinions within unresolved debates as fact, have attracted a great deal of criticism from historians. However, many historians have actually benefited indirectly from this by taking the opportunity to write one of the growing number of books published with the sole purpose of pointing out the novel's historical inaccuracies and false assumptions.

Dean, James

A modern legend that the car in which James Dean died was cursed.

On 30 September 1955, 24-year-old actor James Dean was killed when his rare Porsche 550 Spyder, named by him the 'Little Bastard', crashed

James Dean's Porsche, the 'Little Bastard', after the accident that killed him.
(1999 Topham Picturepoint)

with another car. This was the first in a series of events that have led a number of people to believe that the car and all of its parts were cursed.

The wreck of the car was bought by George Barris, who intended to salvage some of its parts. When the wreck was taken to his garage, the engine came loose as it was being unloaded and broke a mechanic's legs. While popular versions of the following episodes of the legend vary, it is generally said that the engine was then installed in a racing car by Dr William Eschrid, but the car overturned on a bend in its next race and seriously injured the driver. Dr Troy McHenry was taking part in the same race, and his car crashed after he had lost control of it. McHenry died – he had Little Bastard's drive shaft fitted to his car. The curse is also said to have afflicted someone who bought two of the tyres from Dean's vehicle – they both blew out at the same time, forcing the vehicle off the road.

Further instances of the 'curse' are also repeated. It is said that when a teenager tried to steal the car's steering wheel, his arm was badly cut by a piece of metal, and that other potential thieves were thwarted in similar ways. A fire broke out at a garage that later stored what was left of the car, causing a great deal of damage to everything but the wreck itself, and when the car was being displayed as part of a road safety exhibition, it fell off its stand and broke someone's hip. The wreck also seems to have caused problems to those who transported it. One truck driver crashed when he was moving

the Little Bastard. He was thrown from his vehicle, and died when the wreck came free and landed on him. The car vanished in 1960, and has not been seen since.

While some claim that the Little Bastard was truly jinxed, others believe that the incidents associated with it are simply coincidences.

devil dogs *see* BLACK DOGS

Devil's Footprints

An intriguing 19th-century case from Devon involving the appearance of a set of mysterious 'footprints' in the snow that reportedly stretched in an unbroken line across several parishes.

On the morning of 8 February 1855 the residents of parishes in south Devon between Topsham and Totnes awoke to discover a line of what appeared to be footprints, in the fresh snow, following a continuous meandering course for what was claimed to be a distance of over 100 miles (160 kilometres). The tracks were thought to have appeared some time in the early hours, as the last snow had fallen at around midnight.

On 16 February *The Times* reported that:

> The track appeared more like that of a biped than a quadruped, and the steps were generally eight inches in advance of each other. The impressions of the feet closely resembled that of a donkey's shoe, and measured from an inch and a

half to (in some instances) two and a half inches across. Here and there it appeared as if cloven, but in the generality of the steps the shoe was continuous, and, from the snow in the centre remaining entire, merely showing the outer crest of the foot, it must have been convex.

There were reports that the tracks appeared to have been made by something that could travel over rooftops, through or over walls and through narrow drainpipes. The tracks were said to stop on one side of the Exe estuary only to continue again on the other side. At certain points in the journey the tracks appeared to go up to, and then away from, the doors of houses.

The incident certainly caused something of a stir at the time. The newspaper coverage brought forth more claims and a number of theories as to the cause. The scientific community made suggestions ranging from escaped kangaroos to a hot air balloon trailing a rope or chain. However, most of these seem to be almost as far-fetched as the idea amongst some of the more superstitious locals that the footprints were evidence of a visit from the Devil.

The story has gained something of the status of a local legend and it is now very difficult to ascertain whether many of the claims attaching to it have any basis in truth – it is likely that even the original reports were greatly exaggerated. However, to this day,

no widely accepted solution to the mystery has ever been provided.

disappearances

A disappearance is a sudden vanishing of someone or something.

As used in discussions of forteana, the term 'disappearances' applies to the phenomenon of sudden vanishings of people, animals or objects (or the realization that they are no longer present). It is the opposite of the phenomenon of APPEARANCES and both might indicate the beginning and ending of a hypothetical teleportation transaction. This hypothetical process may manifest differently in different sub-categories of phenomena.

There are very few unequivocal observations of disappearances for the obvious reason; while appearances and disappearances can both happen unexpectedly, at least things that appear are available for study. Objects supposedly teleported, or moved by poltergeists, are only referred to as apports if or when they reappear in the same place or at another location. Stories about animals that disappear are more prevalent in folklore, in which they are often regarded as supernatural creatures such as BLACK DOGS.

Uncovering the truth about well-known cases is time-consuming and can sometimes raise more questions that it answers. An example is the alleged disappearance of David Lang, in September 1880, a story that is entrenched in forteana and ufology and which has been researched by many diligent forteans and historians. Variations of the same story sometimes substitute other names for David Lang: eg Oliver Larch, Orion Williamson and Charles Ashmore. Lang, who farmed near Gallatin, Tennessee, is said to have vanished while crossing a field in full view of five people. Researchers found no record of a David Lang or his family in Gallatin. The earliest account is by writer Stuart Palmer, published in 1953. However, it was later proved that Palmer had forged documents in support of his account. The story is also credited to a contemporary character called Joe Mulhatten, famous for winning 'liar's contests' for tall stories. When researchers pointed out the similarity between Palmer's account of Lang and two short stories by US writer Ambrose Bierce (1842–c.1914) – 'The Difficulty of Crossing a Field' and 'Charles Ashmore's Trail' – both published in 1909, Palmer's proponents suggested that Bierce may have heard the story from Mulhatten. This was patently untrue as the names Orion Williamson and Charles Ashmore are the protagonists of Bierce's stories. It was far more likely that Palmer's re-telling was inspired by Bierce's fiction and cleverly exploited the real existence of Mulhatten. Despite this detailed exposé, the various versions of the Lang story have been copied endlessly in the fortean literature without correction or qualification. Curiously, Bierce himself famously disappeared; he was last seen in Chihuahua, Mexico, at the end of 1913, having joined Pancho Villa's army as an observer.

However, there is a considerable body of literature on larger-scale disappearances. Perhaps it is not surprising that many of these are connected with tempestuous storms and dangerous seas. For example, the FLANNAN ISLES MYSTERY, when three lighthousekeepers vanished from a remote island off the west coast of Scotland; the more famous disappearance of the entire crew of the MARY CELESTE; and the loss of Flight 19, a group of five US Navy planes, off the coast of Florida in December 1945, which was inevitably blamed on the BERMUDA TRIANGLE.

Despite the many real-life vanishings for mundane reasons, hoaxes and legends, there are still cases of genuine mystery, largely because of a lack of real evidence one way or another. For example, what happened to the first British colony in America, established in 1587, on Roanoke Island, in what is now North Carolina? When their re-supply ship returned from England in 1590, three years later, there was no sign of more than a hundred men, women and children that had been left there. It is thought likely that, facing starvation if they stayed put, they integrated with native tribes and moved away with them. Similarly, the disappearance of a small battalion of the Royal Norfolk Regiment in August 1915, while fighting at GALLIPOLI during World War I, left wild speculation behind it. The men were last seen advancing into fog behind enemy lines, but this entered the mythology of UFOs as an alien abduction. Military historians believe the group got lost and were massacred, but have not been able to establish it as fact.

Many historical vanishings have been retold in films, and although some would dispute whether it is actually based on fact, the haunting and evocative *Picnic at Hanging Rock* (1975) is one of the most popular. It is based on the alleged disappearance of a party of schoolgirls who never returned from an outing to the HANGING ROCK reserve in Australia's Victoria state on 14 February 1900. Each year on Valentine's Day the film is shown at the picnic grounds after dusk.

dolmen

A megalithic structure consisting of a flat stone on top of two or more standing stones.

'Dolmen' is the name given to the type of prehistoric megalithic structure, common in the British Isles and France, consisting of a relatively flat stone supported on two STANDING STONES. The word seems to be of Celtic origin (probably coming from the Breton *dol* or *taol* meaning 'table' and *men* meaning 'stone' or from the Cornish *tolmēn* meaning 'hole of stone') and is first recorded in English in the 19th century. Dolmens are sometimes also referred to as 'quoits'.

It is thought that dolmens are the remains of tombs, and many grave sites have been found beneath them. When they were built they would probably have been topped by a CAIRN of stones and perhaps a mound of earth, but in many cases these have disappeared,

Lanyon Quoit, near Penzance, Cornwall – an impressive dolmen through which it was apparently once possible to ride a horse. (© TopFoto/HIP)

exposing the giant stones. Many fine examples of dolmens can be found at CARNAC in Brittany. In British folklore they were traditionally known as devil's or fairies' tables, while their enormous size gave rise to legends that they were built by giants.

dragon

One of the most familiar of all mythological beasts, which might have been inspired by real-life animals encountered by early humans.

Described and feared by human

cultures worldwide from the earliest times, the dragon exists in a vast range of forms and abodes in myth and legend.

The classical Western dragon is a malevolent fire-breathing monster encased in an armour of shimmering scales, borne upon four powerful limbs with talon-equipped feet, and sporting a pair of huge leathery wings, plus a long tail tipped with a poisonous barb or arrow-headed sting. Such was the monster reputedly faced by St George, believed to have been a martyr in Palestine, probably before the time of Constantine.

According to a familiar version of the legend (of which there are countless variations), the dragon inhabited a lake near Sylene in Libya, and threatened to lay waste to the town unless it was fed daily with a female virgin. Learning of Sylene's plight, George arrived to do battle with the monster on the day that the king's daughter was due to be sacrificed. Dispatching the dragon after a furious confrontation, George saved the princess's life. Although it is unclear why this Middle Eastern figure became the patron saint of England, in later versions the location of this battle was transplanted to England – the two most popular sites are Brinsop in Herefordshire, and a flat-topped hill near Oxfordshire's famous UFFINGTON WHITE HORSE.

Most British dragons, however, are of the worm variety – lacking wings and legs, with lengthy, elongated bodies, and emitting poisonous vapours rather than fire. Probably the most famous British dragon legend is that of the LAMBTON WORM of north-eastern England, which began as a small newt-like beast thrown into a well by the heir of Lambton Castle during the 14th century, but grew so large that it eventually left the well, wrapped itself around a nearby hill and began devouring the local farmers' livestock to sustain its immense bulk. See also LINTON WORM.

Other tales of Western dragons include the two-legged, winged wyvern; the lindorm (a wingless wyvern); the guivre (a limbless, wingless dragon resembling a monstrous snake); and the amphiptere (a legless winged dragon). Even more bizarre than these was the tarasque. Originating in Asia Minor and said to be the offspring of a famous biblical monster called the leviathan, it was claimed that it was an extraordinary six-legged, lion-headed dragon with a shell of spikes upon its back. Migrating westward, it eventually reached Provence, where it terrorized travellers along or upon the River Rhône – until St Martha tamed it by sprinkling it with holy water.

Equally strange was the shaggy beast or peluda, a water dragon of French lore from the Middle Ages. Allegedly a survivor of the Great Flood, this long-necked monster had a green furry body bristling with poisonous quills, turtle-like feet and a serpent's head. It frequented the banks of the River Huisne, from where it made many forays into the surrounding countryside to kill not only the local livestock but also any maidens or children that it could find – until it was eventually slain by a valiant swordsman who sliced its tail in half, killing it instantly.

Our erstwhile belief in Western dragons was probably inspired at least in part by encounters with real animals, such as huge monitor lizards or gigantic pythons, or even with the fossilized remains of dinosaurs and winged pterosaurs. In his book *The Dragons of Eden* (1977), Cornell University scientist Professor Carl Sagan contemplated a still closer link between fictional dragons and factual giant reptiles – speculating that perhaps some prehistoric reptiles survived into more recent times than currently accepted by science, and that mankind's myths and legends of dragons may stem from ancient inherited memories of our long-distant ancestors' encounters with living dinosaurs.

Oriental dragons are very different from the dragons of the West. Oriental mythology includes many kinds of dragons, and collectively they influence and control every aspect of nature and the affairs of mankind. In stark contrast to their Western counterparts, Oriental dragons are exceedingly wise, are capable of flying without the aid of wings and (apart from spasmodic outbursts of anger) they appear relatively benevolent in their interactions with humanity. They are also revered – to the extent that many of the East's most ancient and august human lineages claim direct descent from a dragon.

E

Earhart, Amelia Mary (1897–1937)

US aviator who disappeared on a round-the-world flight.

Amelia Earhart achieved fame by becoming the first woman to fly across the Atlantic, first as a passenger in 1928, then as a solo pilot in 1932. In 1935, she also made the first solo flight from Hawaii to California. As an inspiring and engaging celebrity, she made use of her fame to advance the cause of feminism as well as to argue on behalf of commercial aviation.

Eager to establish further flying records, she decided to attempt a round-the-world flight, setting off with her navigator, Fred Noonan, from Miami in 1937. After arriving at Lae, New Guinea, Earhart took off on another leg of the journey, aiming to land at a small island, Howland Island, in the mid-Pacific. The aircraft was in radio contact with a US ship throughout the flight but Earhart's communications grew more and more faint until they stopped altogether.

The US authorities immediately initiated an extensive air and sea search, but, after finding nothing, abandoned the attempt after two

Amelia Earhart photographed in 1932 after becoming the first woman to fly solo across the Atlantic. She disappeared five years later while attempting a round-the-world flight.
(© Mary Evans Picture Library)

weeks. No trace of the aircraft or its crew has ever been found on land or beneath the sea, despite several private expeditions, including one as recently as 2004.

Various theories have been advanced to account for Earhart's disappearance, including the idea that she was captured by the then expansionist Japanese and executed as a spy. There have also been unconfirmed sightings of Earhart, and there are those that believe she continued her life anonymously on a South Pacific island. However, the most likely explanation is that, owing to navigational error and changing weather conditions, her plane simply ran out of fuel and crashed into the Pacific, a mere pinprick in that vast ocean.

earth lights

Mysterious displays of light seen in particular areas.

In many parts of the world there have long been descriptions of mysterious lights seen at night in particular places. These lights can be small or large, stationary or mobile, taking a particular form or changing in shape, and can appear in various colours. The thing that they have in common is that they are seen relatively close to the ground rather than in the sky.

In folklore the lights were often attributed to supernatural or magical phenomena such as ghostly spirits, the breath of DRAGONS, sorcerers in flight or dancing FAIRIES, and they were given names like 'spooklights', 'min-min'

(in Australia) or 'the Devil's Bonfires' (Derbyshire). The term 'earth lights' was introduced by the British author and researcher Paul Devereux in the 1980s – it reflects the theory that the lights are the result of processes within the ground.

Many observers had noticed that EARTHQUAKES were sometimes preceded or followed by this kind of anomalous light display, and some suggested that the lights were caused by the earthquakes. This led many people to look for links between earthquakes and reports of UFO sightings. However, others argued that the lights were seen in places where earthquakes were rare. It was in the 1960s that studies of the phenomena began to link them with the presence of geological fault lines and anomalies in the earth's magnetic field. Tectonic strain (the constant subterranean pressure produced by the earth's tectonic plates shifting against one another) coinciding with areas of marked faulting and certain mineral deposits was identified as the cause of earth lights, which are essentially generated through the release of electrons from the earth into the air. One such area was Hessdalen in Norway, where mysterious lights had been seen for generations, often accompanied by subterranean rumbling. A study beginning there in the 1980s produced significant photographs of the light phenomena.

Sceptics claim that many sightings of earth lights are in fact simply effects created by the headlights of unseen distant vehicles or (particularly in hot regions) by light being reflected from another area, along similar lines to the well-known mirages in deserts. However, those who argue against this explanation point out that earth lights have been seen in some places for many years, long before the invention of electric light, and that there have been cases where no potential source of reflected light could be identified. See also ELECTROMAGNETIC PHENOMENA.

earthquakes

Shakings of the earth caused by movements in the earth's crust.

Throughout the ages, earthquakes have been seen as a terrifying and destructive force. The ancient Greeks believed they were caused by giants imprisoned under the earth by Zeus, while other cultures ascribed them to the movements of a giant animal, such as an elephant or a tortoise, on which the world rests.

Modern science has established that most earthquakes are caused by movements in the earth's crust, which is made up of rigid tectonic plates that can shift in relation to one another. When such a shifting occurs great stress is built up until it is suddenly released. Some earthquakes are caused by volcanic activity, which again leads to the build-up and release of stresses in the earth. Earthquakes happen somewhere on the planet every day, but while we tend to think of them as dramatic events, most are so minor that they are only detected

by special monitoring instruments (seismometers).

However, when a major earthquake occurs, the damage caused to buildings and the loss of life can be terrible indeed. Perhaps the worst earthquake in history devastated the Chinese province of Shensi in 1556, resulting in an estimated 800,000 deaths. In 1755, over 70,000 people died when an earthquake all but destroyed the Portuguese city of Lisbon. San Francisco suffered great damage in the very powerful quake of 1906.

Various effects can accompany earthquakes, including more minor tremors either before the main earthquake (foreshocks) or following it (aftershocks). Landslides can be triggered, and the surface of the earth can be liquefied due to the release of underground water. The most terrifying consequence is undoubtedly the tsunami, which is an enormous sea wave or series of waves generated by an undersea earthquake. The destruction caused when such a wave reaches inhabited land can be dreadful. The most recent example of this is the earthquake that took place in the Indian Ocean in 2004, causing a tsunami that devastated coastal regions throughout South-East Asia.

Another effect accompanying some earthquakes is that known as 'earthquake lights' or 'quake lights'. Accounts of strange lights appearing before or during earthquakes go back as far as the ancient Greeks but scientists have always been sceptical of their reality. However, photographs proving their existence were taken in Japan in the 1960s. These light effects vary in colour, duration and intensity and have been compared to the auroras (see AURORA BOREALIS), 'tongues of fire' or glowing balls of light. Particularly dramatic light displays were documented during the 1995 earthquake in Kobe, Japan. Various explanations have been put forward, including the ignition of underground gases or the ionizing piezoelectric effect of rock surfaces grinding against one another, but no completely satisfactory theory has been developed. However, the fact that these lights are often seen to precede a tremor means that many seismologists continue to study the phenomenon in the hope that this may lead to a means of predicting future earthquakes. See also EARTH LIGHTS; ELECTROMAGNETIC PHENOMENA.

earthworks

Ancient fortifications made by digging ditches and heaping up earth.

Earthworks are the most ancient surviving form of structure built by human beings, and examples are found in many parts of the world. The basic method remained the same, whether prehistoric people were constructing religious sites such as HENGES, burial mounds or fortifications: a mixture of earth and stones was dug up to form a ditch and then heaped up to create a bank or mound.

The British Isles contain many impressive examples, including the great mound and ditch at SILBURY HILL and the fortress known as Maiden Castle in Dorset. The latter is an Iron Age site at Fordington Hill, near Dorchester, covering an area of 120 acres. It is thought that a Neolithic barrow was first built there in c.3000 BC and then later adapted into a fort by the digging of further ditches and building of earth ramparts. It survived as a sizeable settlement until, after being stormed by the Romans in AD 43, it was finally abandoned in c.70 AD. The Badbury Rings in Dorset is another fine instance of an Iron Age hill fort, with three concentric ditches and ramparts. The nearby Neolithic barrows suggest that, like Maiden Castle, its occupancy stretches back even further in time.

In North America, substantial prehistoric earthworks have been found, the largest of which are those at Poverty Point in Louisiana, dated c.1800 BC. This settlement was so large in scale (including a main system of concentric semicircles almost 1.6 kilometres (1 mile) wide) that it was difficult to appreciate at ground level. Only with the advent of aerial photography was its complexity revealed. Even earlier are earthworks at Watson Break, also in Louisiana, which were constructed in c.3300 BC. Little is known about the cultures that produced these constructions, but their discovery opened up a tremendously important new chapter in the study of pre-Columbian America.

Some earthworks were built as boundaries rather than fortifications or settlements, and in Britain this continued into Anglo-Saxon times. Offa's Dyke, a ditch and bank running for some 240 kilometres (150 miles), was built by the Mercian king Offa in c.785 to mark his border with the Welsh. This took the place of Wat's Dyke, an earthwork built further east for the same purpose about 80 years before.

The reason for building such earthworks as boundaries and defensive sites is clear enough, but we can only guess at the purpose of many prehistoric constructions – it is generally contended that they had some kind of ritual or religious significance. Whatever the nature, or assumed purpose, of individual earthworks is, their common factor is the phenomenal amount of vision, planning and communal work required in building them. Such efforts can only be justified by a shared belief in the importance of what was being built. The fact that these cultures with comparatively low levels of technology were able to create monuments that endure to this day, and still have the power to impress us with their very scale, remains astonishing.

Easter Island statues

Enigmatic giant stone heads on Easter Island in the South Pacific.

In 1722, the Dutch navigator Jakob Roggeveen (1659–1729) discovered an island in the South Pacific which, as it was Easter Day, he named Easter Island. It was inhabited by a Polynesian people who called themselves the Rapanui. The ancestors of these people had erected a remarkable series of giant stone statues known as *moai*.

While many of the statues take the form of giant heads, a large number also have complete torsos which have sometimes been buried by the natural movement of soil. The number of statues has been estimated at between 800 and 1000, with many unfinished examples still lying in the quarry where they all seem to have been carved. They vary widely in size, from around 180 centimetres (6 feet) tall to an enormous 20-metre (65-foot) specimen that was never completely carved out of its native rock – a volcanic tuff that is relatively easily worked.

Some of the statues were decorated with eyes made from coral and many were surmounted by a circular ornament made from scoria, a different variety of lava from that used to form the main figures. The significance of these 'topknots' is uncertain, with some theories describing them as hats or headdresses, others as stylized hair, but most agreeing that they indicated higher status of some kind.

It is thought that the figures represent gods or sacred chiefs and that they were erected in places that had religious significance. It is difficult to be certain, as much of the native culture and tradition was lost when Easter Island was repeatedly raided by slavers in the 19th century, greatly depopulating the island. Many statues appear to have been toppled by the natives, perhaps as a consequence of

Some of the mysterious giant statues, or *moai*, on Easter Island. (© TopFoto)

disputes and rivalries between chiefs or religious leaders.

How the statues were moved from the quarry when finished cannot be known for certain. It is thought that a system of ropes and rollers would have been used but that this became less possible as the islanders gradually stripped the island of its trees. Local legend has it that the finished statues simply walked to their appointed destinations.

The island's culture was no doubt shaped by its isolation – Chile is over 4,000 kilometres (2,500 miles) away to the east; Tahiti 3,200 kilometres (2,000 miles) to the west – and tablets have been found there inscribed in a script that has never been satisfactorily deciphered. However, it has been shown that the statues are not unique but have resemblances to figures carved by the Polynesian people of the Marquesas Islands.

eclipses

The masking of a heavenly body by another passing between it and an observer.

There are various types of eclipse. When the moon passes between the sun and the earth this is known as a solar eclipse. A lunar eclipse occurs when the earth passes between the sun and the moon. When the eclipsed body seems to be completely hidden this is called a total eclipse. Partial eclipses are, however, more common. An annular eclipse occurs when an outer ring of the eclipsed body remains visible.

Throughout the centuries, and in many countries around the world, eclipses have been interpreted as bad OMENS. The loss of the light from sun or moon could have been terrifying to peoples with no sophisticated grasp of astronomy and no knowledge that the effect was transitory. Some people have suggested that in the past an eclipse may have been interpreted as the end of the world. Some cultures chose to explain the phenomenon by saying that the heavenly body was being eaten by a monster, and they would carry out rituals to drive the beast away.

Various phenomena can be experienced by people from within an area affected by a solar eclipse. Observers report that as the moon begins to pass across the sun there is a strange sensation of a distinct change in the atmosphere. Animals begin to behave as if it were evening, and day-opening flowers close up. As the darkness increases the ambient temperature falls. Where the remaining light of the sun passes through narrow spaces, such as between the leaves of a tree, images of the now crescent-shaped sun will be projected onto surfaces below. Bands of shadows appear on the ground. The sun's corona, or outer atmosphere, becomes visible as a brilliant ring around the black disc of the moon. Bright spots,

like a string of beads, appear in the final few seconds before total eclipse. These spots are in effect the last glimpses of the sun's corona, broken up by the mountainous surface of the moon. They were first documented by the English astronomer Francis Baily (1774–1844) in 1836 and were named 'Baily's beads' in his honour. Elsewhere in the sky some of the brighter stars and planets, particularly Venus, become visible, and solar flares may be seen projecting from the obscured sun.

A lunar eclipse is less spectacular, but one striking effect is a change in the moon's colour, caused by the refraction of light through dust particles.

As mankind's knowledge of astronomy grew, so did understanding of the causes and cyclic nature of eclipses, with the result that the phenomena became predictable. It is said that the explorer Christopher Columbus (1451–1506) used his know-ledge of an imminent lunar eclipse to awe an uncooperative native tribe while stranded in Jamaica in 1503. Whether or not this actually happened, it was certainly an idea that was seized on by writers of fiction and often turns up as a plot device.

Egryn lights
Mystery lights seen in Wales during an early-20th-century religious revival.

The mystery of the Egryn lights appar-ently centres around Mrs Mary Jones, a preacher belonging to a brief Welsh Methodist revival that took place in 1904 and 1905. The lights are named after the chapel at Egryn, a village between the Welsh coastal towns of Barmouth and Harlech. Mysterious lights were reported, both inside and out, when Jones preached in the Egryn Chapel. These lights were first mentioned in the press in early 1905, but apparently they were already well known in the area. It soon became apparent that the lights not only appeared in Egryn, but also seemed to follow Jones around.

A number of journalists reported on the strange case of the Egryn lights, and even those who were sceptical were impressed on witnessing them. One reporter from the *Daily Mail* described a 'ball of fire' that hovered steadily above the chapel roof at Egryn until it suddenly disappeared. Other witnesses described an arch of light, somewhat like the AURORA BOREALIS, and amazing stars that seemed to stay over particular houses. To some of the faithful, the stars indicated the homes of those who were to be converted, as reported by local man Beriah Evans:

> The star has seemed to rest above particular houses, whose roofs are thrown out in bold relief amid the surrounding darkness. When this occurs in the Egryn district a convert or converts invariably turn up at the next meeting from that particular house ... [The star] glows placidly on the roof of the chapel where her service is held, and when it does so the spiritual character of the meeting is very marked.

The lights reportedly manifested in even more different ways, including this description of what was seen by a reporter from the *Daily Mirror*:

> A bar of light quite four feet wide, and of the most brilliant blue. It blazed out at me from the roadway, a few yards from the chapel. For half a moment it lay across the road, and then extended itself up the wall on either side. It did not rise above the walls. As I stared, fascinated, a kind of quivering radiance flashed with lightning speed from one end of the bar to the other, and the whole thing disappeared.

At the time, the mystery lights were very much associated with Mary Jones, and it was reported that they would sometimes be seen hovering around her as she prayed, or would flood a road with light as she walked along it. In more recent times, the lights have been interpreted in a number of different ways. Some have suggested that they were caused by UFOs. Others believe that mystery lights had been seen in the area before Mary Jones started preaching, and were examples of either EARTH LIGHTS or quake lights (see EARTHQUAKES) associated with the Mochras Fault, a fault line identified by geologists on which both Barmouth and Harlech stand.

Egyptian Rite Freemasonry
A form of Freemasonry founded in the late 18th century by Alessandro di Cagliostro and based on the ancient Egyptian mysteries.

Egyptian Rite Freemasonry was founded by Count Alessandro di

Cagliostro (1743–95), a traveller, adventurer and occultist. Most writers agree that this name was an alias, and that his real name was Giuseppe Balsamo. Born of a poor family in Palermo, Sicily, he was said to have learnt a little chemistry and medicine at a monastery in Caltagirone, and subsequently travelled around Europe with his wife, selling an 'ELIXIR OF LIFE'. While in London, Cagliostro was initiated into FREEMASONRY. He claimed that as a youth he had travelled to Egypt, where the temple priests had taken him through palaces never shown to strangers, and passed on ancient esoteric knowledge to him; whether or not this was true, shortly after becoming a Freemason, Cagliostro founded Egyptian Rite Freemasonry in The Hague, the Netherlands. This new order was based on the ancient Egyptian mysteries and incorporated many doctrines which can be found in the *Egyptian Book of the Dead* and other documents of a similar origin. Cagliostro also adopted his own secret sign – a serpent with its tail in its mouth, an ancient Egyptian symbol. The aim of Egyptian Rite Freemasonry was said to be the moral and spiritual reform of mankind, and it was open to both sexes, initiating men and women into separate lodges, with the female lodge headed by Cagliostro's wife, Serafina.

Under Cagliostro's charismatic leadership, Egyptian Rite Freemasonry flourished, attracting members from the highest ranks of society and gaining him entrée to the best social circles in Europe. He persuaded many people to invest in his new form of Freemasonry, and his fame grew as he travelled throughout Russia, Germany and France to promote it. However, while in Rome in 1789, he was arrested by the Inquisition for peddling Freemasonry, and was sentenced to death, although the Pope commuted this sentence to life imprisonment. He died in prison in 1795.

Although Cagliostro's form of Freemasonry cannot be said to have survived him, it nevertheless had an influence on later organizations. During the late 1780s and 1790s, modern Egyptology was enjoying a boom as Napoleon extended the French Empire into Egypt and brought treasures and artefacts back to Europe. The exoticism of all things Egyptian, and the inevitable interest in the long-lost secrets of ancient Egypt, ensured that other styles of Freemasonry based on Egyptian mysteries would soon follow. Two such were the Oriental Rite of Mizraim and the Ancient and Primitive Rite of Memphis, which were combined at the close of the 19th century, and are still practised today.

electromagnetic phenomena
Strange effects associated with the earth's magnetic field.

There are reports of various mysterious effects of light and magnetism going back over centuries. Modern science, however, now categorizes these as electromagnetic phenomena.

This category includes such phenomena as EARTH LIGHTS, earthquake lights (see EARTHQUAKES) and MAGNETIC ANOMALIES. Earth lights have been associated with geological fault lines and the movement of the tectonic plates in the earth's crust. Similarly, earthquake lights are usually seen before or after an earthquake and are often considered to be a forewarning of a tremor. These lights, it is now believed, may well account for some sightings of UFOs.

Magnetic anomalies occur at places where there are marked differences in the composition of the earth's crust, with more magnetic substances being concentrated in particular spots. These are known to play havoc with sea or aerial navigation, especially through their interference with the normal working of compasses.

Instances of localized disruption of electrical equipment in particular places, such as the seemingly automatic switching on and off of lighting or the failure of sound-recording devices to function, have been reported for almost a century. Various explanations have been suggested, from poltergeist activity to the intervention of extraterrestrials. However, many scientists believe that there are 'electromagnetic hotspots' all over the world where the fluctuating electromagnetic energy of the earth can produce surges of power strong enough to affect any electronic device in the area.

Some of the effects of electromagnetism on human beings are only beginning to be understood by science, such as the postulated connection between living close to power lines or telephone masts and certain mental or physical effects in the human body, and there is much to be discovered in this field.

elixir of life

A fabled potion which is believed to give its drinker eternal life or eternal youth.

The elixir of life is a legendary potion which is said to give whoever drinks it eternal life or eternal youth. Throughout the centuries, the magnum opus or 'great work' of countless practitioners of alchemy was the quest for the PHILOSOPHER'S STONE, not only because the stone was said to have the power to turn base metals into gold, but also because it was thought that it could be used to make the elixir of life.

Alchemists also believed that the elixir could be used to create life, as well as to preserve and prolong it. The 2nd-century AD Chinese alchemist Wei Boyang's principal work, *Ts'an T'ung Ch'i* or 'The Convergence of the Three', which is believed to be the earliest known full alchemical text, is largely devoted to a description of the materials and procedures required to produce elixirs of long life and immortality, and there are said to be a thousand known names for these Chinese elixirs, such as 'Grand Concord Dragon Elixir' and 'Roseate Cloud Elixir of the Grand Immortal'. The Elizabethan alchemist Edward Kelley claimed to have discovered

EDW.^DKELLY Prophet or Seer to D.^rDEE.

A portrait of the Elizabethan alchemist Edward Kelley.
(© 2005 Charles Walker/TopFoto)

the philosopher's stone and to have succeeded in making the elixir of life.

entombment

The apparent entombment in rock or wood of living animals.

Insects and other animals trapped in amber thousands of years ago have long provided scientists with insights into evolutionary history. Outside fiction, these long-dead creatures can never be brought to life. However, there have been numerous stories throughout history of the accidental discovery of living animals that seem to have survived being encased in rock,

to be released only when the rocks are broken open.

In 1761, an account appeared in the *Annual Register*, attributed to Ambroise Paré, surgeon to Henry III of France in the 16th century, describing the appearance of a large living toad in the middle of a stone that had been broken open by a labourer. There seemed to be no opening in the cavity for the creature to have entered it, and the labourer claimed to have come across examples of the phenomenon before.

A similar instance was reported in England in 1865, in this case the live toad being released from a block of limestone quarried over 6 metres (around 20 feet) below ground level. As in many such cases, the cavity in which the animal was found was no larger than its body.

Other small animals, such as lizards, have also reportedly been found in similar circumstances, and in some cases the place of 'entombment' is a living tree. Perhaps the most fantastic of these accounts is one maintaining that in 1856 French workers digging a railway tunnel liberated a living pterodactyl from Jurassic-era limestone.

In 1975, American builders in Texas claimed that they found a living turtle inside concrete that had been poured in the previous year. They said that the creature must have been trapped inside the material as it solidified because it left the impression of its form behind when it was set free.

Many of these stories are no doubt hoaxes, some of which will have arisen from making a mistake as to where the creature in question really came from. Was it actually *inside* the split stone or was it merely underneath it when it was broken? In many cases, however, the cavity in which the animal appeared to be trapped is described as being exactly tailored to its size, showing the 'imprint' of its body on the surrounding material. This would suggest that the rock material had actually formed around the creature while still in an incompletely solid state. With some rocks being millions of years old, how could this be possible?

According to current scientific thinking, it would be inconceivable for an animal to be somehow sealed alive into such an airless enclosed space and survive for any great length of time. Also, if it had been trapped in a cramped space with no room to move, how would it be able, as so many accounts relate, to begin to move around in a free and lively way when released? Had it been born there, perhaps from a fertilized egg that had slid into a minute crack in the stone, it would still have been totally cut off from any form of food.

Could it be possible that such animals have undergone a form of hibernation, or suspended animation, lasting for a period of many years? If any of these accounts is true, there seems to be no other obvious explanation. However, conclusive evidence for an actual occurrence is still required.

Exmoor Beast *see* ALIEN BIG CATS

F

fairies

Magical beings, generally of diminutive human form, common in British and European folklore.

The word 'fairy', also spelt 'faery' or 'faerie', is a late derivation of *fay*, which comes via the Old French *feie*, from Latin *fata*, meaning 'the Fates'. Originally 'fairy' (fay-erie) meant 'a state of enchantment', and it was only later that it came to be used for the creatures who caused this enchantment. The term is now broadly used to refer to any supernatural being of human form (and usually diminutive size) which is capable of performing magic.

Stories about fairies tend to be more common in Asian and European cultures than elsewhere in the world, and some folklorists have suggested that, within these cultures, they are all that remains of an earlier belief in animism or that they are a development of beliefs originally relating to the spirits of the dead. In more recent folklore, fairies have become romanticized and are seldom seen as harmful, but in older times they were considered dangerous creatures to be avoided, and placated if encountered. Medieval romances developed the idea of a court of fairies ruled by a king and queen, who liked to ride out in formal processions, especially on May Eve and Midsummer Night, and there has for a long time been a distinction between this aristocratic body of generally benevolent fairies – often known as the trooping fairies, or the seelie (blessed) court – and the malevolent solitary fairies, sometimes identified with the souls of the damned, who are known as the unseelie (unblessed) court.

The realm of the fairies supposedly impinges on that of humans, but it is rarely glimpsed. Fairies are often said to live underground, in hills or mounds, to be able to make themselves invisible and to be fiercely protective of their privacy. In British and European folkloric traditions, there is a vast range of common SUPERSTITIONS and beliefs relating to them.

Anyone who has dealings with fairies must tread very carefully, as they are quick to take offence and will avenge any insult. It is considered unlucky to

Between 1917 and 1920 two young cousins, 16-year-old Elsie Wright and 9-year-old Frances Griffiths, claimed to have taken photographs of fairies in a glen just behind their home in Cottingley, near Bradford, West Yorkshire. This is one of the famous Cottingley photographs, apparently showing Frances Griffiths surrounded by a group of dancing fairies. (©TopFoto/Fortean)

name them, or even to use the word 'fairy' – either because to do so might summon them, or because they dislike being called fairies. Instead, they should be referred to euphemistically by a term like the Good Folk, the Good Neighbours, the Little People or the Gentry. Fairies hate pretentiousness and meanness, but love simple, sincere and generous humans, and will always reward kindness shown to them. They sometimes borrow implements or grain, but will usually return anything they borrow with interest. However, you should never thank them for any gift directly, but should show your gratitude by praising the gift. Care must also be taken if you wish to make them a present in return; clothes should never be offered, and you must never return more than they have given or lent to you. Nor should anyone who has been favoured by the fairies ever mention what has been done for them.

Fairies sometimes steal food from humans, and can extract all the essential goodness from it while leaving its outer form. They love milk and cheese, and any milk which is spilt should be left as their share. Their own food is dangerous to humans; any mortal who eats fairy food can never return to the land of the living, and if he does, he will pine away with the longing to get back to fairyland. Fairy music is unbearably sweet and melancholy, and will haunt any human who hears it till the day he dies; *The Londonderry Air* is said to be of fairy origin. They like to dance in fairy rings, sometimes enticing humans to join them. Fairies are skilled in weaving and spinning, and are said, like humans, to domesticate and breed animals, and they love horses. They hate salt, iron or smoke, so these may be used as protection against them. Fairies sometimes mate and have children with humans, and the offspring from such unions will often have second sight or great musical ability. Fairies will sometimes abduct a human midwife to assist in fairy childbirth, rewarding her richly for her help. They will also sometimes kidnap a human baby and leave a CHANGELING in its place.

fairy light *see* WILL-O'-THE-WISP

falls

Unexplained instances of strange things falling from the sky.

Human history is full of instances of things that appeared strange and inexplicable to our ancestors coming to be understood as science advances. However, one phenomenon that has been reported for centuries and still resists explanation is that of weird objects falling from the sky, also known as 'mystery rains'.

One of the more common themes in this is that of falling fish or other aquatic animals. Many cases are on record, including a shower of sprats landing on the Norfolk seaside town of Great Yarmouth in 2002, a rain of frogs in Llanddewi, Wales, in 1996, and another in Croydon, London, in 1998. The usual explanation of such occurrences is that the creatures were sucked up into the air by a localized whirlwind or waterspout to be deposited elsewhere. This theory is given credence by the fact that reports also exist of ponds and their contents disappearing overnight or lakes being suddenly empty of fish.

However, not all falls are as easy to account for. In *Mysterious Worlds* (1980), Arthur C Clarke (1917–2008) gives an account of hundreds of hazelnuts falling from the sky in Bristol in 1977. Puzzling enough in itself, the event was made even more mysterious by the fact that it occurred in spring, when no nuts would be in season. Similarly baffling was the experience claimed by one W G Grottendieck in Sumatra in 1903 of small, hot stones raining down in his bedroom during the night, without appearing to damage his roof and seeming to fall at a much slower speed than would be expected.

Also common are falls of ice, not as mundane hail or sleet but as often dangerously large lumps. One modern-day explanation attributes this phenomenon to water, or waste, falling from jet aircraft flying so high that any liquid leaving them must freeze in the atmosphere. However, many accounts of ice falls predate the invention of the aircraft, including a block of ice about 6 metres (20 feet) in diameter, estimated at half a ton in weight, that dropped on a farm in the Scottish Highlands in 1849. This ice was reportedly perfectly clear, but other falling chunks have been described as being milky, of various colours and containing rocky debris. Such large pieces of ice cannot be attributed to weather conditions, nor could they be debris from a comet as they would not survive as ice long enough to hit the earth.

Other strange falls include a red rain that fell in 2001 on Kerala in India. The liquid was analysed and found to contain fungal spores. While this accounted for the unusual colour, it didn't explain how the spores came to be there. In various states of the USA showers of corn husks or kernels have been reported in places where no such crops were being farmed nearby. Stories of showers of stones peppering the roofs of isolated houses with no apparent culprit to be found are not uncommon and many of these have been attributed to the activity of poltergeists.

The suggested explanations for this range of phenomena, from freak weather to a kind of volcanic activity hitherto unknown to science, really belong to the realm of conjecture and a convincing theory remains to be found.

fireballs
Particularly bright meteors.

The International Astronomical Union defines a fireball as a meteor brighter than magnitude –4, which in lay terms means one as bright as the planet Venus in the night sky. Essentially, a fireball is caused by the entry into the earth's atmosphere of a larger-than-usual object, anything from a few centimetres in size. Fireballs generally have a long glowing tail and observers have occasionally reported hearing a roaring sound to accompany their flight. They are both rare and unpredictable and never fail to have a striking effect on those lucky enough to see one.

An unusually well-documented incident took place at Peekskill, a suburban town in New York State, on 9 October 1992. The fireball was observed by many people attending an evening football game, and several of them recorded the event in photographs and video footage. A large rocky fragment was later found to have landed on a parked car.

In earlier times, fireballs were variously interpreted as stars falling to earth, expressions of the anger of gods or the travelling of the spirits of the dead. In many cultures they were taken as evil OMENS. In more recent years they have generated UFO reports or sparked claims that the military are testing 'Star Wars' weaponry in space.

Fátima *see* MARIAN APPARITIONS

fish, falls of *see* FALLS

Flannan Isles mystery

The strange disappearance of three lighthousemen from the Flannan lighthouse in December 1900.

On 26 December 1900, the lighthouse tender *Hesperus* arrived on a routine visit at Eileen Mor, the largest of the Flannan Isles, a remote group of islands off the west coast of Scotland. However, when it arrived, the lighthouse was found to be deserted.

A telegram sent by the master of the *Hesperus*, taken from the records of the Northern Lighthouse Board, reads:

> A dreadful accident has happened at Flannans. The three Keepers, Ducat, Marshall and the occasional have disappeared from the island. On our arrival there this afternoon no sign of life was to be seen on the Island. Fired a rocket but, as no response was made, managed to land Moore, who went up to the Station but found no Keepers there. The clocks were stopped and other signs indicated that the accident must have happened about a week ago. Poor fellows they must been blown over the cliffs or drowned trying to secure a crane or something like that.

The conclusion in the reports of the time was that the keepers had left the lighthouse buildings for some reason during bad weather and been swept out to sea by an unexpected wave. However, there were some intriguing circumstances surrounding the disappearance which, fuelled by press speculation and the Wilfrid William Gibson poem 'Flannan Isle', have continued to keep the mystery alive in the public imagination. The fact that the iron railings around the west landing and the crane platform were displaced and twisted, as noted in Superintendent Muirhead's report following the incident, led to suggestions of the involvement of some 'unearthly' force. It was also noted by Mr Moore that the coat of one of the keepers remained inside, although the oilskins and sea boots of the other two keepers were missing. The very fact that all three must have left the building together has also been taken to be unusual – normal practice would require one keeper to remain inside to tend the light at all times.

As with that other famous maritime disappearance, the MARY CELESTE, some accounts state that a half-eaten meal was discovered on the table. In the Gibson poem, the discovery is related as follows:

> Yet, as we crowded through the door,
>
> We only saw a table, spread
>
> For dinner, meat and cheese and bread;
>
> But all untouch'd; and no one there:
>
> As though, when they sat down to eat,
>
> Ere they could even taste,
>
> Alarm had come; and they in haste
>
> Had risen and left the bread and meat:
>
> For at the table-head a chair
>
> Lay tumbled on the floor.

This certainly doesn't agree with the eyewitness reports. It was partly from the discovery that (among other morning work) the meal things had been cleared away that the time of the incident was placed in the afternoon of 15 December 1900, the day on which the last entry appeared on the slate (where notes were made before being transferred to the log). Indeed, everything was found to be in order at the lighthouse buildings, even to the extent that the gate had been secured. This in itself might be considered odd if the loss of all three keepers was due to a situation, occurring during a severe storm, which induced such a state of panic that one of those involved did not have time to put on his oilskins.

Suggested explanations over the years have included insanity on the part of the keepers, an attack by a sea serpent, the Devil and the inevitable alien abduction. However, it seems likely that this was simply a tragic accident behind which were left too few clues for certainty.

Flight 19 *see* BERMUDA TRIANGLE

foaflore *see* URBAN LEGENDS

foaftale *see* URBAN LEGENDS

folklore

A term loosely describing a body of popular traditions and beliefs.

Although most of us can easily name several stories, customs, songs or superstitions that we would describe as items of folklore, it is a term that is notoriously difficult to pin down to a definition that would be accepted by all the people with an interest in the field. Folklore is generally considered to consist mainly of oral tradition (at least historically) and to be characterized by repetition leading to a constant, dynamic variation. This could be further developed by recognizing that in preliterate societies and groups, folk tales, rhymes, songs, SUPERSTITIONS and sayings were (and still are) used as a way to pass on customs, skills, knowledge and warnings from one generation to the next, helping to underpin and preserve value systems and a sense of identity. However, to restrict a definition to this would ignore the fact that in all of these forms there is also an element of pure entertainment.

The boundaries between the figurative narratives that form much of what would be described as folklore and those that might be described as myths or legends are, at the very least, blurred. In general terms, 'folklore' is usually reserved for those that do not form part of a religious belief system (as is usually the case with MYTHOLOGY) or that are not intended (at least partly) to describe real historical events or characters (as with LEGEND). However, in practice, it is extremely difficult to separate the three, and 'folklore' is often used as a catch-all term. Within the academic study of folklore, the working definitions employed have tended to become very wide in recent years – for example, after tackling the question, the US folklorist Dan Ben-Amos settled on 'artistic communication in small groups'.

The word 'folklore' was coined by the English antiquary W J Thoms in 1846, as an alternative name for what had generally been described until then as 'popular antiquities'. The dramatic rise in academic interest in folklore during the 19th century was due in part to the rise of romantic nationalism throughout Europe, which encouraged interest in popular stories and traditions as a means to establish or reinforce national identities. This was paralleled within the Romantic literary movement, which drew on folklore, particularly fairy tales, as one of its sources of inspiration – as can be seen in poems such as Shelley's 'Queen Mab' (1813) or Keats's 'Eve of St Agnes' (1820). Much of the poetry of Sir Walter Scott grew out of his extensive knowledge of traditional ballads and stories, and the same source informed many of his novels.

Many traditional folk tales are clearly fictional and employ characters that are archetypal. Stories about wicked step-parents, mysterious strangers or witches were wholly fictional, but may have acted as cautionary tales, giving warnings against the many types of folly to which human beings are prone, or containing other kinds of life lessons. Others gave homely explanations for seemingly mysterious phenomena in everyday life, such as the MAN IN THE MOON.

A common characteristic of many strains of folklore is the suggestion (possibly sometimes believed, possibly sometimes only figurative) that there are other worlds that exist in parallel to our own and occasionally interact with it – whether at certain 'magical' times of the year or at the behest of their strange inhabitants. All around the world, everyday events that seem to be unexplained have been attributed to the activities of mysterious non-human (but often human-like) magical creatures such as brownies, elves, djinn, FAIRIES, little people and leprechauns, who may be helpful or troublesome, kindly or malevolent. These otherworldly beings may also be of a more directly terrifying aspect, and take the form of ghosts or spirits – such as the BANSHEE, BLACK DOGS or the wild huntsman known in parts of England as HERNE THE HUNTER.

Although many people tend to think of folklore as something that belongs to the distant past, it is still very much alive in the modern world. Indeed, new folk tales and beliefs are being created and spread far more quickly than ever before – oral repetition having been joined by the mass media, the photocopier and the Internet. In the modern world, cunning or foolish peasants, vain or cruel kings and wicked stepmothers have given way to alien abductions, web wizards, VANISHING HITCH-HIKERS and disappearing mothers-in-law. Perhaps the best-known current form of folklore is the genre usually described as URBAN LEGENDS. Like traditional stories, these contemporary folk tales were largely spread by word of mouth until the arrival of the Internet allowed them to be disseminated worldwide with extreme rapidity. Such stories exhibit an important feature of folk tales in that they mutate and grow in the telling, allowing the narrator to add or subtract details according to their local relevance or the expectations of the audience.

Similar to these are the conspiracy theories and other stories that spring up alongside the 'accepted' versions of events – such as the supposed non-accidental death of Diana, Princess of Wales, or the belief that man has never really landed on the moon. In the popular imagination, certain real people have undergone a trans-formation into larger-than-life, almost mythical figures, not so very long after their (real or assumed) deaths. Examples include ELVIS PRESLEY, who continues to be sighted by the faithful in the most unlikely of places despite having died in 1977. Places and inanimate objects have also undergone a similar process – examples are the famous BERMUDA TRIANGLE, HANGING ROCK in Australia, the HOPE DIAMOND with its legendary curse and the ill-fated TITANIC.

foo fighters

Strange aerial lights seen by pilots during World War II.

During World War II, Allied aircrews reported encounters with mysterious balls of light during the course of

Mysterious lights encountered by World War II fighter pilots. (© 2005 TopFoto/Fortean)

combat missions over both Europe and the Pacific. The luminous forms would apparently fly near to, or with, their aircraft and then manoeuvre suddenly away. The phenomena were dubbed 'foo fighters' after a catchphrase belonging to a 1940s cartoon character: 'Where there's foo there's fire'.

Speculation was rife – a popular concern was that foo fighters were a secret weapon deployed by the Axis powers. However, the lights did not fire upon, attack or otherwise interfere with Allied aircraft. Alternative theories included balloons, artillery flak or St Elmo's fire but, as a contemporary commentator remarked, 'no explanation stood up' and they remain an unsolved mystery of World War II. The Nazi secret weapon theory still circulates, but ufologists cite them as pre-1947 examples of UFOs. An alternative suggestion is that foo fighters were an unrecognized electromagnetic effect generated by the intense use of military radar during wartime.

footprints *see* DEVIL'S FOOTPRINTS

Fountain of Youth

A legendary spring whose water has the power to restore health and youth or to confer immortality.

The legend of a spring which can restore health and youth, and even give immortality to the drinker, appears in various mythologies. In the Hindu fable of Cyavana, an elderly priest reveals religious secrets to two demigods in exchange for rejuvenation in the Fountain of Youth, and the theme of this miraculous water source is expanded on in a number of ancient Hebrew, Greek and Roman writings. In Celtic folklore, it is said to be situated in the magical otherworld of Tir Na Nog. The Fountain of Youth is also mentioned in the 3rd century in *The Alexander Romance*, in which Alexander the Great is described as crossing the Land of Darkness in search of it. Arabic versions of this work were very popular in Spain during and after the period of Moorish rule, and the Spanish explorers who went to the New World would have been familiar with the legend. When they arrived in the Americas, they heard native stories of a Fountain of Youth which was said to be located in the mythical land of Bimini, somewhere north of present-day Cuba, and these tales also reached Europeans in the Caribbean. Adventurers therefore sought the legendary spring. One Spanish explorer, Juan Ponce de León, was said to have heard tales of the fountain from the natives of Puerto Rico when he conquered the island, and to have gone in search of it. It is unlikely that this was the motive for his explorations, especially as his name was not associated with the legend until after his death, but there is no doubt that whatever he had been looking for, he discovered Florida in 1513, and ever since, some of the most persistent myths associated with the state relate to its being the location of the Fountain of Youth.

fox fire *see* WILL-O'-THE-WISP

Freemasonry

The institutions, rites and practices of the Freemasons, members of a secret male fraternity.

Freemasonry is the term used to refer to the institutions, rites and practices of the Fraternity of Free and Accepted Masons, widely known as Freemasons or Masons. The oldest-known branch of this worldwide organization, the Grand Lodge of England, dates back to 1717, with a continental branch, the Grand Orient de France, being founded in 1728.

The historical origins of Freemasonry are a subject of much speculation and debate, with some claiming that it is directly descended from the KNIGHTS TEMPLAR, and others that it was an offshoot of the ancient mystery religions of the Egyptians and Babylonians (see also EGYPTIAN RITE FREEMASONRY). But the most commonly held view is that it was an institutional outgrowth of the medieval guildsmen and craftsmen called masons, who formed primitive trade unions known as lodges for their mutual protection. It is widely believed in occult circles that these men, who travelled throughout Europe building the great cathedrals, incorporated esoteric knowledge into the sacred architecture of these cathedrals. As the lodges gradually opened up to admit people from other professions and walks of life, it is said that their purpose changed, and the various grades which workers had originally gone through in learning their craft were replaced by degrees of advancement in esoteric knowledge, eventually resulting in the form of Freemasonry practised today. Modern Freemasonry is sometime referred to as 'speculative' Masonry, because it speculates on the true meanings behind the original symbolism employed by the earlier form, known as 'operative' Masonry.

Whatever its real origins, Freemasonry relies heavily on architectural and geometrical symbolism, with one of its prime symbols being the square and compasses, tools of the stonemason's trade, arranged to form a quadrilateral; the square is often said to represent matter, and the compasses spirit or mind. Sometimes in the space between these, a blazing star or other symbol of light is incorporated to represent truth or knowledge. Alternatively, a letter G may be used to represent God and/or Geometry, and the Supreme Being, or God, is sometimes referred to in Masonic ritual as the Grand Geometer, or Great Architect of the Universe.

There is no central Masonic authority; instead, there are independent jurisdictions, which normally correspond to a single country, although their territory may be bigger or smaller than this – for example, in North America each state and province has its own jurisdiction. The ruling authority of the jurisdiction is usually called a Grand Lodge or Grand Orient, and the smaller geographical areas in the jurisdiction each have their own lodge, which meets in a building known as a temple or Masonic centre, each lodge being governed by a Worshipful Master or Right Worshipful Master.

This painting shows a meeting of the Masonic Lodge in Vienna, to which Mozart reportedly belonged, in the 18th century. (© TopFoto/HIP)

Freemasonry upholds the principles of brotherly love, faith and charity, and accepts members from almost every religion, including Christianity, Judaism, Hinduism and Buddhism. Although most branches require that candidates must profess their belief in a Supreme Being, this phrase is often given a very broad interpretation, and a principle of non-dogmatism and tolerance is stressed. Freemasons are taught moral lessons through rituals, and members progress through 'degrees', the three initial ones being Entered Apprentice, Fellow Craft and Master Mason. However, the organization continues to be open only to men.

Freemasonry is often called a secret society, but the level of secrecy about its membership and practices varies widely around the world. However, precise details about the rituals are not made public, and Freemasons have a system of secret modes of recognition – the best known being the secret grip used in handshakes. This secrecy, combined with speculation as to the exact nature and level of commitment that members make to the organization and each other, has led to a great deal of suspicion over the years – particularly the suggestion that it can affect the partiality of members who hold high positions in the public services. Freemasons would counter that the organization is committed to community and charity work and that the meetings are simply a social outlet.

One of the most famous Freemasons in history was Mozart, whose opera *The Magic Flute* makes extensive use of Masonic symbolism. See also SECRET SOCIETIES.

Freemasonry, Egyptian Rite

see EGYPTIAN RITE FREEMASONRY

Friday the 13th

The superstition that Friday the 13th is the unluckiest day in the calendar.

The belief in many parts of the Western world that Friday the 13th is the unluckiest day is probably the most widespread of all superstitions. Children born on Friday the 13th are said to be unlucky and short-lived, while if a funeral procession passes a person on this day, they are likely to be condemned to death. There are numerous other superstitions relating to the date – for example, it is unlucky to be married on the day or to cut your hair or go out at night. More generally, Friday the 13th is just assumed to be unlucky for almost everything, and believers in the tradition often spend the day at home, rather than risk an expedition.

The superstition is often said to

have ancient origins, and a number of theories have been proposed to explain it. The most common comes from the Christian tradition, and combines the separate fears that both Fridays and the number thirteen are unlucky. Friday is the day on which Jesus was crucified, and some theologians have suggested that Adam and Eve ate the forbidden fruit on a Friday. Friday was also considered a bad day to start any new undertaking and, in the medieval Christian tradition, may have been considered unlucky because it was the Muslim Sabbath. Added to this, there were thirteen people at the Last Supper (Jesus and his twelve disciples), and Judas Iscariot is said to have been either the thirteenth to arrive at the feast or the first leave it, on his way to betray Jesus. However, thirteen was considered unlucky before this by the Romans, for whom twelve was a number of completeness (for instance, there are twelve months in a complete year, twelve signs of the zodiac, and so on). Thirteen was one beyond this, and thus beyond the pale. Thirteen is also the traditional number of members of a coven: sometimes said to be twelve witches and Satan.

Another theory relates the belief to the KNIGHTS TEMPLAR, the chivalrous order suppressed by King Philip IV of France in 1307 on charges of heresy and homosexuality – although the true motive was almost certainly to impound the order's wealth. A series of well-coordinated raids was carried out at dawn on Friday, 13 October, resulting in a large number of arrests and eventual executions, including that of the Templars' Grand Master, Jacques de Molay, since when the day has been considered unlucky.

Unfortunately for theories such as these, there appears to be no evidence that Friday the 13th (as a particular combination of day of the week and date of the month) was believed to be unlucky before the end of the 19th century. As late as the 1898 edition of E Cobham Brewer's immense *Dictionary of Phrase & Fable*, there are separate entries for Friday as unlucky and thirteen as unlucky, but nothing about the combination of the two.

Recent research by Nathaniel Lachenmeyer has shown that while the separate superstitions were strong in the 19th century, the combination of the two only really began to affect public consciousness from 1907 onwards. In that year, the Boston financier Thomas W Lawson published his novel *Friday, the Thirteenth*, a mixture of romantic love-story and polemic against the stock market, which cemented the connection between day and date by using the title phrase as both the opening and closing words of the story. Thanks to Lawson's massive self-promotion, the book sold 60,000 copies in its first month and was even filmed in 1916 as a feature-length silent movie. The novel is almost entirely forgotten today, while the film no longer exists, but it appears that Lawson's book is the primary origin of the modern fear of the date. That being the case, the fact that Philip IV moved against the Templars on Friday the 13th,

while true, starts to look coincidental, with only retrospective significance.

Sometimes the superstition is combined with others, such as that it is bad luck to meet a black cat. On Thursday, 12 October 1939 the town of French Lick, Indiana, passed a law, beginning at midnight and running throughout the following day, to the effect that all black cats should be belled so the population could avoid them. Off and on, the law remained in force for the ill-omened Fridays until 1942.

Surprisingly, there is some evidence to suggest that Friday the 13th can actually be unlucky. An article called 'Is Friday the 13th bad for your health?' appeared in the *British Medical Journal* in 1993. This compared traffic volumes and hospital admissions for transport accidents on Friday the 13th with those for the preceding Friday. The results showed that, while the numbers of shoppers weren't significantly different on the two days, there were far fewer vehicles on the road on the 13th than on the 6th. At the same time, a far greater number of people were taken to hospital after traffic accidents on the 13th than on the 6th. Both results can probably be explained by public fears about the 13th: fewer people are prepared to drive on that day because it's considered unlucky, while those who do are probably more nervous than usual, and thus more prone to getting involved in accidents. Such an explanation is supported by recent research carried out by the psychologist Professor Richard Wiseman, who surveyed 4,000 people and found that people who generally considered themselves unlucky in their daily lives were far more likely to believe in bad-luck superstitions, such as Friday the 13th, than those who thought themselves lucky.

Beliefs surrounding Friday the 13th still persist, and in recent times the date has been used as a title for the popular series of *Friday the 13th* 'slasher' films. In the story the central character, Jason Vorhees, is a serial killer who was born on Friday the 13th. The series began in 1980 and Jason has so far slaughtered his way through eleven films.

The main reason for the survival of the superstition into the 21st century is, perhaps, the attention of the mass media, ever hungry for material. Topical newspaper, magazine or television features frequently appear when the 13th day of the month falls on a Friday and, whether they provide examples of apparent bad luck, examine the origin of the belief or take an anti-superstition stance, they continue to keep the idea in the public consciousness.

However, if you still can't be persuaded that the superstition is unfounded, you could try any one of a number of folk remedies for avoiding bad luck on the day – such as standing on your head and eating a piece of gristle …

frogs *see* FALLS

G

Gallipoli

*Site of the alleged disappearance
of a battalion of the Royal Norfolk
Regiment during World War I.*

A major but ultimately unsuccessful
Allied campaign of World War I was
fought on the Gallipoli Peninsula in
Turkey. Its aim was to secure passage
of the Dardanelles for Allied shipping,
aid Russia and possibly even remove
Turkey from the war. After a promising
start, with amphibious landings of
thousands of troops in April 1915, the
campaign soon degenerated into the
kind of trench warfare and stalemate
that characterized the Western Front
in Europe.

One of the elements of the British
Army sent to Gallipoli was E Company
of the 5th Territorial Battalion of the
Royal Norfolk Regiment. Like many
bodies of soldiers raised to fight in the
Great War, this battalion differed from
regular army units in being composed
exclusively of men of the same
occupation or from the same area, in
this case all employees on the royal
estate at Sandringham. For this reason

they were known unofficially as the
King's Own Sandringhams.

In their very first engagement, on 12
August 1915, the Sandringhams went
forward to attack the Turkish lines.
Moving resolutely under artillery and
machinegun fire into a wooded area,
they disappeared into the smoke and
confusion of battle and were never
seen again. Not a single man returned
to the Allied lines.

Their families were simply notified
that the men were missing in action;
not even King George V (1865–1936)
himself could find out any more
information. Enquiries made through
the Red Cross to discover if any of them
were in Turkish prisoner-of-war camps
drew a blank. It was as if they had
vanished from the face of the earth.

The mystery took on a romantic tinge
when in 1965 a New Zealand veteran
of Gallipoli, supported by a few others,
claimed to have witnessed oddly
shaped clouds hovering at a low level
over the area where the Sandringhams
were making their attack. According to
this account, the company advanced
into one of these clouds and did not

re-emerge. The cloud then rose up into the sky. In the popular imagination, the brave Sandringhams had been carried bodily out of the blood and mire of battle and up to heaven. An alternative theory was that the oddly shaped cloud was in fact a UFO, and this was a case of alien abduction. However, military historians believe that the group became lost and were massacred – while this has not been thoroughly established as fact, it is taken by many to be, although tragic, the most likely explanation.

giants

Mythical human beings of huge size.

The folklore of most cultures around the world contains references to mythical giant human beings.

In Greek mythology they were considered to be the sons of Gaia (the earth-goddess) and Uranus (the sky-god), and were so strong that only a god could kill one of them. They were said to have waged a war against the Olympian gods (the gigantomachy) but on being defeated were buried beneath Mount Etna. The Cyclops were a race of one-eyed giants, one of whom, according to Homer, fell foul of Odysseus, illustrating a common quality often ascribed to giants: that of being rather dim-witted.

The existence of large-scale prehistoric constructions all over the world, such as STONEHENGE or the 'Cyclopean' masonry of ancient Greece, gave rise to the common idea that they must have been built by giants. Similarly, giants are traditionally given credit for constructing natural formations like the volcanic Giant's Causeway in Northern Ireland.

In many cases this type of belief reflects the widespread idea that humankind has undergone a process of degeneration from prodigious ancestors. The Bible, for example, includes a reference to the mighty predecessors of ordinary men:

> There were giants in the earth in those days. (Genesis 6:4)

Another biblical reference is to Goliath, the champion of the Philistines, 'whose height was six cubits and a span' (approximately 3.4 metres or 11 feet). This daunting and seemingly invincible enemy is, of course, killed by David with the help of the Lord and a slingshot.

Perhaps the most famous giants in British mythology are Gog and Magog, the last two survivors of a giant race said to have been defeated by the legendary King Brutus. They were taken prisoner and made to work as porters, and their images were often commemorated in buildings, represented as massive figures bearing the weight of great lintels on their shoulders.

Giants also feature in folk tales, such as 'Jack and the Beanstalk' and 'Jack the Giant-killer', and one was immortalized by the Irish writer Oscar Wilde (1854–1900) in his children's fairy story 'The Selfish Giant' (1888).

Do giants exist in reality? Throughout the ages there have been reports of taller-than-average human beings, usually men, but substantiating such claims has always been difficult. However, there are some giants whose existence can be proven. Among these is Charles O'Brien, or Byrne (1761–83), known as the Irish Giant, whose height was 2.5 metres (8 feet 4 inches) and whose skeleton is preserved in the Royal College of Surgeons in London.

In the USA, Robert Pershing Wadlow (1918–40) of Illinois topped 1.8 metres (6 feet) by the age of ten, and eventually grew to a height of 2.7 metres (8 feet 11 inches), making him the world's tallest recorded person, a record still unsurpassed.

The woman documented as the world's tallest was Zeng Jinlian, of China (1964–82), who measured almost 2.5 metres (8 feet 2 inches).

In many cases of modern giantism it is known that the condition is caused by the excessive production of growth hormone by an overactive pituitary gland. It is possible to treat this problem medically, but basketball teams might be denied many a star player if this remedy were universally applied.

giant waves

Sailors have reported encounters with giant waves since ancient times. These were originally dismissed as tall stories, but recent satellite studies have confirmed that the waves are real.

It is extremely difficult to estimate the size of waves, and in rough seas waves often appear bigger than their actual size. A Victorian scientist calculated that any wave greater than 18 metres (60 feet) high would collapse under its own weight, and it was generally thought that the giant waves described by sailors could not be real. Tsunamis or tidal waves which are caused by earthquakes are no more than a few feet high in deep water, only reaching a larger size as they approach land. The giant waves that the Victorians dismissed were clearly in another category entirely.

Some instances of giant waves were recorded by reliable observers, and meteorologists were forced to reconsider whether some of the reports were accurate. In 1861 the bell of the Bishop Lighthouse in the Scilly Isles was broken by a wave which reached more than 30 metres (100 feet) above sea level, and a wave of 34 metres (112 feet) was measured from the USS *Ramapo* in 1934.

Giant waves were then considered to be freak occurrences that would only come about once in a thousand years or more at any given spot. However, a detailed satellite survey carried out by the EU-funded MaxWave programme, which started in 2000, found this was not the case. In 30,000 images the researchers found ten waves with a height in excess of 24 metres (80 feet), making them far more common than anyone had previously thought.

Further scientific work modelling the waves revealed that they can be created when smaller waves combine to form a larger one. Research continues on identifying the geographical areas where these combinations are likely to occur and the weather conditions that produce them.

Giant waves are now believed to have sunk some 22 supercarriers – ships more than 200 metres (650 feet) long – between 1969 and 1994. They are no longer regarded as mythical but are treated as a real threat to shipping.

Gimlin, Bob *see* BIGFOOT

Glastonbury Tor

A teardrop-shaped hill situated at Glastonbury in Somerset, England, which has for thousands of years been regarded as a place of great magical power; it is associated both with the legend of King Arthur and with Gwyn ap Nudd, King of the Fairies, and is identified with the mystical Isle of Avalon.

Glastonbury Tor has for thousands of years been regarded as a place of great magical power. Situated at Glastonbury in Somerset, the tor (a local word of Celtic origin, meaning 'conical hill') is strikingly located in the middle of a plain called the Summerland Meadows, which is recovered fenland. Neolithic flint tools have been found on the site, and the remains of a lake village show that there was a Celtic settlement there some time between 300 BC and 200 BC, while Roman remains and earthworks provide evidence of later occupation. Stones from a 5th-century building, thought to have been a monks' retreat or a fort, were used to build the 12th-century Church of St Michael on the tor;

in 1275 this church was demolished by an earthquake, and although it was rebuilt, all that now remains of it is its tower, which has been restored in recent times and is the only standing architectural feature of the tor. The church's stones were then used to build an abbey on its site in the 1360s, but this, too, was destroyed as part of the Dissolution of the Monasteries in 1539, when the last abbot of Glastonbury was hanged there.

The tor was once known by the Celtic name of *Ynis Witrin*, or 'Isle of Glass'; it is thought that thousands of years ago the plain was flooded, and the hill was one of only a few islands left unsubmerged, remaining for centuries afterwards an islet which became a peninsula at low tide. The tor's slopes appear to be fairly regularly terraced, and some believe their formation to be the remains of an ancient, possibly Neolithic, sacred spiral maze or labyrinth – a ceremonial way dedicated to the Goddess (sometimes referred to as the Great Goddess, the Mother Goddess and the Moon Goddess, among other names). Indeed, it has been suggested that the tor itself is a representation of the Goddess's body.

Glastonbury Tor has, for centuries, been the focus of legends and folklore that all point to its being a site at which the veil between this world and the next is thin. The tor has long been associated with Gwyn ap Nudd, first Lord of the Underworld and King of the Fairies, and is widely believed to be the entrance to Avalon or Annwn,

Glastonbury Tor in Somerset, England, long held to be a place of great magic and mystery. (© TopFoto/Fortean)

the land of the FAIRIES. It is also said to have been one of the strongholds of the legendary Celtic hero KING ARTHUR, and on Christmas Eve Arthur's ghost is believed to lead a spectral procession of knights along a ley (see LEYS) which links Cadbury to Glastonbury. According to one story, the young Arthur visited Avalon and was given a cauldron of rebirth and power; after being mortally wounded, he was taken to the isle in a sacred boat, and he is rumoured to be buried on the site of the abbey, where he awaits the time when he will rise again as 'the Once and Future King' to aid Britain in its time of greatest need.

The tor is also reputed to be the hiding-place chosen by JOSEPH OF ARIMATHEA for the HOLY GRAIL, which he is said to have buried near the Chalice Well, a natural spring at the tor's foot. Another claim relates to the GLASTONBURY ZODIAC, a giant astrological zodiac believed by some to have been carved into the land around Glastonbury. According to legend, the tor once boasted a stone circle like that at STONEHENGE, and recent archaeological work has led to the discovery of foundations of what appears to be an ancient stone circle temple. The tor is also believed to be a highly powerful energy centre and the converging point of a number of geomagnetic power lines; there have been many reports of sightings of strange balls of light in the area and, in recent years, of UFOs.

Glastonbury Zodiac

A vast physical representation of the zodiac in the countryside around Glastonbury.

In 1927 the English artist Katherine Maltwood (1878–1961) claimed to have discovered that a system of landmarks and prehistoric earthworks around Glastonbury could be interpreted as a gigantic zodiacal chart imprinted on the landscape. Having been asked to illustrate a book on the HOLY GRAIL, she found that places mentioned as being in the Vale of Avalon (which some associate with the Glastonbury area) could be identified on a map and that the figures representing the signs of the zodiac were then revealed. The makers of this zodiac, which Maltwood believed dated from c.2700 BC, dug earthworks in such a way that they incorporated natural features such as rivers, hills (including Glastonbury Tor) and roads to form images of the signs of the zodiac, which cover a circular area some 16 kilometres (10 miles) in diameter.

Maltwood linked this to the Round Table of KING ARTHUR, who had long been associated with Glastonbury, as well as to the Grail legends, believing that initiates had both kept the secret of the zodiac and maintained the earthworks over the centuries of the Christian era.

Sceptics, however, question whether the ancient culture that is supposed to have created the earthworks involved would have had the same idea of the zodiac as that which came down to us via the Greeks and Romans.

Glozel mystery

A mystery relating to the discovery of a subterranean chamber full of mysterious artefacts in Glozel, near Vichy, France; some have suggested a link to the Knights Templar.

The initial discovery which led to the Glozel mystery was made in the tiny French hamlet of that name in 1924. A teenager called Émile Fradin was working on the family farm when a cow slipped into a hole in the pastureland. When the cow was freed the Fradins discovered an unknown subterranean chamber, lined with bricks. Among the artefacts in this chamber were a number of clay tablets that seemed to be inscribed with an unknown alphabet, carved bones and antlers, statuettes and fragments of ceramics.

Fradin showed the artefacts to the local school teacher, Adrienne Picandet, who in turn showed them to another teacher, Benoit Clément. Eventually, Dr Morlet, a physician and amateur archaeologist from Vichy, heard of the finds, and went on to excavate the site, discovering numerous further objects. Morlet described the finds in a series of articles and booklets, crediting Fradin as co-author, and causing controversy within archaeological circles – Morlet

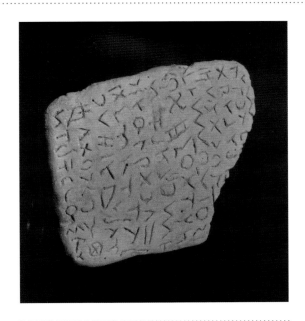

One of the clay tablets, inscribed with 'Glozelian'
characters, discovered at the site in Glozel.
(© Roger Viollet/TopFoto)

was dismissed as an amateur and Fradin as a 'peasant'. Morlet claimed that the Glozel finds were Neolithic, but the establishment disagreed with him. Morlet invited a number of scholars to visit the site, some of whom claimed that the site was a fake and hinted that Fradin had perpetrated a hoax.

The site became increasingly popular, and two tombs were discovered there in 1927. These contained more artefacts, which were put on display in the farmhouse – the start of a museum that still exists. Glozel was the topic of increasingly heated debate in academic circles. In February 1928 the president of the French Prehistoric

Society filed a complaint of fraud against Émile Fradin, and some of the artefacts were confiscated. Soon after, further excavations were carried out by a group selected for their objectivity. They found more tablets inscribed with 'Glozelian' characters, as well as other objects. The group attributed their finds to the Neolithic period, and believed the site was genuine. However, the police judged the artefacts to be recent forgeries, although the case was eventually dismissed.

In the 1970s the artefacts were tested using thermoluminescence dating techniques. The results suggested that some of the finds were indeed thousands of years old, while others were hundreds of years old – but why would objects from such a wide range of time have been collected together on a farm in Glozel?

Some believe that the 'treasure' at Glozel, described as 'only two or three days' swift ride' north of RENNES-LE-CHÂTEAU, is linked to the KNIGHTS TEMPLAR, and that the Glozel tablets are inscribed in Templar code, which, if it were correctly deciphered, might reveal the location of the treasures that the Templars allegedly discovered. For some the mystery of Glozel continues.

Golden Dawn *see* HERMETIC ORDER OF THE GOLDEN DAWN

grail *see* HOLY GRAIL

Great Pyramid

The largest of the Egyptian pyramids, built by Cheops.

The Great Pyramid at Giza was built by Cheops (or Khufu), the 26th-century BC king of Memphis. It is the largest of the PYRAMIDS of Egypt and one of the legendary Seven Wonders of the World.

The statistics of its dimensions alone reveal it to be a colossal feat of engineering. It occupies an area of 5.3 hectares (13 acres) and its original height has been calculated at 147 metres (481 feet) – its apex is missing and it has been suggested that it was never actually completed. It is square

in cross-section at every level and the length of the base of each side is 229 metres (751 feet). It is constructed of limestone blocks, over two million of them, each weighing more than two tonnes. Even more massive are the blocks used to form the ceiling of the 'King's Chamber', each of which weighs more than nine tonnes. Originally, it was covered in a smooth casing of stone but this has been lost over the centuries, particularly since earthquakes in the 14th century dislodged much of it. Local Arabs are said to have pillaged the stones for use in building their own mosques and palaces. For thousands of years it was the highest construction in the world, until the builders of the 19th century began to outstrip it.

No one can be certain as to how it was built, but most theories involve the construction of an enormous ramp of bricks and earth, which may have been lubricated with water, to allow the enormous blocks to be hauled or pushed into position. One theory suggests that hoists using counterbalancing baskets of sand may have been employed. It has been estimated that the construction of the pyramid would have taken at least 20 years, even given a massive force of labour. The precision of the building is remarkable, with less than 0.1 per cent of error in the alignment of the sides, and the fitting together of the blocks is extremely tight.

Why was the Great Pyramid built? The generally accepted explanation is that it was designed as the tomb of Cheops. This has led to the naming of the various chambers within the structure. The King's Chamber is the largest of these and contains a red granite structure identified as a sarcophagus. A smaller chamber has been labelled the Queen's Chamber, although it contains no similar structure. Scientists have studied the pyramid throughout the ages (Sir Isaac Newton thought that finding its dimensions would allow him to calculate the ancient Egyptian cubit) and various surprising discoveries have been made. The siting of the building has been shown to suggest a deliberate alignment of its four sides with the cardinal points of the compass. It has also been argued that the various passages inside it are aligned with the stars of the constellation of Orion. It is claimed that the pyramid's proportions give it unexplained qualities. In particular, some say that objects placed inside a scale model of it will be physically affected, with food being preserved and dull razors becoming sharp.

Some theorize that the Great Pyramid was not built as a tomb at all but as a kind of ideal structure in which now unknown religious or cult observances would be carried out. Others believe that it is an elaborate astronomical observatory, aligned with significant points in the heavens, or a giant sundial whose shadow indicates the solstices and equinoxes. Yet others maintain that there must be further undiscovered chambers within the structure that will one day provide the key to its proper purpose.

Great Zimbabwe

The remains of a mysterious stone city in south-east Zimbabwe which legend says was the capital of the Queen of Sheba.

When Portuguese traders first encountered Great Zimbabwe in the 16th century, they believed they had discovered the legendary capital of the Queen of Sheba. For centuries after, various travellers attributed its construction to the Egyptians or Phoenicians, and it was not until the 20th century that it was finally, and correctly, recognized as having African origins. It is now generally thought that Great Zimbabwe was built by ancestors of the Shona, between the 12th and 15th centuries. But while the question of who built it seems to have been settled, the question of why has not.

Great Zimbabwe is an impressive complex of ruins. The Great Enclosure, built on the valley floor, is the most famous feature of the ruins. It is surrounded by roughly circular double walls, with a circumference of over 240 metres (800 feet), making it the largest ancient structure south of the Sahara. Inside the wall are enclosures and passageways, and a conical tower. All the structures are built from granite, with no mortar, suggesting highly developed stone-working skills. The site was described by Portuguese captain Viçente Pegado in 1531:

> Among the gold mines of the inland plains between the Limpopo and the

The Great Enclosure is arguably the most impressive of the ruins at Great Zimbabwe. (© 2004 TopFoto/Imageworks)

Zambezi rivers [there is a] ... fortress built of stones of marvellous size, and there appears to be no mortar joining them ... This edifice is almost surrounded by hills, upon which are others resembling it in the fashioning of stone and the absence of mortar, and one of them is a tower more than 12 fathoms high. The natives of the country call these edifices Symbaoe, which according to their language signifies court.

Archaeologists disagree as to why this great city, which it has been estimated might have had a population of up to 18,000 people, was built, obviously flourished, but was subsequently abandoned.

Green Children of Woolpit

The legend of two green-skinned children, said to have appeared in the Suffolk village of Woolpit in the 12th century.

The legend of the Green Children of Woolpit was first described by the chronicler Ralph of Coggeshall, writing at Coggeshall Abbey in Essex at the beginning of the 13th century. In his account, 'within living memory' a boy and a girl with green skin were found near one of the wolf pits (trenches dug for catching wolves) which gave Woolpit its name. The villagers who made the discovery were unable to understand the speech of the two strange children, and took them to the home of Sir Richard de Calne, the lord of the manor. The children were greatly distressed, and initially refused to eat, although on seeing some freshly cut beans they showed signs of interest in them, and for a time ate nothing else. Although tenderly cared for, the boy became ill and died within a year. However, the girl thrived, gradually losing her green tinge and learning to speak in a manner that her new friends could understand. She told them that she came from a land where the sun did not shine and where it was normal to be green. She and her brother had inadvertently stumbled upon the sunny Suffolk village of Woolpit when they were out tending their flocks. They had found a cavern and heard the ringing of bells from within it. By following the sound they had eventually emerged in the sunlight and after a time they had been found by the kind villagers.

The chronicler William of Newburgh (died c.1198) also tells the story of the Green Children. He places the events slightly earlier, in the reign of King Stephen (1135–54) rather than King Henry II (1154–89) – the 'within living memory' of Ralph of Coggeshall. In William of Newburgh's account, the children emerged from the pits at harvest time, and were found by the villagers who were working in the fields. Both children learned English, and explained that they were from St Martin's Land, a Christian place where the sun didn't shine, but which was separated from a sunnier place by a broad river. According to William, the girl eventually married a man from Norfolk.

The peculiar story of the Green Children of Woolpit has been subject to numerous interpretations. It has been suggested that many elements of the legend, such as the bells ringing, the land of twilight, and the river, equate to the standard themes of fairylore and that it is simply a story in this tradition. More sensationally, it has also been suggested that the children were aliens, or that they were from a race of green people who lived at the hollow centre of the earth. One of the more respected theories comes from researcher Paul Harris, who suggests that the children were actually from the nearby village of Fornham St Martin, and the river they referred to was the River Lark. Harris believes that the children's parents could have been Flemish merchants or weavers, persecuted by Henry II. He suggests that the parents may have been killed, and that the children fled to Thetford Forest, becoming lost in underground mine passages, slowly starving and eventually stumbling into Woolpit. Harris believes that the children would have been disorientated by the sunlight after their dark adventures, and that their Flemish language would have confused the villagers. Their greenish colour he attributes to malnutrition.

Grim Reaper

A personification of death as a dark or skeletal figure in a monk's robe, usually carrying a scythe and sometimes also an hourglass.

The personification of death exists in the mythology of almost every culture and religion. In the West, Death is seen as one of the four horsemen of the Apocalypse. Since medieval times Death has been portrayed in European-based folklore as a male figure who usually carries a scythe (to symbolize his task of harvesting the souls of the recently dead), and sometimes also bears an hourglass (to remind us of the inexorable passage of time and the fact that death must come to us all). He appears as one of the cards of the major arcana in the tarot. He is often shown as a skeletal being, and especially in later times is depicted as wearing a black monk's robe. Sometimes he has no discernible features, with a black void instead of a face and no visible extremities. This figure is known as the Grim Reaper, and his function is that of a 'psychopomp' – a spirit whose task it is to conduct the souls of those who have recently died into the afterlife. Since he is believed to be present at the point of death to assist the dying person with the transition to the other side, it is perhaps not surprising that many seriously ill hospital patients have claimed that they have seen an apparition of the Grim Reaper standing at the foot of their bed. In most accounts, his appearance causes a sudden drop in temperature in the room; he rarely speaks, and glides rather than walks, but he fades away if the patient decides it is not yet time for them to go with him. However, few people who have had near-death experiences claim to have seen the Grim Reaper, and many of the recorded sightings of this apparition do not in fact result in the death of the observer or of a close friend or relative; instead, his alleged manifestations have sometimes been interpreted as a warning of imminent danger. The Grim Reaper has become an iconic figure in literature, art and popular culture, and nowadays is sometimes portrayed as a somewhat sympathetic character.

Guadaloupe *see* MARIAN APPARITIONS

Hanging Rock

Geological formation in Australia associated with a mysterious disappearance.

Hanging Rock is the popular name for an unusual geological formation, also known as Mount Diogenes, in a rural area of Victoria, Australia. It is an example of a volcanic plug, a mass of solidified lava blocking the vent of an extinct volcano.

In 1967 the Australian writer Joan Lindsay (1896–1984) published a novel telling the story of a group of schoolgirls taken by their boarding-school teachers for a picnic at the rock on 14 February 1900. Several of the girls and one accompanying teacher apparently vanish in mysterious circumstances and are never seen again. One girl from this group is later found in a dishevelled and disturbed state, entirely unable to give a coherent account of what happened to her companions. The novel ends tantalizingly with no explanation offered for the disappearance.

The novel was popular in Australia but was not widely known elsewhere until it was made into a film in 1975 by the Australian director Peter Weir. The film was a great international success, establishing Weir's reputation and bearing the allusive style and atmosphere of mystery that were to become recognized as his hallmarks. The film's publicity claimed that it was based on a true story, leading to a widely held belief that it portrayed actual events.

While the novel was grounded in the author's own experience, describing locations that she knew well, Lindsay never explicitly claimed that the story was anything other than a product of her imagination – although (as with the film) there was an implication that the story was based on real-life events. Those who believe the story to be entirely fictional have pointed out that, in the story, St Valentine's Day falls on a Saturday, although, in reality, 14 February 1900 was a Wednesday. Also, while such an event, if true, would have been certain to become a news item, researchers have combed Australian newspaper archives in vain for any mention of an unexplained disappearance at Hanging Rock at around that time. However, this has not stopped speculation as to what might have caused the DISAPPEARANCES, and in 1980 Yvonne Rousseau's *The Murders at Hanging Rock* was published, offering several hypothetical explanations for the mystery. Again, this added to the general perception that book and film were based in fact.

In the original manuscript of her novel, Lindsay apparently included a final chapter in which she hinted that the victims of the disappearance had entered a 'time warp'. However, her publisher advised her to drop this chapter in favour of leaving the reader with an entirely unexplained mystery.

Hauser, Kaspar
(c.1812–1833)

A German foundling, apparently a 'wild boy'.

Kaspar Hauser came to public attention as a strange youth found wandering in the marketplace of Nuremberg, Germany, in May 1828. Witnesses estimated his age as around 16, but his behaviour was that of a much younger child and he could give no explanation of his origins or of how he had come to be there. Later, he told a story of having lived in a hole in the ground, completely isolated from the world apart from a mysterious man who looked after his needs but had eventually abandoned him in the marketplace.

He seemed to be completely unused to human contact and walked with the unsteady gait of a toddler. While he was able to speak and understand German, his vocabulary and grasp of grammar were childish. He was carrying two letters, one purportedly written by his mother, saying that his name was Kaspar and explaining that he was the illegitimate son of a cavalry officer. The writer claimed to be too poor to care for him and asked for him to be taken in by a peasant family until he was old enough to join the cavalry like his father. The other letter, from the family who had raised the baby, asked that he be enrolled in a cavalry regiment. It was later argued that both documents were forgeries.

Hauser would eat only bread and water at first, claiming that these had been his only form of nourishment throughout his life. However, he did not exhibit the effects of the malnutrition he would undoubtedly have suffered if this had been the case. Rumours about his origins soon spread, one of the most persistent being that he was a scion of a noble family. In particular, it was claimed that he was the son of Karl, Grand Duke of Baden (1786–1818), whose title had passed to an uncle after he had died without a living son. The theory was that a dying baby boy had been substituted for Kaspar, thus cheating him of his inheritance. Presumably those responsible lacked the hardness of heart to murder the boy. On the other hand, many believed Hauser to be a fake.

The youth's story became famous throughout Europe and he was looked after and studied by various eminent men. He was educated and gradually made to be more at home in society but never lost an air of strangeness and other worldly innocence. His senses were said to be more acute than normal, especially his sense of smell and his eyesight, which allegedly allowed him to see in the dark.

In 1829 he was the victim of a knife attack by a hooded man which left him with a serious head wound. While some accused him of having inflicted the injury on himself, others took the incident as proof that vested interests were concerned with having Hauser put out of the way or frightened into silence.

Whatever the truth of the first incident, four years later Hauser was fatally stabbed by an unidentified assailant, dying after three days in which he was often accused of having attempted suicide. Hauser died insisting that he had not harmed himself.

The story was brought to a wider audience in 1974, when the German director and screenwriter Werner Herzog (1942–) filmed it as *The Enigma of Kaspar Hauser*.

In 2002 DNA-matching tests were carried out on samples from Hauser's clothing and from the royal family of Baden. The results appeared to show that the boy was indeed related to them. However, the truth behind his short and sad existence remains a mystery.

Hell Hole *see* SIBERIAN HELL HOLE

henges
Prehistoric enclosed circular or oval areas.

'Henge' is the name given to two types of prehistoric construction. The first is a circular or oval plateau enclosed by an earthen bank and an internal ditch; sometimes it contains a burial chamber. It seems that the material excavated to make the ditch was usually used to form the outer bank. Sometimes a second encircling ditch is found, and occasionally there is no ditch at all. The second type of henge is again a circular or oval plateau, but in this case surrounded by a construction of large standing stones, such as at STONEHENGE or AVEBURY, or wooden posts, such as at WOODHENGE. Each type had at least one formal entrance leading to the central enclosure. The word itself is a back-formation from Stonehenge, which literally means 'stone gallows'.

The purpose of henges is still a matter of conjecture, but it is assumed that they had some sort of religious or ritual function. The fact that the ditch is always inside the bank would indicate that they were certainly not intended as fortified sites. Some henges are believed to have been built with a deliberate alignment of the axis (and the entrance) towards a particular point of the compass or the position of sunrise or sunset on important days. However, many do not fit into this category and it is thought local geographical conditions often determined the siting. See also MEGALITHS.

Hermetic Order of the Golden Dawn

An occult society founded in 1888 which incorporated elements of Rosicrucianism, Freemasonry and the kabbalah, and focused on both practical and ritual magic; although short-lived, it was probably the most influential Western magical order of modern times.

Originally titled the Fraternity of the Esoteric Order of the Golden Dawn, the occult society better known as the Hermetic Order of the Golden Dawn was founded in 1888 by three members of a group called the Societas Rosicruciana: Dr William R Woodman, Dr Wynn Westcott and MacGregor Mathers. The founders compiled and developed a system of philosophy, rituals, magical incantations and symbols that incorporated elements from the kabbalah, Rosicrucianism (see ROSICRUCIANS) and FREEMASONRY, as well as material from the Egyptian Book of the Dead. Its concepts and works were also influenced by theosophy, Éliphas Lévi and late medieval grimoires. The stated purpose of the order was to test, purify and exalt the spiritual nature of the individual, and to further what it called 'the Great Work', which was to obtain control of the nature and power of one's being. The Outer Order of the Golden Dawn was controlled by an Inner Order of which only Westcott, Woodman and Mathers were members and the self-appointed chiefs. Mathers claimed to receive his orders and teachings from a third order of superhuman adepts called

MacGregor Mathers, co-founder of the Hermetic Order of the Golden Dawn, is seen here performing his rites of Isis.
(© 2006 TopFoto/Fortean)

the secret chiefs, thought to be entities of the astral plane. The structured hierarchy was based upon the Tree of Life of the kabbalah, with ten grades corresponding to the Tree of Life's ten sephiroth. The order taught three magical systems: the Key of Solomon, Abramelin, and Enochian. It also gave instruction in astral travel, scrying, alchemy, the tarot and astrology.

Commonly referred to as the Golden Dawn, this organization was probably the single greatest influence on 20th-century occultism. In it, most of the concepts of magic and ritual that have since become core elements of Wicca, Thelema, Western Mystery Schools and other forms of magical spirituality were first formulated. From its very beginnings, it wrapped itself in a cloak of manufactured legend and secrecy; members took an oath not to publicly reveal its teachings, on pain of being struck down by spirits. It attracted a membership which included a number of prominent poets and artists, notably the authors Algernon Blackwood and W B Yeats, who in later life stated that all of his work derived from his study and practice of magic. One of its most revolutionary aspects was the admittance of women to its ranks, unlike Masonic and Rosicrucian lodges, which were exclusively male.

Its Outer Order focused on practical magic, while its Inner Order, which was also the organization's repository of Rosicrucian knowledge, dedicated itself to experimental ritual magic. In 1891, Westcott founded the Westcott Hermetic Library as an alchemical resource for its members. One of its best-known and lasting legacies is the Golden Dawn Tarot, designed by Mathers.

When Woodman died in 1891, he was not replaced within the organization. Westcott resigned to protect his position as the London coroner, leaving Mathers in effective control of the order. Aleister Crowley joined the society in 1898, quickly rising through its ranks, but then he and Mathers fell out; the antagonism between them is said to have led to their engaging in a psychic war which went on for years. In any event, both were eventually expelled from the order, which subsequently fragmented, with various members claiming leadership. Some members left to form a society which retained the name of the Golden Dawn, but was more focused on mysticism than magic, and this underwent further splits; the followers of Mathers founded one spin-off organization, the Alpha et Omega Temple, and another main splinter group was called the Stella Matutina. Today, numerous societies exist which claim heirdom to the Golden Dawn tradition. Although it only lasted 15 years, it remains one of the most influential Western magical orders of modern times.

Herne the Hunter

In folklore, a spectral huntsman wearing a pair of stag's antlers who is said to haunt Windsor Great Park. According to legend, he appears when the monarch is about to die or at other times of national crisis.

The first recorded reference to Herne the Hunter, a ghostly figure wearing a pair of stag's horns who is said to haunt Windsor Great Park, is from around 1597, in Shakespeare's play *The Merry Wives of Windsor*:

> There is an old tale goes that Herne the Hunter
>
> Sometime a keeper here in Windsor Forest,
>
> Doth all the winter-time, at still midnight,
>
> Walk round about an oak, with great ragg'd horns ...

You have heard of such a spirit, and well you know

The superstitious idle-headed eld

Receiv'd, and did deliver to our age,

This tale of Herne the Hunter for a truth.

There are several versions of the legend of Herne the Hunter, but the traditional story is that he was one of many huntsmen employed by King Richard II on the Windsor Castle estate. During a hunting party, Herne saved the King's life when he was attacked by a wounded stag, but in doing so was mortally injured himself. A local wizard called Philip Urwick appeared from nowhere and offered to help, and he ordered that the dead stag's antlers should be removed and placed on Herne's head. He then took Herne to his hut and tended him for a month, and when he was restored to health, Herne returned to court and the King made him his favourite, giving him magnificent gifts such as a gold chain. But Herne's fellow foresters, jealous at his rise, went to Urwick and persuaded him to use his powers to remove Herne's hunting skills. He did so, and the King was forced to dismiss Herne from his service. In one version of the story, Herne's rivals also framed him for poaching. In shame and despair, Herne hanged himself from an oak tree in the forest, and the tree was blasted by lightning during a terrible thunderstorm.

Herne's rivals were at first delighted, but soon they too lost their hunting abilities and, consulting Urwick, they were told that they would have to appeal to Herne's spirit for mercy. They went to the oak and called on him, and he appeared, wearing his antlers, and ordered them to bring the royal horses and hounds to him and ride out to hunt with him the next night, and every night following. They obeyed, and soon the deer herds were depleted and the King demanded to know the cause. The huntsmen confessed their story. That night, Richard walked through the park, and Herne's spirit appeared and told him that the huntsmen who had brought about his death must be hanged from his oak. After this was done, the deer returned to the park as if by magic, and Herne never appeared again during Richard's reign, until the King's murder. Every winter, he is said to ride out at midnight on a black horse, accompanied by fierce hunting dogs and a horned owl, carrying a hunting horn and his golden chain, and still wearing his antlers. The hanged huntsmen are compelled to ride with him for all eternity, and he leads a wild hunt through the forest at the mid-winter solstice, collecting damned souls to join him. He is said to appear at the tree now known as Herne's Oak whenever the monarch behaves unjustly, or is about to die, or when the nation is in danger, and is said to have been sighted before such historic events as the execution of Charles I in 1649, the eve of both World Wars in 1914 and 1939, the abdication of Edward VIII in 1936 and George VI's death in 1952. It is generally believed that the Herne's Oak of Shakespeare's time was felled by accident in 1796, and that replacements have been planted on or around the original site since then.

Some people have suggested that certain motifs in the story – the wearing of stag's horns, the significance of the oak tree and the reference to the Wild Hunt – are echoes of much older myths of a Horned God, as worshipped in Britain in pagan times, and that these elements, retained as a distant folk memory, were combined with a local ghost story to create a legend that has become part of British folkore.

hill figures *see* CHALK FIGURES

hollow earth theory

The idea that the earth is not solid but hollow.

The idea that the planet earth is not a solid mass but is hollow inside was first given scientific credence by the English astronomer Edmond Halley (1656–1742). Halley was interested in magnetic variations of the compass and he developed the theory that these could be accounted for by the existence of more than one magnetic field. He came to believe that there were several spheres, one inside another, that were filled with a luminous gas. Quantities of this gas escaping at the North Pole where the outer crust was thin were, he thought, the explanation of the AURORA BOREALIS.

The hollow earth theory was also supported by the American businessman John Symmes (1780–1829), who also believed that there were entrances to another world of the interior, thousands of miles wide, at each of the poles. He dreamed of mounting an expedition to explore the Arctic and discover the 'Symmes' Hole' there. This never happened, but some of those who took part in a US expedition to Antarctica (1838–42) were aware of the theory, though, of course, no such hole was found.

Other followers of the theory included Cyrus Read Teed (1839–1908), a US physician who believed not only that the earth was hollow but that the interior was populated and illuminated by its own sun. Teed went on to found his own religious cult, centred on belief in his theories.

When a frozen woolly mammoth was found in Siberia in 1846, believers in the hollow earth hypothesis took this as proof, arguing that the creature was not extinct in the centre of the earth and had emerged from there only to freeze to death relatively recently.

The idea perhaps found its most lasting 19th-century exposition in the science fiction of the French novelist Jules Verne (1828–1905). In his *A Journey to the Centre of the Earth* (1872), he describes explorers descending inside a volcano to discover a prehistoric world, complete with dinosaurs, at the earth's core.

In the 20th century, the hollow earth theory became linked to belief in aliens, as the idea became popular that the centre of the earth was populated by extraterrestrials. These beings were said to emerge from the poles from time to time in spacecraft, thus providing an explanation for some sightings of UFOs. Some people apparently believe that the Nazis were aware of an entrance to the centre of the world at the South Pole and that Hitler and his immediate retinue escaped there at the end of World War II.

Aircraft flights over both poles, beginning with that of US admiral Richard Byrd (1888–1957) over the North Pole in 1926, and the photographic evidence they provided failed to convince believers that there were in fact no vast entrances to the hollow interior of our planet. The advent of space flight and the photographs of earth taken from space would also seem to add weight to the argument against the existence of such enormous holes in the earth's surface.

However, the hollow earth theory still has its adherents, and not only in the world of science fiction and fantasy.

Holy Grail

In Christian mythology, the dish or cup said to have been used by Jesus at the Last Supper and, in some accounts, to have been used by Joseph of Arimathea to catch the blood of Jesus as he hung on the cross. This legendary vessel featured prominently as the object of a quest by the Knights of the Round Table in the medieval Arthurian romance cycle, and belief in its existence, and speculation as to its whereabouts, persist to this day.

The Holy Grail, also known as the Sangraal, is the legendary subject of several late-medieval Arthurian romances. This dish or cup, which possessed magical powers such as the ability to heal all wounds, was said to have been used by Jesus at the Last Supper and, in some versions of the story, to have been used by Joseph of Arimathea to catch the blood of Jesus as he hung on the cross. The origin of the Grail legend is obscure, but it is thought that much of its setting and imagery draws from pagan Celtic mythology, which includes a number of stories featuring magical cauldrons which can restore life. The Grail romances started in the 12th century in France (the word 'grail' comes from the French *graal*), and were translated into other European languages.

A common theme in the Grail cycle is that it is a symbol of God's grace, which can only be attained by someone who is spiritually pure. In some accounts, the Grail was brought to GLASTONBURY TOR in Britain by JOSEPH OF ARIMATHEA, who established a dynasty of custodians to guard it, but it was lost because of their unworthiness. A number of Christian revisionists have claimed that the identification of the Grail of Joseph with the Holy Chalice used by Christ at the Last Supper is erroneous, but this remains historical practice.

Belief in the Grail's existence, and speculation as to its whereabouts, persist to this day. It is rumoured by some to have been brought to Britain and hidden by the KNIGHTS TEMPLAR, or to have been thrown into the Chalice Well at Glastonbury. Books such as *THE DA VINCI CODE* have also popularized the idea that the Grail is hidden in ROSLYN CHAPEL, in Scotland.

homing animals
Animals that travel long distances to be reunited with their owners.

Every so often, an article appears in the press that tells the story of an animal reunited with its owner after a long and perilous trek, not entirely dissimilar to the plot of the 1963 Disney film *The Incredible Journey*. A typical example is the story of Doug Simpson of Selah, Washington, and his Alsatian, Nick. Simpson was on holiday with Nick in the Arizona desert when the dog went missing. Simpson searched for the dog, but eventually had to return home, more than 1,000 miles away. Four months later, Nick arrived at Simpson's home in Selah, battered, emaciated and exhausted, but definitely alive. The terrain the dog had apparently covered included desert and mountains. Numerous such examples have been collected over the years. But while Nick the Alsatian 'simply' managed to find its way home, what about animals that find their owners when their owners have moved house?

In 1952, retired schoolteacher Stacy Wood moved from her home in Anderson, California, to Gage in Oklahoma, some 1,500 miles away. She had a two-year-old Persian cat called Sugar, but Sugar had a hip deformity and did not enjoy travelling, so Wood arranged for the cat to live with a neighbour, rather than undergo the long journey. After two weeks with her new owners, Sugar disappeared, only to appear 14 months later at Wood's new home. The hip deformity seemed to confirm that the cat was the same one. Another homing animal apparently authenticated by a bone deformity was the cat of New York vet Michael W Fox. Fox left his cat to be cared for in New York when he moved to California, 2,500 miles away. Months later, a cat that looked just like the one he had left in New York appeared at his new house. He examined the cat, finding the same deformed bone growth in the fourth vertebra of its tail as he had found when he had examined the cat in New York, months earlier.

Sceptics dismiss stories of homing animals, saying that owners unintentionally claim other animals for their own simply because they miss their pets so much. However, stories such as those of the cats mentioned above seem to be authenticated by veterinary evidence. Many suggestions have been made to explain how animals might manage to do this, including teleportation or telepathy, but as yet no satisfactory answer has been found.

Hope Diamond
A blue Indian diamond which is said to be cursed.

The Hope Diamond is the world's

Socialite Evalyn Walsh McLean wearing the Hope Diamond on a necklace; some claim that the misfortunes in her life were consequences of the jewel's curse. (© Bettmann/Corbis)

largest blue diamond, currently in the possession of the Smithsonian Institution in Washington, DC. Apart from its size and beauty, it is famous for the legendary curse said to befall those who own it.

The stone is believed to have originated in India, as part of a much larger diamond bought in the 17th century by the French traveller Jean Baptiste Tavernier (1605–89), who subsequently sold it to Louis XIV (1638–1715). As part of the French crown jewels, it became known as the 'French Blue' until it was stolen in 1792 during the French Revolution.

It reappeared as a smaller stone in England, and its owners included George IV (1762–1830). In 1839 it appeared in the catalogue of the collection of the banker Henry Philip Hope (d.1839), from whom it acquired its lasting name. The gem remained in the Hope family until it was sold in 1901 to pay off debts, eventually becoming the property of the French jeweller Pierre Cartier (1878–1965).

In 1911 Cartier sold the diamond to US socialite Mrs Evalyn Walsh McLean (1886–1947), who had it set in a necklace. Sold after her death, it was donated to the Smithsonian Institution in 1958 by New York diamond merchant Harry Winston (1896–1978).

The legend of a curse seems to derive from an article published in *The Times* in 1909 while the jewel was being sold at auction in Paris. The journalist related a history of untimely deaths suffered by people through whose hands the diamond had passed. According to this, the curse arose from the original diamond having been stolen from a Hindu temple, where it had formed one of the eyes of an idol of the god Siva.

The first victim was said to be Jean Baptiste Tavernier, who, on another journey to India, was apparently torn to pieces by wild dogs. Among other unlucky owners were Louis XVI (1754–93) and his queen Marie Antoinette (1754–93), who were executed during the French Revolution. The last Sultan of Turkey, Abd-ul-Hamid II (1842–1918), was said to have owned the gem for a time before being deposed in 1909.

The legend grew in 1929 when the American actress and singer May Yohe (1869–1938), who was married to Lord Francis Hope, the last of the Hopes to own the diamond, published her book *The Mystery of the Hope Diamond*. This volume recounted the well-known stories and added a few more, although some of the protagonists seem to be fictional.

Is there any truth in the notion of a curse? Much of the evidence does not stand up to scrutiny. It is unlikely that the diamond was ever the eye of an idol, being the wrong shape according to descriptions and sketches by Tavernier (who died, an old man, in his bed and not between the teeth of savage dogs). Any student of history could point out reasons for the fate of the French king and queen that are quite independent of their jewellery collection. The same is true of the Turkish Sultan, whose empire was on its last legs before backing the losing side in World War I finished it off.

As for Mrs Evalyn Walsh McLean, it has to be said that her life was afflicted with misfortunes. Her son was killed in a car accident while still a child, her estranged husband died an alcoholic in an asylum and her daughter succumbed to a drug overdose at the age of 25. However, hers is not the only family to find wealth no guarantee of happiness.

I

ice circles
Mysterious circles found in frozen ponds and rivers.

In various parts of the world, but most commonly in North America, northern Europe and Russia, people have discovered and photographed mysterious circle patterns that have appeared in frozen bodies of water overnight. Like CROP CIRCLES, these ice circles are usually perfectly geometrical in shape but, unlike crop circles, no more elaborate patterns or complex designs have been found. Again like crop circles, there is considerable variation in the size of the ice circles: some occur on thinner ice than others; some appear smooth and contained within the ice; others seem to have been scored into the surface with a sharp implement, leaving shards.

In the absence of skating FAIRIES, some link these formations with UFO activity, and speak of seeing strange glows in the sky or briefly glimpsed silvery craft hovering over the site. Unfortunately, no photographs have appeared to back up these claims.

Sceptics point to circles that have obviously been scored into the surface and detect the hand of hoaxers, but in some cases these scored circles have appeared on ice too thin to support the weight of a person. It has been pointed out that in rivers rotating ice sheets often form and freeze where the river turns, but this obviously fails to explain circles formed in still water.

ice falls *see* FALLS

Illuminati
A name adopted by various philosophical or religious societies which claim enlightenment, and especially used to refer to an 18th-century group of German freethinkers known as the Bavarian Illuminati. Since its abolition in the late 18th century, this organization has been the focus of numerous claims that it survives and continues to work towards a goal of world domination.

The word *illuminati*, which is Latin for 'the enlightened ones', was originally used by the Ante-Nicene clergy to refer to those who underwent Christian baptism, on the grounds that they then had an enlightened understanding. The name was subsequently adopted by a number of secret or mystical societies which claimed special enlightenment, such as the Alumbrados, a 16th-century Spanish sect. However, it is now most commonly associated with the Bavarian Illuminati, a short-lived movement of German republican freethinkers that was founded in 1776 by ex-Jesuit Adam Weishaupt and Baron Adolph von Knigge.

Originally calling itself the Order of Perfectibilists, the group aimed to discuss and disseminate the radical philosophies of the day; to combat religious superstition and encourage rationalism; to increase morality and virtue and oppose evil; and thus to lay the foundations for the reformation of the world. While there is some dispute as to whether or not its members were principally Freemasons (see FREEMASONRY), or former Freemasons, it certainly incorporated or adapted much Masonic ritual, although its approach was of a rationalistic rather than an occult nature. This offshoot of the European Enlightenment attracted a considerable membership, including literary men such as Goethe and Herder, and in its heyday it had branches in most countries on the continent of Europe. However, it soon became subject to internal splits and factions, and an edict issued by the Bavarian government in 1785 led to its abolition. It had officially ceased to exist by 1790.

However, it was not long before its opponents began to suggest that the organization had survived abolition and continued to operate in secret. In 1798 the British author John Robison and the French author Abbé Augustin Barruél both published works making these claims; Barruél stated that the French Revolution of 1789 had been engineered and controlled through the Jacobins by the Illuminati, and later theorists also claimed that they were responsible for the Russian Revolution in 1917. The movement has been the subject of various conspiracy theories alleging its ongoing influence on world affairs. Some say that the Illuminati are in league with the KNIGHTS TEMPLAR and the ROSICRUCIANS, and that their conspiracy leads back to the Vatican; some that the organization is much older than its Bavarian incarnation, and that it dates back to ancient Egyptian times, while others go further and claim that it is of extraterrestrial origin. The common theme which runs through all of these theories is that its aim is world domination. It is generally said to be working towards the replacement of all religions and nations with humanism and a single world power – employing such methods as blackmail, assassination, the control of banks, the infiltration of government, wars, revolution and even mind control in order to move its members into positions of power.

This notion of an all-powerful secret society controlling world affairs has captured the imagination of many writers, and has had a distinct influence on popular culture; a number of science fiction authors have used it as a theme, and Umberto Eco's novel *Foucault's Pendulum* (1989) includes references to the Illuminati, as does Dan Brown's 2000 novel *Angels and Demons*; several video and computer games are also based on storylines involving them, and the villains of the 2001 film *Lara Croft: Tomb Raider* are a group called the Illuminati, whose plan is to rule the world, and who claim to have existed for millennia for this purpose.

Although there is little or no reliable evidence to support the claim that the Bavarian Illuminati survived after the end of the 18th century, one possible reason for the persistence of conspiracy theories about them may be the fact that a number of groups have used the name since then, many of which claim to be descended from the Bavarian Illuminati. See also SECRET SOCIETIES.

images, bleeding

Apparently miraculous images that appear to 'bleed'.

In the classical Greek period, there were stories of sacred groves of trees which yielded wood for crafting divine effigies, which bled when attacked. While it may not be the origin of modern accounts of statues and pictures that bleed, it shows that the pious belief that sacred images may 'come alive' when a divine spirit inhabits them is quite ancient. That this tradition is persistent is demonstrated by the occasional historical example, such as the 'miraculous painting' of the Virgin Mary of Mantua, in Lombardy, Italy. According to legend, it was looted in the 17th century and hung on a tree for target practice. It is said that when a bullet rebounded off the icon, blood spurted from the damaged painting. It is now on display in the Church of Maria and St Anthony of Padua, in Prague, and supposedly still bleeds to this day.

Since the 1980s, there has been an unprecedented rise in the number of reports of bleeding images, nearly all of them in a Catholic context. The phenomena exhibited include bleeding from the wounds of the crucifixion, sweating blood, a flow of tears of blood from the eyes (see also IMAGES, WEEPING) and, more rarely, bleeding from a Eucharistic host held by a statuette. Many of the images involved were bought on visits to shrines of earlier 'miracles' or visions, so there is also an element of 'transmission' in this phenomenon.

The majority of cases are never properly investigated. Of those that are, most are quickly unmasked as simple, if pious, frauds, and bishops have not shrunk from condemning them. A very few cases have been tentatively authenticated and hotly contested. One of the most famous of these, which illustrates the difficulties involved in investigation, occurred in the Italian port of Civitavecchia in 1995. The small plaster statuette of the Virgin Mary had been bought at Medjugorje (a town in Bosnia-Herzegovina associated with MARIAN APPARITIONS) and installed in the garden of the Gregori family home. One day, blood-like tracks that streamed

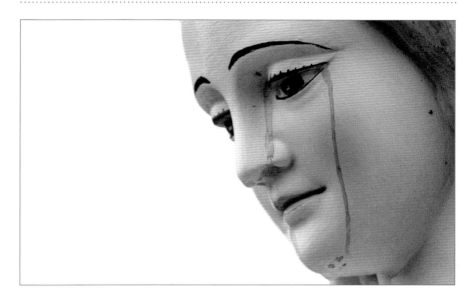

This weeping statue of the Virgin Mary in Sacramento, California, is said to cry tears of blood. (© Corbis)

from its eyes were found. This was quickly proclaimed a 'miracle', and thousands came to see the 'tears of blood'. The local bishop, Girolamo Grillo, a renowned sceptic in matters of superstition, ordered an investigation by civil and forensic authorities. However, instead of revealing a hoax, as the bishop hoped, the study by the Institute for Forensic Medicine at the University of Rome established that the statue was solid and had no mechanism for delivering a fluid to the eyes, and that the red fluid was all or partly male human blood. A theological commission, set up to consider the implications of at least 60 eyewitness testimonies, judged that the male blood on the female statue indicated the unity of the Holy Mother and Son. During these investigations the statue was locked away in Bishop Grillo's possession and, he claims, it once cried tears of blood in his hands. Now convinced of its authenticity, he placed it on public display in Civitavecchia's Church of San Agostino. Since then, the numbers of miracle cures, conversions and pilgrims attributed to it have grown each year.

Almost immediately, one of Italy's largest consumer groups brought a formal complaint against 'unknown persons' under a 1930s law prohibiting fraudulent magicians and hoaxers, which was followed by allegations of fraud from other sources. In 2001, the ongoing inquiry by police and other authorities was hindered by the Gregori family's refusal to provide DNA samples. The case was eventually dismissed by a judge on the grounds of failure to come up with any evidence to support the allegations within a period of six years. Since then, the phenomenon seems to have received some unofficial approval from senior clergy.

Proper sceptical inquiry can also be fraught with conflicting ideologies. For example, in Cochabamba, Bolivia, a statue of the crucified Christ is believed by many to bleed from wounds, shed tears of blood and sweat blood. The phenomenon began in March 1995 and has apparently returned each Easter Holy Week since then. Later that year, film-maker Ron Tesoriero and Dr Ricardo Castanon twice took samples of the blood-like liquid for DNA analysis at Gentest in the USA and at a state forensic laboratory in Australia. Both confirmed the presence of human female blood products. Michael Willesee, who included this account in the documentary he made for Fox, the US TV network (*Signs From God: Science Tests Faith*, first aired in the USA in July 1999), was not fazed by the discovery of female blood exuding from the statue of a male deity – the opposite of the situation at Civitavecchia. A born-again Catholic, Willesee suggested that the blood was either the Virgin Mary's or, as Jesus had a single human parent, he somehow shared her female genetic make-up.

Inevitably, this creative interpretation failed to impress the Committee for the Scientific Investigation of Claims of the Paranormal-school of sceptics who commented on the documentary. Not only did they propose a number of ways in which statues and icons can, surreptitiously, be made to appear to weep or bleed, but they raised the suspicion that, as the owner of the statue was female, the blood might be hers. The doubts were not resolved because no proof was offered to support these claims. To complicate matters, the 'bleeding' statue of Cochabamba is also closely associated with two female 'mystics' – Catalina Rivas (who herself developed stigmata) and Nancy Fowler – who both claim to receive messages from Jesus and who both have their own devout followers.

The most bizarre claim in this category is the menstruating statue of the Hindu goddess Bhagawati, at a temple in Kerala, India. The temple is built on the site of a visit by the god Shiva, and his wife Parvati, to a local sage. During the visit, the goddess began to menstruate and, according to tradition, went into seclusion for three days. The statue of Bhagawati is made of iron and said to be a replica of an ancient one, lost in a fire. The statue wears a napkin which is periodically examined for signs of menstruation; if present, the statue is removed for a three-day cleansing ritual, following which it is reinstated in a grand ceremony.

images, spontaneous
Meaningful images which apparently appear without human intervention.

Human beings have an exceptional

visual sense. Once the mind is engaged, the simple act of looking (ie merely directing the eyes towards something) becomes the immeasurably greater and more complex act of perception – involving consideration, deduction, extrapolation, memory, understanding, curiosity and especially imagination. The organizational processes the mind applies to our perceptions, particularly vision and hearing, allow us to quickly detect patterns in the sensory input. Among these processes are *apophenia* (perception of connections between seemingly unrelated data) and *pareidolia* (perceptions in which vague stimuli can be overlaid with distinct meaning or details). In effect, humans are predisposed to see meaningful images wherever they look.

Forms, figures and scenes occurring spontaneously through natural or accidental processes come under the general fortean heading of SIMULACRA. Typical examples would include the shapes of animals in clouds, faces in the bark of trees or grain of wood, or abstract landscapes in rock formations or polished sections of stone (such as those Richard Shaver saw as signs of an ancient civilization inside the earth). Other such images, claimed by some to be divinely created, are called *acheiropoieta* (see TURIN SHROUD). There are no certain boundaries to these definitions. Many spontaneous images cross categories and are interpreted according to the opinions of the viewer – such as marks that resemble holy script or symbols.

We might also include within the category of spontaneous images some of the photographs said to contain images of ghosts, saints or Jesus and the Virgin Mary; these are often said to have occurred when the camera 'went off by itself'.

More problematical cases involve religious images that seem to move, weep or bleed, because they usually occur within a fervent atmosphere of devotion and expectation (for examples, see IMAGES, BLEEDING and IMAGES, WEEPING).

images, weeping
Apparently miraculous images that appear to 'weep'.

While there has been an unprecedented rise in the number of reports of bleeding statues and pictures since the 1980s (see IMAGES, BLEEDING), reports of statues and pictures of Jesus and of his Mother weeping, oozing or sweating clear or oily liquids began increasing in the 1970s.

The antiquity of this phenomenon is well established by relatively isolated events. From the time of the Middle Ages, accounts of pilgrimages to the Holy Land sometimes mentioned locations of weeping icons. The Madonna and Child icon of Marijapovch, in north-eastern Hungary, which has reportedly been weeping since 1715, is itself a copy of an earlier icon which apparently began weeping in 1696, and was appropriated by the Austrian emperor Leopold I. A similar weeping icon was venerated in the Slovakian village of Klokochovo in 1670. Another typical example is the statue of the scourged Christ, once used during processions in Steingaden, Germany – until it was put away in 1735 because it appeared 'uncomfortably pitiful'. When it was found again in 1738 in a farmhouse in Wies, it was said to be wet with tears. St Gregory of Tours (538–94) described the practice by some religious communities of using weeping statues to convert non-believers, but it is not clear whether these were examples of pious fraud or supposedly authentic occurrences.

The overwhelming majority of weeping images are representations of the Virgin Mary and, like the bleeding images, have often been bought at the shrines of earlier miracles. The theological explanation for the phenomenon is that it represents Mary's desolation at the sins and sufferings of this world. Many are associated with the initial mystical experience of a nun or pilgrim – such as Sister Agnes Sasagawa at Akita, in Japan, who, in the throes of her own stigmatization in July 1973, heard a voice from a wooden statuette of Mary. Like the statuette, Agnes bore a cross-shaped wound on one hand, from which blood flowed. In January 1975 the nature of the exudations changed; they became clear and more like tears or sweat, and continued like that for the next six years. Bishop Ito of Niigata ordered a sample of blood and tears from the statue to be sent to the Faculty of Legal Medicine of the University of Akita for scientific analysis. This confirmed that the samples were of human origin but from three different blood groups, which was interpreted as a sign of the Holy Trinity being present rather than indicating a hoax. In 1984 Bishop Ito declared the phenomenon to be 'of supernatural origin', and in June 1988 Cardinal Ratzinger (then Prefect of the Congregation for the Doctrine of the Faith, later to become Pope Benedict XVI) judged the phenomenon at Akita 'reliable and worthy of belief'.

Some sceptics remain unconvinced. It is all too easy to fake the weeping or bleeding of a statue. A leading Italian sceptic, Dr Luigi Garlaschelli of Pavia University, has recreated one using 'a hollow statue made of a porous material … glazed or painted with some sort of impermeable coating'. The statue is filled with liquid which then seeps out through a tiny hole or scratch in the head. 'When I put it to the test, this trick proved to be very satisfactory, baffling all onlookers', he wrote.

This hypothesis accounts well for some cases, such as the plaster statuette of the Virgin Mary at the Inala Vietnamese Catholic Centre in Brisbane, Australia, which was said in May 2002 to be exuding a scented oil. The Archbishop of Brisbane, John Bathersby, convened a commission, headed by an agnostic chemistry professor, which subjected the statue to X-ray examination and the oil to gas chromatography and mass spectroscopy tests. They found the oil was similar to a commercial product, a red substance which was not blood, and that 'two small-diameter holes had been drilled through the statue through which liquids could have been injected'. The archbishop promptly declared that the exudations were 'not, within the proper meaning of the word, a miracle' and that the statue should be removed from public veneration, and ordered an inquiry into the funds and donations it had generated.

On the other hand, Dr Luigi Garlaschelli's hypothesis does not seem to explain the instances where statues involved are solid or non-porous, where the phenomenon persists over a long period or where the liquids contain identifiable human blood. It leaves many questions still unanswered. Parapsychologists and forteans have speculated as to whether, if any authentic phenomena were proved to be involved, these cases might be related to those poltergeist cases which are alleged to include mysterious flows of liquids, teleportations of liquids and so-called 'persistent stains'.

J

jack-o'-lantern *see* WILL-O'-THE-WISP

Jeffries, Anne
(c.1626–c.1698)

A Cornish woman who, in 1645, claimed to have been spirited away by fairies and taken to fairyland. On her return, she apparently possessed healing powers and the gift of clairvoyance.

The story of Anne Jeffries has passed into West Country legend. This Cornish woman was said to have gone into service with a family living in St Teath at the age of 19. Intelligent but illiterate, Anne had always been fascinated by FAIRIES, and in her free time she often searched for them. In 1645 she fell into a fit, and was ill for some time afterwards, but later, when she had recovered, she began to make prophecies, and apparently demonstrated healing powers. She said that while she was suffering from her fit, she had been taken to fairyland, and that the fairies had given her these new powers.

Anne claimed she had been sitting knitting in the bower of the garden when she had heard tinkling sounds, rustling and laughter, and six beautiful little men dressed handsomely in green had appeared before her. They scrambled onto her lap and began to kiss and stroke her affectionately, much to her delight, and then one had put his hands over her eyes. She felt a sharp stinging and everything went dark. Then she was lifted into the air and carried away, and when she was set down again and her sight was restored, she found herself, dressed in magnificent clothes, in a wonderful land full of fairies who appeared to be human-sized. Her six companions were there, also now full-sized, and they continued to court her. She would have happily stayed there forever; she was particularly enamoured of their leader, and presently the two of them stole off together to make love. However, they were interrupted by her other suitors, who were accompanied by an angry crowd, and in the fight which ensued, her lover was struck down and fell wounded at her feet. The fairy who had blinded her once again put his hands over her eyes, and she felt herself being transported back to the bower, where she woke to find herself surrounded by anxious friends.

Although Anne never returned to fairyland, she said the fairies were with her constantly, although only she could see them. Word of Anne's healing touch and her curative salves and medicines soon spread, and people came to seek her help. But although, after her fairy experience, Anne became very devout in her religion, her powers brought her to the attention of a local Justice of the Peace, John Tregeagle, who had her arrested and imprisoned, first in Bodmin Jail and later in the house of the Mayor of Bodmin, for six months. During this time, she was apparently not fed, but she did not complain and remained in good health until her release.

In 1696, while Anne was still alive, Moses Pitt, the son of her old master and mistress, sent a letter to the Bishop of Gloucester which gives an account of Anne's later life and his own early memories – he was still a child when Anne had come to work for his family. He recalled seeing her dancing in the orchard, and her telling him that she had been dancing with the fairies. She said they fed her fairy food, and Moses related how she had once given him a piece of fairy bread, and it had been the most delicious bread he had ever tasted. While composing his letter, Moses Pitt sent an old friend of the family to speak to Anne, but, not wishing to repeat her experiences at John Tregeagle's hands or draw further attention to herself, Anne refused to say anything. She never took any payment for her alleged cures, and is thought to have died in 1698.

Joseph of Arimathea, St (1st century AD)

A wealthy Jew who, according to biblical lore, took Jesus's body down from the cross and laid it in the tomb he had prepared for himself. In medieval times he became connected with the Arthurian cycle as the first keeper of the Holy Grail, which he is said to have brought to Britain.

According to the New Testament gospels, a wealthy Jew called Joseph, who lived in the Judean city of Arimathea and may have been a member of the Sanhedrin, was a secret follower of Jesus. After the crucifixion, he went to Pontius Pilate and asked for Jesus's body; on being granted it, he purchased a fine linen cloth and wrapped the body in it, then placed it in a tomb which he had prepared for his own burial. Further details of his story appear in several New Testament Apocrypha, such as the Acts of Pilate, known in medieval times as the Gospel of Nicodemus or the Narrative of Joseph; this book tells of how the Jewish elders, angered by Joseph's burial of Jesus's body, had him imprisoned, and of how he miraculously escaped and testified to the elders that Jesus had risen from the dead and ascended to Heaven. Christians often interpret Joseph's role as fulfilling Isaiah's prophecy that the grave of the Messiah would be 'with a rich man'.

During the Middle Ages, a series of

This 19th-century stained-glass window from Kilkhampton Church, Cornwall, depicts Joseph of Arimathea carrying the Holy Grail and the flowering Glastonbury Thorn. (© 2004 Charles Walker/TopFoto)

legends came to be attached to Joseph, most of which first appear in Robert de Boron's epic romance of c.1200, *Joseph d'Arimathie*. Joseph is said to have been held in a Roman prison for twelve years, and while there to have received the HOLY GRAIL from an apparition of Christ, becoming its first keeper; after his release he travelled to Britain, and hid the Grail near the Chalice Well at GLASTONBURY TOR. Later works also describe him as being a founder of Christianity in Britain, building the first church and converting the Britons even before the new religion had become established in Rome, and the legend of the Glastonbury Thorn tells of how he planted his hawthorn staff in the ground at Glastonbury, where it flowered for many years afterwards every 5 January (the old Christmas Eve). According to some accounts, he was the uncle of Jesus's mother, Mary, and Jesus is even said to have visited Britain with him as a boy – a legend which inspired William Blake's mystical poem, later to become the hymn 'Jerusalem'.

Joseph of Arimathea is venerated as a saint by the Catholic and Eastern Orthodox Churches, and his feast day is 17 March in the West and 31 July in the East.

K

Keel, John *see* MOTHMAN

Ker-Îs

A mythical lost city, said to lie beneath the sea in the Bay of Douarnenez, off the coast of Brittany, France.

In Breton tradition, Ker-Îs, or Ker-Ys, is a city in the Bay of Douarnenez, now lost beneath the sea. According to the legend, the city was built by Gradlon, a Cornish king, for his daughter Dahut. To prevent it being flooded by the sea, an enormous stone wall was built around it, and the only keys to the gate of this dam were held by Gradlon himself. The city became known as a place of decadence and excess. One night, a storm rose to punish the people of the city. Satan, or one of Dahut's many lovers, encouraged her to steal the keys from her father. Gradlon was saved when a saint warned him to leave, and he took a horse and galloped to safety before the city was engulfed by the sea. Everyone else, including the wicked Dahut, perished. King Gradlon is said to have established Quimper as his capital following the loss of Ker-Îs, and

a statue of him riding his horse stands at Quimper's cathedral, the Cathédrale St-Corentin.

Some believe that Ker-Îs will one day re-emerge from the ocean, and that the first person who sees it will become its king.

The story of Ker-Îs shares many elements with the legendary LYONNESSE, an inundated land off the coast of Cornwall.

King Arthur
Semi-legendary 6th-century king of the Britons.

Enduring legends have ensured a place in British tradition for King Arthur, but was there ever such a person in reality, and how much of the legend is true?

If a historical Arthur existed, he was probably a war leader (not necessarily a king) of the British people who, both Romanized and Christian, resisted the encroachments of the pagan Saxons in the 6th century. He is supposed to have won a great victory at Mount Badon (c.518), to have met his death in a further battle at Camlan (c.539) and to have been buried at Glastonbury. In fact the sites of these battles have not been comprehensively identified and there is no firm evidence to connect Arthur with Glastonbury.

As far as historical chronicles are concerned, the first appearance of Arthur is in the *Historia Britonum* ascribed to the Welsh writer Nennius (fl.769). It might have been expected that he would merit a mention in the Anglo-Saxon Chronicles, which are usually dated to the reign of Alfred the Great (849–99), but no such personage is included.

It has been suggested that Arthur is based on a legendary Celtic hero, as shown by the widespread occurrence of traditional tales about him throughout the former Celtic strongholds, from Cornwall to Scotland and from Wales to Brittany.

Whether or not a real Arthur existed, it is the legend that has become more important, especially as it was elaborated at the hands of writers such as Geoffrey of Monmouth (c.1100–c.1154) and Sir Thomas Malory (d.1471). It is to these later authors that we owe the tradition of his being the son of a high king of Britain, Uther Pendragon, as well as the famous tales of Camelot, the Knights of the Round Table and their quest for the HOLY GRAIL, the magical sword Excalibur, Lancelot and Guinevere, and MERLIN. The post-medieval themes of chivalry and the purity of the knight would certainly not have made much sense to a war

King Arthur and Queen Guinevere sit at a table set for a banquet; Sir Lancelot kneels before them. From a 14th-century French manuscript, 'Romance of the Holy Grail'. (© The British Library/HIP/ TopFoto)

leader fighting for the survival of his people against the Saxons.

According to the stories, after a glorious career of winning battles and righting wrongs, Arthur was mortally wounded at the battle of Camlan by his nephew Mordred. From there he was carried to Avalon, whence in his people's hour of greatest need he will return to save them. Support for this notion is lent by the alleged inscription on his grave: *Hic iacet artorius rex quondam rexque futurus* ('Here lies Arthur, the once and future king'). However, the magnitude of the disaster awaiting the British people that would be severe enough to summon Arthur from his rest must be cataclysmic indeed, given that World War II was not enough to inspire his reappearance.

It is essentially impossible to say for sure whether or not there was a historical Arthur. The chronicles on which we depend for evidence were known to 'print the legend' as well as recount fact. Perhaps Arthur is really a composite figure made up of attributes of several real or legendary heroes and the battles and sites associated with his name belong to more than one individual.

Knights Templar

A religious and military order founded by Crusaders in c.1119 for the protection of the Holy Sepulchre and pilgrims visiting it; suppressed 1307–14.

The Knights Templar was the largest and most powerful of the Christian military orders. Founded in c.1119 in the aftermath of the 1096 Crusade, its purpose was to help the new Kingdom of Jerusalem to defend itself against its hostile Muslim neighbours, and to protect the large numbers of pilgrims who travelled to Jerusalem after its conquest by the Crusaders. Its members took a vow of poverty, and this vow was reflected in the order's seal, which depicted two knights riding on one horse; the order's full

name was originally the Poor Knights (or Fellow Soldiers) of Christ and the Temple of Solomon, although it soon came to be referred to as the Order of the Knights Templar, or simply the Templars. The name derived from the temple, supposedly built by Solomon, near which the Templars were assigned quarters in Jerusalem.

They quickly became a powerful force in the international politics of the Crusades period, and were permitted by various papal bulls to levy taxes and exact tithes in all the areas under their control, being officially exempted from having to answer to any authority except the Pope's.

Because they regularly transported money and goods between Europe and Palestine, the Knights Templar came to develop a highly efficient banking system, and became very successful investors and moneylenders. But it was this success, and their great power, which was probably the cause of their downfall. Having been refused a loan by the order to finance his wars, King Philip IV of France waged a campaign to have them discredited and excommunicated so that he could get control of their wealth for himself, and in 1307 he had most or all of the Templars in France arrested. Interrogated under torture, some confessed to sacrilegious acts, and to the worship of a demonic figure known as Baphomet, and when their leaders denied these admissions, they were executed. A papal inquiry into the practices of the order followed, and by 1314 it had officially ceased to exist,

Life-sized marble effigies of Knights Templar in the Temple Church, London, dating from the 13th century. (© 2006 Charles Walker/TopFoto)

its banking system broken up and its property either seized or turned over to the Hospitallers, a rival military order. As he burned at the stake, Jacques de Molay, the Grand Master of the Knights Templar, is said to have cursed both King Philip and the Pope, and when they both died within a few months of his execution, this added to the legends which later built up around the order.

The Knights Templar figure strongly in the foundation and ritual of FREEMASONRY, and several self-styled orders have claimed to be descended from, or to be a revival of, the Templars. Conspiracy theorists have suggested that the motives for their suppression went far beyond simple jealousy of their wealth and power. Over the centuries, they have been surrounded by stories of secrets and mysteries, with some claiming that the Templars were the repository for secret knowledge which linked them to the ROSICRUCIANS, the Priory of Sion, the Gnostics, and lost relics and teachings of Jesus. The best-known of these theories is that the Templars found the HOLY GRAIL, and after their suppression took it to Scotland, where it was hidden somewhere in ROSLYN CHAPEL. Others say that they found the Ark of the Covenant, a chest containing sacred objects, such as the stone tablets on which God inscribed the Ten

Commandments. The mythos of the Knights Templar as the keepers and guardians of the Holy Grail has captured the imagination of writers and has had a number of influences on popular culture; it forms a central plot point in Umberto Eco's *Foucault's Pendulum* (1989) and, more recently, in Dan Brown's THE DA VINCI CODE, and also figures prominently in the storyline of the 1989 film *Indiana Jones and the Last Crusade*. See also FRIDAY THE 13TH.

kraken

A legendary Scandinavian sea monster, stories of which are now thought to have been inspired by sightings of giant squid.

For many centuries, sailors reported terrifying encounters with the kraken, a sea monster that was said to attack ships, wrapping its tentacles around seamen and dragging them to their deaths in the sea below, or crushing the entire ship in its tentacles, leaving it a wreck. The kraken was said to be such a size that it could be mistaken for an island before it attacked, and Erik Pontoppidan, Bishop of Bergen, described the beasts as 'floating islands' in his *Natural History of Norway* (1752–53), where he also describes a typical encounter with a kraken:

> [Our fishermen's] lines, they say, are no sooner out than they may draw them up with the hooks all full of fish; by this they judge that the kraken is at the bottom ... There are sometimes twenty boats or more got together, and throwing out their lines at a moderate distance from each other; and the only thing they have to observe is, whether the depth continues the same, which they know by their lines, or whether it grows shallower ... If this last be the case, they find that the kraken is raising himself nearer the surface, and then it is not time for them to stay any longer ... When they ... find themselves out of danger, they lie upon their oars, and in a few minutes after they see this enormous monster come up to the surface of the water ... though his whole body does not appear, which, in all likelihood, no human eye ever beheld ... Its back or upper part, which seems in appearance about an English mile and a half in circumference ... looks at first like a number of small islands ... At last several bright points or horns appear, which grow thicker and thicker the higher they rise above the surface of the water, and sometimes they stand up as high, and as large, as the masts of middle-sized vessels. It seems these are the creature's arms, and, it is said, if they were to lay hold of the largest man-of-war, they would pull it down to the bottom.

Zoologists dismissed such stories of the kraken as legend, until some remains from a creature very similar to a kraken were washed ashore near Albaek, Denmark, in 1853. The remains were formally documented and the giant squid gained scientific recognition. The biggest specimen of giant squid so far recorded (and the creature, though now acknowledged, remains elusive) was stranded in Newfoundland in 1878. From tail to beak it measured 6.1 metres (20 feet), and the longest of its tentacles measured 10.7 metres (35 feet). While it is not thought possible that a giant squid could wreck a ship or drown a sailor, many now think that the myth of the kraken grew from genuine sightings of the giant squid.

L

ladders

That it is bad luck to walk under a ladder is one of the most widely known, and acted upon, superstitions of today.

Almost everyone knows that it is 'bad luck' to walk under a ladder, and many people who claim not to be superstitious will still act upon this warning. The earliest known written reference to this superstition dates to 1787, when it was included in Francis Grose's *A Provincial Glossary*. Grose noted that to walk under a ladder 'may prevent your being married that year'. Another specific prediction for the fate of someone who walked under a ladder was that they would end their life on the gallows, but in most instances, and certainly in modern times, to walk under a ladder is simply unlucky.

Should you inadvertently walk under a ladder, it is said to be possible to reverse the bad luck by spitting through its rungs, by crossing your fingers or by not speaking until you see a four-legged animal.

Numerous suggestions have been made to explain why we believe it is unlucky to walk under a ladder. Some have claimed that the ladder, wall, and ground form a triangle which represents the Trinity in Christianity, and to walk through this triangle would be disrespectful. It has also been said that the ladder represents the gallows, or the ladder used at the Crucifixion. There is no evidence to support any of these explanations, and some believe that the superstition arose for purely practical reasons. The fate of one unfortunate pedestrian who recklessly walked under a ladder was described in *Notes & Queries* in 1866:

> A friend of mine, who objected on principle to such superstitious nonsense, had a paint-brush dropped right on his head while passing under a ladder in Cornhill. He has since been a devout believer in the ill-luck of the proceeding.

Lambton Worm

A legendary dragon said to have terrorized the area around Lambton

Castle, north-east England, in the 14th century.

The Lambton Worm is probably the most famous British DRAGON legend. The story centres around Lambton Castle, family home of the Lambtons, in County Durham, and the standard version of the legend follows that outlined by Robert Surtees in his *History, &c., of Durham* (1820):

> The heir of Lambton, fishing, as was his profane custom, in the Wear, on a Sunday, hooked a small worm or eft, which he carelessly threw in to a well, and thought no more of the adventure. The worm (at first neglected) grew till it was too large for its first habitation, and, issuing forth from the Worm Well, betook itself to the Wear, where it usually lay a part of the day coiled round a crag in the middle of the water; it also frequented a green mound near the well (the Worm Hill), where it lapped itself nine times round, leaving vermicular traces, of which, grave living witnesses depose they have seen the vestiges. It now became the terror of the country, and, amongst other enormities, levied a daily contribution of nine cows' milk, which was always placed for it at the green hill, and in default of which it devoured man and beast.

Meanwhile, the 'profane' heir had mended his ways by repenting and joining the Crusades. On his return he was dismayed by the reign of terror that the wickedness of his fishing on a Sunday had unleashed. He set forth to fight the dragon, but it soon became clear that it possessed the power of reuniting its body parts each time it was sliced through. Eventually, after consulting a witch, the heir equipped himself with a special suit of armour, studded with numerous razor blades, and lay in wait for his prey on a crag above the river. When the dragon attacked it wrapped its body around the heir to crush him, but through its own effort the dragon was cut to pieces by the blades. The pieces fell into the river and were carried away by the water, the current keeping the pieces apart so that they were unable to rejoin. Thus the dragon was finally defeated.

Surtees continues by telling of a curse, a further part of the legend of the Lambton Worm:

> There is still a sequel to the story: the witch had promised Lambton success only on one condition, that he should slay the first living thing which met his sight after the victory. To avoid the possibility of human slaughter, Lambton had directed his father, that as soon as he heard him sound three blasts on his bugle, in token of the achievement performed, he should release his favourite greyhound, which would immediately fly to the sound of the horn, and was destined to be the sacrifice. On hearing his son's bugle, however, the old chief was so overjoyed, that he forgot his instructions, and ran himself with open arms to meet his son. Instead of committing a parricide, the conquerer again repaired to his adviser, who pronounced, as the

alternative of disobeying the original instructions, that no chief of the Lambtons should die in his bed for seven, or, as some accounts say, for nine generations – a commutation which, to a martial spirit, had nothing probably very terrible, and which was willingly complied with …

Some claim that the curse held true. See also LINTON WORM.

lands, lost *see* LOST LANDS

legends

Traditional stories distinguished from myths or folk tales by the fact that they are attached to a historical event, person or place and are often claimed to be true (or are at least thought to contain an element of truth).

The word 'legend' (from the Latin *legenda*, meaning 'to be read') was originally used in connection with mottos or inscriptions, but it came to be understood more widely to mean a traditional story of a saint's life, and later as a general description of stories lying somewhere between myths and folk tales. Legends are usually understood to be distinguished from MYTHOLOGY or FOLKLORE by the fact that they are connected to a historical event, person or place, are often told as true stories and are believed to contain a kernel of truth and to be based, however tenuously, on historical fact. However, there is often a blurring of the myth/folk tale/legend distinction, since some myths (such as those from

ancient Greece) include references to historical figures and places like Achilles and Corinth, as well as to gods and mythological creatures. It could also be argued that all are examples of folklore.

Before the advent of the printing press, legends were often passed on orally, sometimes by professional storytellers. Some, such as the legends of KING ARTHUR and his knights, were handed down through poems and ballads. The earliest surviving complete epic poem written in English, the Anglo-Saxon story of the southern Swedish hero Beowulf, is dated at around 1000, but it is thought to have been originally composed some 300 years earlier. Although the poem is a work of fiction, which relates the hero's slaying of the monster Grendel and his mother and, later, a DRAGON, it also mentions a historic event – King Hygelac's raid on Frisia, which took place around 516 – and many scholars believe some other people and events in the legend were also real. Another legend which comes to us through ballads is that of Thomas the Rhymer (known as 'True Thomas' for his gift of prophecy), a 13th-century poet who was said to have been swept away by the Faerie Queen into fairyland, to be her lover for seven years.

Legends usually involve a heroic character, a fantastic place or a fabulous beast. The most famous British legendary character is King Arthur, whose historical basis is the subject of many theories. In medieval times, the Arthurian legend became entwined

'Sir Galahad, Sir Bors and Sir Percival Receiving the Sanc Grael' by Dante Gabriel Rossetti. This painting shows the knights receiving the Eucharist in the holy vessel. The Arthurian legend has remained one of the best-known through the ages.
(© 2006 TopFoto)

with another legend, that of the HOLY GRAIL, which became the object of a quest by Arthur's knights. The next most prominent British legendary hero is ROBIN HOOD, although the only source for his historical existence is a ballad cycle thought to have begun in the 14th century, and he may be an entirely fictitious character. Other legendary characters are the BRAHAN SEER, Faust, HERNE THE HUNTER and Roland, the 8th-century Frankish commander in Charlemagne's service, whose legendary status was established in an 11th-century poem called *The Song of Roland*.

Many cryptozoological creatures of which stories are told in relation to specific locations might be regarded as legendary – the stories are offered as truth but, in the absence of indisputable evidence, they have something of the status of folklore. The story of the LOCH NESS MONSTER, which began with the tale of a sighting by St Columba in the 6th century, is a long-standing example. The same can also apply to places, such as ATLANTIS, the ancient island said by Plato to have been destroyed by a natural disaster 9,000 years before his time; El Dorado, a golden city believed to be located somewhere in

South America, and which inspired many expeditions to find it (notably by Sir Walter Raleigh); and, more recently, the BERMUDA TRIANGLE, in which a number of ships and planes are said to have 'mysteriously' disappeared.

The enduring appeal of fantastic, but allegedly true, stories is attested to by the popularity and pervasive nature of the modern URBAN LEGEND.

Lemuria
Legendary lost land beneath the Indian Ocean.

In 1864, the British ornithologist Philip Sclater (1829–1913) published his theory that a stretch of land had at one time connected Madagascar with South-East Asia. In his opinion this would explain the existence of lemurs in both Madagascar and India but not in Africa. In honour of this humble mammal he named the lost land, which had presumably sunk beneath what is now the Indian Ocean, Lemuria.

The German biologist E H Haeckel (1834–1919) took this theory further, suggesting that the sunken land was where the human race had begun (the site of the Garden of Eden) and that its inundation would explain gaps in the fossil record of mankind.

Nineteenth-century occultists took up the idea of Lemuria and suggested that survivors of the original inhabitants still existed, possessed of superhuman qualities and living secretly in various parts of the world. The theosophist Madame Blavatsky believed that ATLANTIS was peopled by inhabitants

who succeeded those of Lemuria. Some people also used the name MU for Lemuria.

The study of plate tectonics, with its concept of the movement of continental plates, nowadays gives a more likely explanation for the widespread distribution of similar species than a legend of lost continents.

ley lines *see* LEYS

leys
Supposed alignments of ancient sites, originally described by the English antiquarian and photographer Alfred Watkins.

In 1921, the English antiquarian scholar and pioneer photographer Alfred Watkins (1855–1935) first lectured on his discovery of old straight tracks across Britain. He believed that vestiges of these tracks remained, primarily in the alignment of various ancient sites, including STONE CIRCLES, STANDING STONES, barrows, CAIRNS and burial mounds. He called these lines 'leys'. The word derives from 'lea', meaning 'open country' or 'pasture'. *The Old Straight Track*, Watkins's key work on this subject, was published in 1925.

Over time Watkins's observation became endowed with fantastic accretions, so that by the 1960s leys had become 'ley lines', variously interpreted as being lines of occult force, magnetic lines in the ground facilitating the trajectories of UFOs or dowsable lines

Two of the six points on this 18.5-mile ley in Wiltshire
are visible in this photograph: Old Sarum in the
foreground and Salisbury Cathedral in the distance. The
ley also passes through Stonehenge and Clearbury Ring.
(© 2006 TopFoto/Fortean)

of unspecified energies. The latter is the popular understanding of the term even today. Much that was written and said about leys was hearsay, and most people were unaware that there had never been such an archaeological entity as a 'ley line'.

In the 1970s, there was intense debate about the statistics associated with drawing straight lines on maps linking points representing ancient sites, much of which was conducted in the pages of *The Ley Hunter* magazine (published 1969–98). From the late 1980s onwards some 'ley hunters' began researching actual, archaeological linear features, such as the pre-Columbian straight landscape lines in the Americas (like the NAZCA LINES), which ethnographical and archaeological evidence indicates were spiritual geographies related to shamanism. The research-based ley hunters also became aware of linear features like Neolithic cursuses (mysterious earthen avenues sometimes running for kilometres across country) in Britain, and Bronze Age STONE ROWS (see also MEGALITHS) in Britain and continental Europe. They further discovered that in medieval Europe there were specialized routes (both actual, visible paths and 'virtual' ways, ie geographically located routes but invisible, existing only in folklore) apparently relating to an archaic agrarian shamanism and spirit lore that probably had its roots in pre-history.

light, wheels of *see* WHEELS OF LIGHT

lightning, ball *see* BALL LIGHTNING

Linton Worm

A legendary dragon from the Scottish Borders, said to have destroyed both animals and people in the town of Linton in the 12th century.

The story of the Linton Worm was detailed in a late-17th-century manuscript written for the Somerville family, who claimed that their ancestor, John Somerville, had killed this DRAGON:

> In the parochene of Lintoune, within the sheriffdome of Roxburghe, ther happened to breede ane hydeous monster, in the forme of a worm … in length three Scots yards, and somewhat bigger than ane ordinarie man's leg … This creature, being a terrour to the country people, had its den in a hollow piece of ground, on the syde of a hill … which unto this day is knowne by the name of Worme's glen.

One day John Somerville was visiting the town of Jedburgh when he heard reports of the beast – some claimed that it grew larger each day, and that as it continued terrorizing the neighbourhood of Linton, it was also developing wings. The story is taken up by 'WE' in *Notes & Queries* (February 1866):

> Somerville determined to see the monster, and accordingly, rode to the glen about sunrise, when he was told it generally came forth … Satisfied that the beast was not so dangerous as reported, he resolved to destroy it, but as everyone declared that neither sword nor dagger had any effect on it, and that its venom would destroy any one that came within its reach: he prepared a spear double the ordinary length, plated with iron, four feet from the point, on which he placed a slender iron wheel, turning on its centre. On this he fastened a lighted peat, and exercised his horse with it for several days, until it shewed no fear or dislike to the fire and smoke. He then repaired to the den, and, on the worme appearing, his servant set fire to the peat. The speed at which he advanced, caused the wheel to spin round, and fanned the peat into a blaze. He drove the lance down the monster's throat full a third part of its length, when it broke, and he left the animal writhing in the agonies of death.

The manuscript claims that Somerville was knighted for his valiant deed, receiving the barony of Linton, and the area was no longer troubled by dragons. See also LAMBTON WORM.

Loch Ness Monster

A mysterious giant creature thought to inhabit Loch Ness in Scotland.

Prior to 1933, Loch Ness, a large expanse of fresh water – approximately 38.6 kilometres (24 miles) long, 1.61 kilometres (1 mile) wide and at least 297 metres (974 feet) deep – in the Highlands of Scotland, was relatively secluded, but during the early part of that year a vast amount of earth and forest overlooking its northern shore-line was removed to make space for a new motor road, the A82, which has since offered motorists driving along it some spectacular views of the loch – and its most celebrated inhabitant.

On the afternoon of 14 April 1933, Mr and Mrs John Mackay became the first two post-A82 eyewitnesses of a mysterious entity soon to become known around the world as Nessie, the Loch Ness monster. Driving southwards alongside the loch, the couple were approaching Abriachan on its north-western shore when Mrs Mackay called out to her husband to look towards the centre of the loch. They later said that to their amazement they saw an enormous animal rolling and diving amid a turbulent mass of water, and watched this extraordinary spectacle for several minutes before the creature in question finally plunged beneath the surface. Their account was published in the local newspaper, the *Inverness Courier*. Other reports followed soon afterwards, and the great British monster story was up and running.

Since as far back as the 6th century,

A photograph allegedly of 'Nessie', taken in 1977. (© 2004 Fortean/TopFoto)

when St Columba supposedly repulsed an attack from a water monster at the mouth of the River Ness, there had been local reports of a giant creature inhabiting Loch Ness itself, but it was not until 1933 that it attracted international interest – an interest that shows no sign of waning more than 70 years later. During those years, countless sightings, photographs, films and other material allegedly substantiating the existence of such a creature have been obtained. Most have been discounted outright by sceptics, or damned plausibly or otherwise by claims of hoaxes – as with the classic 'Surgeon's Photograph' of 1934. The 'monster' in this photograph, taken by a doctor, was later revealed to have been a model constructed using a toy submarine. However, there are some items of evidence that remain sufficiently compelling to merit serious attention.

A prime example of such evidence came from aeronautical engineer Tim Dinsdale's success in filming what appears to be a huge water creature in the loch on 23 April 1960. This was the last day of his six-day monster-hunting expedition, and Dinsdale claims that as he was driving along the Foyers Bay stretch of road in the morning he saw a hump-like object on the surface of the loch. He estimated that the object was approximately 1.2 kilometres (0.7 miles) away. Getting out of the car, he focused his binoculars upon the object, which was oval in shape and mahogany in colour with a dark blotch on the left side, but as he stood watching, it began to move.

Convinced that it was a huge living animal, Dinsdale started filming it with his tripod-mounted cine camera, and shot about four minutes of black and white film. It seemed to show something throwing up a conspicuous V-shaped wake as it swam towards the opposite shore, submerging slowly, but then changing direction and swimming south, parallel to the shore and almost

lost beneath the water surface. This film was analysed by the Royal Air Force's Joint Air Reconnaissance Intelligence Centre (JARIC), which announced that the hump was 3.7–4.9 metres (12–16 feet) long, a cross-section through it would be no less than 1.53 metres (5 feet) high and 1.83 metres (6 feet) wide, and its speed was 11.3–16 kilometres per hour (7–10 miles per hour). Most significantly, JARIC deemed that rather than the hump being a surface craft or submarine, '… it probably is an animate object' – that is, part of a living creature.

In more recent times, sonar traces recording the presence of huge, seemingly solid, animate bodies under the water have been obtained by many expeditions, including those led by Dr Robert Rines from the Academy of Applied Science in Boston, Britain's own 'Operation Deepscan' of 1987 and investigators aboard the *MV Nessie Hunter* in July 2001. However, by far the most exciting sonar-related piece of evidence favouring the existence of Nessie was obtained in 1972. Indeed, it is still widely held that this is the most important evidence of any kind for the Loch Ness monster's reality.

In August 1972, Rines's team was using underwater cameras and sonar equipment positioned in Urquhart Bay. On the morning of 8 August the sonar detected a flurry of movement that appeared to be a shoal of fish swimming frantically away from something coming up behind. From the sonar readings obtained, this latter object seemed to be a very large solid body, moving purposefully through the water (rather than merely drifting), and measuring 6.1–9.2 metres (20–30 feet) long. At the same time that the sonar was recording the moving body, the cameras were taking photographs of it, and when their film was developed, some frames revealed an extraordinary flipper-like object, diamond in shape and estimated to be 1.22–1.83 metres (4–6 feet) long. Some believed that it resembled a diamond-shaped, paddle-like limb, attached to a much larger body.

What makes these results note-worthy is that whereas eyewitness reports are subjective (and thereby open to criticism and doubts concerning their precise interpretation and reliability), here were two independently obtained results that not only convincingly supported one another but, in addition, were obtained by wholly objective, disinterested witnesses – machines. Based upon the evidence of these photographs, Rines and British naturalist Sir Peter Scott formally christened the Loch Ness monster *Nessiteras rhombopteryx* – 'monster of Ness with diamond fin', in December 1975.

Even the most hardened Nessie sceptics were baffled by these 'flipper' photographs – especially as the creatures whose limbs most closely resemble such flippers are those long-necked aquatic reptiles of prehistoric times, the plesiosaurs, believed extinct for more than 65 million years. Even before the flipper photos were obtained, the numerous

reports of a long-necked four-limbed monster with humped back had made the plesiosaur identity by far the most popular contender for the solution to the Nessie mystery. Moreover, as it is known that plesiosaurs used to swallow large stones for ballast purposes, this would even explain why dead Nessies do not float to the surface. Other cryptozoological identities proposed over the years include a highly specialized long-necked seal, a giant newt or salamander, a huge form of eel and even a massive worm, but none corresponds as closely and comprehensively with the Loch Ness monster's appearance (as described by those who believe they have seen it) as a plesiosaur (especially one of the long-necked elasmosaur forms). Sceptics favour such varied possibilities as diving birds, floating algal mats, swimming deer, stray seals, optical illusions, boats, sturgeons, otters and tree trunks or branches cast adrift on the loch surface.

In recent years, an additional but equally perplexing category of evidence has been forthcoming from the loch – unexplained animal sounds recorded by submerged microphones. These include a series of pig-like grunting noises recorded by a sonic survey of the loch in 2000, whose frequency (741–751 Hz) was comparable to sounds produced by various known aquatic species such as killer whales, walruses and elephant seals.

Yet if sizeable animals of any kind do exist in the loch (and there would need to be at least 30 or so to sustain a viable breeding population), why have they not been discovered by now, after decades of intense investigation? The following claim is often made as an insight into the problems faced by Nessie-seekers. It has been said that the volume of Loch Ness is such that if all of its peat-filled water could be removed, the chasm remaining would be so vast that the entire human population of the world could be fitted into it three times over. In short, some would say that a number of monsters could live concealed in Loch Ness with no more risk of being found than a moving needle in a visually impenetrable haystack. As for the oft-cited statement that there is insufficient food in the loch for any such creatures, it has been claimed that at any given time Loch Ness contains an estimated 27 tonnes of fish alone (mainly char, trout and salmon), not to mention all manner of smaller sources of nutrient; so should Nessie and its kin exist, they are certainly not going to starve!

London Monster

A case that revolved around allegations that a stalker was abroad in 18th-century London carrying out bizarre attacks on women; it is often cited as a historical example of mass hysteria.

Between 1788 and 1790 there were 30 recorded cases of attacks by a criminal that the press referred to as the London Monster. A man was said to stalk his female victims, shout obscenities at them and then slash or cut their dresses (and often their buttocks too) with a sharp blade. In some instances the attacker was said to force a small bunch of artificial flowers into the face of his victim, before completing his usual crimes. Hysteria grew, alongside sensationalist reporting in the press, and many women are said to have attempted to safeguard themselves from the monster's attentions by investing in brass or copper armour to protect their buttocks (for the wealthy) or cooking pots and 'cork rumps' (for the poor). Pickpockets are thought to have used the panic to their advantage, shouting the word 'monster' to distract everyone's attention. Also, many men were said to have been attacked and falsely accused simply for looking 'suspicious'.

Law enforcement was, at this time, in its infancy, and the police force of the day, the Bow Street Runners, was unable to apprehend this confident criminal. A philanthropist called John Julius Angerstein offered a reward of £100 for information leading to the capture of the monster. Soon afterwards the Bow Street Runners were flooded with new allegations of attacks (with many women claiming to be the 'latest' victim) and with vigilantes who claimed that they had found the man. Eventually, one John Coleman accused an artificial-flower maker called Rhynwick Williams of stabbing his fiancée, Anne Porter. Porter is said to have fainted when confronted with Williams, and a number of other women agreed that he was the monster.

The trial of Williams was somewhat bizarre. The charge first brought against him was that of assault with the intention to deface someone's clothing, judged to be the most serious law on the statute books which fitted this unprecedented crime – this little-known charge related to a felony, whereas common assault was only judged as a misdemeanour. It was clear that the judges wanted the London Monster to receive the death penalty or transportation at the very least. Also, the main witnesses for the prosecution in the trial were Coleman and Porter, who still hoped to receive the £100 reward. Williams was granted a retrial, and in this instance was represented by an Irish poet called Theophilus Swift. Swift attempted to discredit the prosecution (and their desire for the reward) but he handled the case badly and Williams was convicted – albeit for a misdemeanour this time, which carried the maximum penalty of six years' imprisonment. The attacks ceased.

It is impossible to know the truth behind the London Monster, and whether Rhynwick Williams was simply a scapegoat. It has been suggested that MASS HYSTERIA led women to fabricate monstrous attacks, or to believe that they had narrowly escaped an attack when they had not. Some have said that the monster was never anything more than a rumour, and certainly, as distressing as the attacks might sound, no grave injury was ever done.

lost cities

Once-thriving cities that experienced terminal decline.

History and folklore contain many accounts of cities that were once thriving and vibrant communities but which entered periods of decline leading not only to their abandonment but to their being all but erased from human memory.

Some are known to have been destroyed in war, such as Troy or Carthage. Others succumbed to natural disaster, such as Pompeii, buried for centuries beneath the volcanic ash from an eruption of Vesuvius. Some were simply abandoned by their inhabitants when changes in such conditions as climate or water supply ended their viability.

A city in the last category was Ubar (also known as Iram of the Pillars), a legendary wealthy trading centre in the Rub' al Khali desert of the Arabian Peninsula. According to Muslim tradition, its decadence earned it divine punishment and it was buried in the sands. It was not known whether or not this city had actually existed until modern scientific techniques were employed by expeditions searching the area. Ground-penetrating radar revealed a buried fortress and the remains of an underground water cistern, the destruction of which was thought to have caused the abandonment of the city.

Other lost cities are considered to be purely mythical, such as King Arthur's Camelot, or the city of KER-ÎS, portrayed in Breton legend as having been

The ruins of the city of Troy, excavated by Heinrich Schliemann.
(© Ullsteinbild/TopFoto)

swallowed up by the sea in the Bay of Douarnenez. However, for centuries Troy was thought to exist only in the epic poems of the ancient Greeks until the German archaeologist Heinrich Schliemann (1822–90) excavated its site in the 1870s and 1880s. Perhaps other legendary lost cities will in future years be shown to have a basis in fact.

lost continents

Continents believed to have sunk beneath the sea.

Many civilizations have traditional tales about continents that once existed but were said to have been swallowed up by the sea. By far the most famous of these is ATLANTIS, a name that inevitably appears whenever mysterious UNDER-WATER RUINS are discovered in any part of the oceans. Other famous examples are LEMURIA and MU.

Some of these myths may have had a basis in reality as inundations by the sea are known to have happened throughout history. However, as life in these lost continents is inevitably portrayed as being one of abundance and perfection, it may be that they simply reflect a deep human need to believe in a 'golden age' when society was more wonderful than in the world of today.

lost lands

Lands mentioned in history or fable and now unknown.

Like LOST CONTINENTS, lost lands form an element in many bodies of traditional folklore. One of the best-known is LYONNESSE, a land said to have existed between the Scilly Isles and Land's End, reputed to be the birthplace of KING ARTHUR.

In South-East Asia, the Tamil tradition speaks of Kumari Kandam, a land to the south of India which was submerged in the sea by a great flood. It is not out of the question that such a place did exist, as the great tsunami of 2004 showed the destructive power of the seas of the region.

Ancient Greek geographers wrote of an island they called Thule, located somewhere north of the Orkney Islands. It is not known for certain whether or not this refers to an actual island (Shetland has been suggested), an island that is now under the sea or part of the mainland of Scandinavia. Unromantic as it may seem, it is likely that many supposedly lost lands were simply the creation of incomplete or misinformed geography.

lost tribes *see* TEN LOST TRIBES OF ISRAEL

luminous phenomena

Strange lights or glows seen in places or around people or objects.

For centuries, various types of luminous phenomena have been observed in nature and considered to be mysterious or paranormal. Some are now known to be produced by electrical or electromagnetic effects, and these include EARTH LIGHTS, quake lights (see EARTHQUAKES), BALL LIGHTNING, aurora (see AURORA BOREALIS) and St Elmo's fire. It is thought that certain of these effects are still responsible for many reported sightings of UFOs.

Another luminous phenomenon is the WILL-O'-THE-WISP. This is the common name for the ignis fatuus (Latin, 'foolish fire'), a glowing light produced through the combustion of marsh-gas over swampy areas, believed in the past to be created by FAIRIES or evil spirits in order to lead travellers astray.

Foxfire is another form of naturally generated glow, in this case the phosphorescence generated by certain types of fungus on rotting wood. In the 19th century it was also discovered that the phosphorescence often seen by sailors in the wake of ships was caused by microscopic animals, such as *Noctiluca*, present in the water.

lycanthropy

The power to transform magically into a wolf; also, a psychological condition in which the patient believes himself to be a wolf.

The word 'lycanthropy' comes from

the Greek *lykos*, meaning 'wolf', and *anthrōpos*, meaning 'man'. The belief that under certain circumstances a human can transform into a wolf (or 'werewolf') has been found all over the world since ancient times. Possibly the first written reference to lycanthropy is in the Old Testament book of Daniel, in which King Nebuchadnezzar is described as displaying symptoms of werewolfism for several years. A Greek legend tells how Lycaon was transformed into a wolf by the god Zeus after serving him a dish of human flesh, and in the 5th century BC, the Greek historian Herodotus told of the Neuri, a strange people who became wolves for a short time each year. The Roman poet Virgil also wrote in the 1st century BC of a necromancer called Moeris who could transform himself into a wolf. During the Middle Ages, the rise of witch-hunting was accompanied by a rise in the number of accounts of werewolves, which were also attributed by the Church to demonic influence; in 1257, torture was officially sanctioned as a means of forcing werewolves to confess to their crimes, and alleged werewolves received the same punishment as those found guilty of witchcraft. The most notorious werewolf case of the 16th century was that of a French peasant called Gilles Garnier, accused of killing four children and devouring their flesh; he was said to have been seen in his half-man, half-beast state by many witnesses, and was burnt alive. One theory suggests that the explosion of werewolfism in the Middle Ages was caused by the contamination of rye bread with ergot, a fungal parasite which grew on the rye and was ingested with the bread made from it; ergot induces LSD-type hallucinations, and may have caused people to think they were seeing werewolves.

However, since early times, lycanthropy has also been recognized as a medical or psychological disorder. The Greek physician Galen, in the 2nd century AD, considered it to be a melancholic state, and in the 7th century Paulos of Aegina described the condition in detail and recommended treatments for it, which included massive bloodletting, baths of sweet water and milk whey, and purging with various herbs. And despite the links between werewolfism and demonic influence made by the Inquisition, some 16th- and 17th-century writers maintained that it was a medical or mental affliction. The word 'lycanthropia', as used to describe this disorder, first appears in English in Reginald Scot's 1584 book *The Discoverie of Witchcraft*, and Robert Burton's *The Anatomy of Melancholy* (1621) also describes the affliction of lycanthropia or wolf-madness, in which the sufferer runs howling about graves and fields at night and believes himself to be a wolf. During the Inquisition the terms 'lycanthropy' and 'werewolfism' were used more or less interchangeably, but after then the word 'lycanthropy' was generally restricted to the medical sense rather than the supernatural one. With the emergence of psychology as a scientific field, the term almost disappeared from medical literature, the behaviour of the patient tending to be diagnosed as another condition such as schizophrenia, bipolar disorder, multiple personality disorder or necrophilia.

According to folklore, there are a number of ways in which an individual can become a werewolf: being bitten by a werewolf; being put under a curse; heredity; being conceived on the night of a full moon; being possessed by a demon; eating the flesh of a rabid wolf; or drinking water from a puddle formed in a wolf's footprint. A person can also voluntarily become a werewolf by putting on a wolf's skin, a special belt or a magical ointment. Signs that someone is a werewolf include hairy palms, eyebrows which meet in the middle, an index finger considerably longer than the middle finger and hair between the shoulder blades. It is said that a werewolf can be made to return to his human form by calling him by his human name, or by extracting three drops of blood while he is in his animal state. Also, if a werewolf can restrain himself from eating human flesh for nine years, he is said to be cured of the curse. The 1941 film *The Wolf Man*, starring Lon Chaney Jnr, introduced additional elements which have now become part of popular werewolf lore, although they were only created for this film: the vulnerability of werewolves to silver, the fact that a werewolf must transform at the full moon and the mark of the pentagram on the palm, which identifies a werewolf or his next victim.

Lyonnesse

A legendary lost land, said once to have connected Cornwall, in south-west England, with the Isles of Scilly.

In William of Worcester's 15th-century *Itinerary*, reference is made to 'woods and fields and 140 parochial churches, all now submerged, between the Mount [St Michael's Mount] and the Isles of Scilly'. Sixteenth-century topographer John Norden named this lost land as 'Lioness', and Richard Carew also discussed Lioness in *The Survey of Cornwall* in 1602:

> That such a Lioness there was, these proofs are yet remaining. The space between the Land's End and the Isles of Scilly, being about 30 miles, to this day retaineth that name, in Cornish Lethowsow, and carrieth continually an equal depth of 40 or 60 fathom ... save that about midway there lieth a rock, which at low water discloseth his head ... Fishermen also casting their hooks thereabouts, have drawn up pieces of doors and windows.

Cornish tradition has it that when Lioness or Lethowsow was inundated by the sea, one man, called Trevilian, escaped on horseback, galloping ahead of the waves on a white horse.

Some claim that Lethowsow's association with Lioness, or Lyonnesse, came from a mistaken association of it with the birthplace of Tristan in legends of KING ARTHUR – Thomas Malory has Tristan de Liones in his *Morte d'Arthur*. Lyonnesse has also been suggested as the birthplace of King Arthur, and Tennyson had Arthur dying there. But this does not answer where the legend of Lethowsow, or Lyonnesse, came from.

Breton tradition has its own sunken land in KER-ÎS, said to lie under the Bay of Douarnenez. As the monks of the monastery on St Michael's Mount looked to the monks of Mont-St-Michel as their mother house, the tradition of Ker-Îs could have travelled from France to Cornwall and been adapted to become Cornwall's own lost land. It has also been suggested that the original legend arose among coastal people who could see the physical evidence that the land had, in the past, extended further. In either case, local lore still holds that on certain days the muffled bells of the submerged churches can still be heard, and it is said that as late as 1780 an old Cornishwoman threw herbs into the sea at Land's End, reciting an incantation as she did so, in the hope that Lyonnesse would rise from the sea in front of her.

Mad Gasser of Mattoon

A mysterious attacker who 'gassed' his victims.

The Mad Gasser of Mattoon was one of the names given by the press to a mysterious prowler said to have plagued the US town of Mattoon, Illinois, in September 1944. He was also known as 'the phantom anaesthetist', and was said to spray unsuspecting victims with an incapacitating gas.

The first 'gassing' that was reported to the police came on the night of Friday 1 September, when a Mrs Kearney claimed that an unseen intruder had opened a window of her house and sprayed a gas into the building that had left her and her daughter feeling dizzy and sick. The police found nothing, but the next day the Mattoon *Daily Journal-Gazette* had a front-page report on the incident, with the headline '"Anesthetic Prowler" on Loose: Mrs Kearney and daughter first victims'.

More reports followed. On 6 September, the *Daily Journal-Gazette* reported that Mrs C Cordes was 'overcome after picking up cloth found on porch' and by 9 September the *Charleston Daily Courier* reported that 25 people had fallen victim to the Mad Gasser and that:

> Demands for a citizens' mass meeting to plot the capture of the 'Madman of Mattoon' grew today as an 11-year-old girl, three women and an eight-year-old boy reported to police that they were victims of the phantom prowler whose trail is marked by a sweet-smelling anesthetic that causes nausea and temporary paralysis.

The police were no nearer to apprehending the gasser, and the townspeople were awaiting further attacks, when on 13 September the *Daily Journal-Gazette* carried the headline '"Gas Calls" at Vanishing Point'. Reports of the gasser ceased.

Various theories to explain the phenomenon of the Mad Gasser have been put forward over the years, with the most commonly accepted being that this was a classic case of MASS HYSTERIA, more than helped along by the sensationalist reporting of the time. It has been noted that the first headline

A picture of the Mad Gasser of Mattoon, which appeared on a set of 'Myth or Real?' collectors' cards. (© TopFoto/Fortean)

in the *Daily Journal-Gazette* implied that there would be further incidents – 'Mrs Kearney and her daughter first victims' – and reports such at that in the *Chicago Herald-American* of 10 September were hardly objective:

> ... bewildered citizens reeled today under the repeated attacks of a mad anesthetist who has sprayed a deadly nerve gas into 13 homes and has knocked out 27 known victims.

Mass hysteria has also been given as the explanation for a series of similar, although less well-known events in two counties of Virginia between December 1933 and January 1934, where reports of a figure spraying gas into homes at night also caused a sensation. As the *New York Times* reported on 22 January 1934:

> Farmers' families of Botetourt County, terrified by a stealthy marauder who hurls gas into rooms, overcoming

his victims or making them violently ill, are locking doors and windows securely these nights. Men keep their shotguns ready to guard their homes.

Less well-regarded explanations for the Mad Gasser of Mattoon have included toxic pollution from nearby factories (although how the pollution affected individual homes rather than the whole town is not explained) and an actual assailant, who was even named as a disgruntled local chemistry student called Farley Llewellyn by the writer Scott Maruna in his *The Mad Gasser of Mattoon: Dispelling the Hysteria* (2003).

Maeshowe
A Neolithic passage tomb on the Orkney Islands.

The TUMULUS, or burial mound, of Maeshowe, or Maes Howe, is located in the parish of Stenness, in Orkney's West Mainland. Possibly built around 2800 BC, the grass-covered mound is around 30 metres (100 feet) in diameter. Entered through a long, low passage, the tomb contains one large main chamber, with three side chambers leading off it. When the site was excavated in 1861, the passage was inaccessible, and an entrance was made by digging down through the roof of the main chamber from the top of the mound above, a section now replaced with a concrete roof. When the archaeologists entered the tomb, they discovered that it had earlier been broken into by Vikings, who left runic graffiti around the walls, carved there in

the 12th century. Translations of these runic inscriptions reveal the graffiti to range from the boastful, 'These runes were carved by the man most skilled in runes in the western ocean', to the banal, 'Arnfithr the son of Stein carved these runes'. Other inscriptions include: 'It was long ago that a great treasure was hidden here. Happy is he that might find that great treasure' and 'Ingigerth is the most beautiful of women' (next to a crude drawing of a panting dog).

Although renowned for its collection of Viking runes, Maeshowe is perhaps most famous for its solar alignment. While at NEWGRANGE it is the first rays of the mid-winter sun that light up the burial chamber, at Maeshowe the final rays of the setting sun, around the time of the winter solstice, shine through the entrance passage and light up the tomb inside. While we will never know for certain why Maeshowe was built in this way, numerous theories have been put forward. Some have suggested the alignment served as nothing more than a reminder of the calendar – that the darkest part of the year was over and the days would begin to lengthen again. Others believe that the entry of the sun into the tomb was tied to fertility rites, or belief in life after death.

magnetic anomalies
Areas where the earth's normal magnetic field is distorted.

The magnetic field of the earth follows a fixed and predictable pattern overall. However, in some areas this pattern is distorted, causing localized, untypical magnetic effects to be experienced. For centuries, sailors have reported the existence of regions where, for no apparent reason, their compasses become inaccurate. Such magnetic anomalies are believed to occur within the BERMUDA TRIANGLE, and regularly form part of the theories offered for the allegedly mysterious nature of the area.

In recent times it has been possible to identify and map these anomalies – particularly through the use of magnetometers and satellite detection. A number of suggestions have been offered as to their cause. It is now generally accepted that magnetic anomalies are the result of variations in the magnetic properties of the types of rock making up the earth's crust, with some rock strata being more magnetized than others. However, claims that there are some highly localized and incredibly strong magnetic anomalies have led to some slightly more controversial theories, ranging from the idea that they indicate the sites of giant meteorite strikes through to the suggestion that they are evidence of the implantation by extraterrestrials of secret observatories or tracking stations.

magnetic hills
Places where objects appear to roll uphill.

A so-called 'magnetic hill' is a slope where the normal action of gravity

The 'Electric Brae' in Ayrshire, Scotland. (© 2004 Firth/TopFoto)

appears to have been cancelled out by some mysterious force, leading objects to apparently roll uphill instead of down. If a motor vehicle is brought to a halt and placed in neutral on such a hill, it will seem to roll uphill when its brakes are released.

In such instances, the apparent mystery is actually the result of an optical illusion brought about by the topography and other geographical features of the area. This is usually attributed to the human brain attempting to gain a sense of up and down, when there is no level horizon visible, by looking to things it expects to be vertical. If nearby trees are at an angle (perhaps having been affected by the prevailing wind), or if field walls and fences are not completely vertical, the brain can mistakenly interpret a slight downward slope as an uphill one. In many cases the illusion can be appreciated by moving away from the road to a point where the broader configuration of the land can be seen.

Cases of this phenomenon are found all over the world – possibly the most famous being Spook Hill in Lake Wales, Florida. In local legend, this site is the burial place of a great chief of the Seminole people who killed a giant alligator in a nearby lake. Years later, when the Seminoles had been displaced by white settlers, mail riders began to notice that their horses were labouring hard on what looked like an easy downward trail and the place soon garnered its superstitious nickname. Scotland is home to another well-known example – the 'Electric

Brae' in Ayrshire (on the A719 between Dunure and Croy Bay), where local legend holds that an 'electric' force within the hill is responsible. The effect has become such a tourist attraction that a marker stone has been erected to explain the illusion.

magpies

Omens about magpies date back to medieval times, and a divination rhyme about these birds is one of the most widely known, if not necessarily believed, superstitions.

In general, magpies have a rather bad reputation. Since at least the 1500s there are records that show that it was thought an ill omen to see magpies, and they are still often considered to be an 'evil' bird. However, the most familiar superstition relating to magpies comes in the form of a rhyme, which apparently divines the future according to the number of magpies that are seen. The earliest form of this rhyme dates to around 1780, and it exists in several versions today, with perhaps one of the most common being:

One for sorrow

Two for joy

Three for a girl

Four for a boy

Five for silver

Six for gold

Seven for a secret never to be told

Another fairly common version is:

One for sorrow

Two for mirth

Three for a death

Four for a birth

Five for silver

Six for gold

Seven for a secret never to be told

Some versions continue up to ten, and refer to the Devil in the last line:

Eight for heaven

Nine for hell

And ten is for the Devil's own sel'

Various procedures can be followed which the superstitious would claim will help you to avoid the bad luck of seeing a solitary magpie. These include tipping your hat to the magpie; addressing it with 'Good morning' or 'Good day', and in some versions then enquiring after its wife and family; turning around three times; shooting and saluting it (using your fingers as though they were a gun, followed by a salute); or saying the rhyme:

I cross the magpie,

The magpie crosses me;

Bad luck to the magpie,

And good luck to me.

Man in the Moon

The supposed likeness of a man's face or figure seen on the surface of the full moon.

The various cultures of the world interpret the markings on the face of the full moon in different ways.

In many countries, they are thought to represent a man's face, or the figure of a man. In Inuit legend, it is believed that the Man in the Moon is the keeper of the souls of men and animals. In Malaysia, he is seen as an old hunchback sitting under a banyan tree, plaiting bark into a fishing line to catch everything on earth. The moon markings are also said to show a rat which gnaws through the fishing line and a cat which chases the rat. As long as the equilibrium between the man, the rat and the cat continues, the world is safe, but if the man ever finishes making his fishing line, the world will end. On Florida Island in the Solomon Islands, the Man in the Moon is known as Ngava, and at the full moon people say, 'There is Ngava sitting.' In Europe, while many people see the markings as a friendly face, others see the figure of an old man carrying a bundle of sticks on his back and sometimes bearing a lantern and a forked stick; there are a number of legends explaining how he came to be there, one version of which relates how, instead of resting on the Sabbath like a good Christian, an old man once went to the woods to cut a bundle of sticks. On his way home he met a stranger who chided him for working on a Sunday, and he replied laughingly, 'Sunday on earth, or Monday in heaven, it's all the same to me'. The stranger replied, 'Since you do not value Sunday on earth, yours shall be a perpetual moon day in heaven; you shall bear your burden for ever and stand in the moon for eternity, as a warning to all Sabbath-breakers.' And the old man was banished from earth, to become the Man in the Moon.

man-eating tree

A legendary man-eating plant.

In 1878, the German explorer Carle Liche wrote a letter to a friend that included an account of his travels in Madagascar, and of an incredible man-eating tree that he had seen while he was there. The letter was subsequently published in various journals. Liche had apparently spent time with a tribe called the Mkodos, and he claimed that they had shown him the tree and explained that they used it for human sacrifice, a practice he had apparently witnessed, describing the death of a woman in gory detail:

> The atrocious cannibal tree that had been so inert and dead came to sudden savage life. The slender delicate palpi, with the fury of starved serpents, quivered a moment over her head, then fastened upon her in sudden coils round and round her neck and arms; then while her awful screams ... rose widely to be instantly strangled down again into a gurgling moan, the tendrils one after another, like green serpents, with brutal energy and infernal rapidity, rose, retracted themselves, and wrapped her about in fold after fold, ever tightening with cruel swiftness and the savage tenacity of anacondas fastening upon their prey. And now the great leaves slowly rose and stiffly erected themselves in the air, approached one another and closed about the dead and

hampered victim with the silent force of a hydraulic press and the ruthless purpose of a thumb screw.

Chase Salmon Osborn, a former Governor of Michigan, was so impressed by Liche's account (which many now agree was simply a hoax, published under a pseudonym) that he travelled to Madagascar to seek out the carnivorous plant himself. He did not find it, but he claimed that he discovered that it was well known to natives there, and stories of its existence were also believed by some Western missionaries. He published *Madagascar, Land of the Man-eating Tree* in 1924.

An account of a Nicaraguan man-eating tree was published in the *Illustrated London News* in 1892. A vine-like plant of the swamps is described, capable of eating small animals (a dog is rescued from it in the course of the article) and of attempting to take humans. As the author concludes:

> If correct, it is very clear we have yet to add a very notable example to the list of plants which demand an animal dietary as a condition of their existence; and our sundews, Venus flytraps, and pitcher plants will then have to 'pale their ineffectual fires' before the big devourers of the Nicaragua swamps.

Other man-eating trees have been described, and the legends of such trees persist. While carnivorous plants are known that can devour frogs, and other small creatures, no man-eating tree has ever been discovered, or at least not by anyone who has lived to tell the tale.

Marfa lights
Mysterious lights visible in the sky near Marfa, Texas.

The Marfa lights can appear in the sky, on any clear night, between Marfa and Paisano Pass in Presidio County, Texas. The earliest report of the lights is often cited as being from 1883, from a cowhand called Robert Reed Ellison, who thought he had seen an Apache campfire, but could find no evidence of this upon investigation. Ellison apparently told his family what he had seen, and his story became known through oral tradition. Legend has it that the lights were seen again in 1885, and in 1919 cowboys who had seen them went in search of their source, but found nothing.

In the mid 20th century, the first reports of the lights appeared in the press, and such reports continue to this day, with a number of sightings each year – many from the specially built viewing platform that has been erected. The lights seem to appear at random, although they are only ever seen on clear nights. They are described as glowing balls of light, sometimes multicoloured, that can either hover above the ground, appear high in the sky, or move slowly or rapidly in any direction. Inevitably, many suggestions have been made as to what the lights really are.

Some describe the Marfa lights as 'ghost lights' or 'spook lights', and believe that they have a supernatural origin. Others regard them as UFOs, and refer to Marfa as a 'window area' – a place from which UFO sightings are reported far more frequently than would be expected. It has also been suggested that the lights are caused by swamp gas or electrostatic discharge or, more recently, that they are examples of BALL LIGHTNING or EARTH LIGHTS. Sceptics claim that there are more mundane explanations for the lights. They point out that the early reported sightings are only hearsay and local folklore, and that genuine sightings, backed up by evidence, only began in the motorized age. This is significant to their theory, because many sceptics claim that the lights are simply car headlights distorted by atmospheric phenomena. The conclusions of a 2004 investigation into the Marfa lights, conducted by the University of Texas Society of Physics Students, backs up this theory, although the study has been criticized for being too limited – the students concentrated on too small a portion of the sky, and only for four nights.

While it is certain that the Marfa lights exist, which is unusual in the world of mysterious phenomena, their cause remains a subject of debate.

Marian apparitions
Visions of the Virgin Mary experienced by various people throughout the ages.

From the early days of the Christian

Church, various people around the world have experienced visions of the Virgin Mary, the first recorded being her appearance in c.40 AD to the apostle James in Saragossa, Spain.

The apparitions have been experienced by individuals and by small or large groups (as at the village of Knock in County Mayo, Ireland, where a group of 15 people reported experiencing visions of the Virgin Mary). They have occurred not only in Europe but worldwide. In the New World, for example, a poor Aztec peasant (a convert to Christianity) called Juan Diego had visions in 1531 of a beautiful woman surrounded by light who said she should be called Our Lady of Guadaloupe, after the town near which the visions were said to have taken place.

One of the best-known cases took place in 1917, at Fátima, a rural village in Portugal. Three young shepherds reported experiencing a series of visions over a period of six months. They described seeing angels, but most of the apparitions involved the Virgin Mary, who enjoined the children to urge the world to repent and focus upon herself as the way to God.

The children said they had been entrusted with three secrets: the first was a vision of hell and the eternal punishment that awaited unrepentant sinners; the second was a prediction of another world war that would follow the one currently raging unless mankind repented; the third secret was not revealed at the time but written down from the children's accounts

The three young shepherds, Jacinta, Francisco and Lucia, who reportedly saw a series of visions of the Virgin Mary at Fátima, Portugal, in 1917.
(© Mary Evans Picture Library)

and kept hidden away from the public in the Vatican.

After a period of investigation, the Roman Catholic Church declared that the visions were worthy of belief in 1930, and the site has become a place of pilgrimage for millions of Catholics from around the world.

The third secret entrusted to the children was revealed by the Vatican in 2000, although some Catholics hold that this revelation was incomplete and that more knowledge (of presumably momentous significance) remains to be disclosed. It concerned a vision of a bishop dressed in white being cut down by a hail of bullets while making his way to the Cross. The Vatican claimed that the vision related to the attempted assassination by a gunman of Pope John Paul II in St Peter's Square in 1981, on an anniversary of one of the original visions. The Pope himself believed that the Madonna of Fátima saved his life by ensuring that he was not fatally wounded, and he ordered that one of the bullets fired at him should be placed in the crown of the statue of the Virgin at Fátima.

While the faithful may accept these manifestations as genuine divine events, what is the non-believer to make of them? It is easy for sceptics to dismiss visions appearing to single individuals as psychological or delusional, and even to attribute those experienced by small groups as being the products of MASS HYSTERIA or mass hypnosis. Strong faith and eagerness to believe are well known to affect human beings both mentally and physically, as with the placebo effect or faith healing.

Another explanation offered is that these apparitions are attributable to pareidolia (from Greek, meaning 'wrong appearance'), which essentially means that the mind interprets a random visual image as being something known and recognized, as when people staring into a fire seem to detect forms or even faces in the flames.

Some suspect hoaxes or 'publicity stunts' by the Church, designed to renew faith at times of political upheaval or decline in everyday

religious belief. It has been pointed out that most of the documented apparitions are experienced by the very young or unsophisticated, who are most likely to be credulous. However, the response to this by religious believers would be that it is because faith is at its strongest and most uncorrupted in these people that they are chosen to communicate divine messages.

marine mysteries
Mysterious phenomena occurring at sea.

The seas of the world have always exercised a fascination for humankind, and their sheer size and power bring with them danger and a sense of isolation unparalleled elsewhere in human experience. In ancient times, the elemental force of the sea was worshipped as a god – for the ancient Greeks this was Poseidon and for the Romans it was Neptune.

In addition to the terrifying physical phenomena that can be manifested by the waters themselves (such as GIANT WAVES and whirlpools), seafaring lore is littered with accounts of the strange creatures to be found in the oceans of the world. One of the most famous of these sea monsters or sea serpents is the KRAKEN, which was once believed to haunt the shores of Norway and was said to be able to seize a ship in its tentacles and drag it beneath the water. It is now thought that the legend might have been inspired by a giant squid. Giant squid were rumoured to exist long before they became known to science, when badly decomposed specimens were washed up on beaches around the world.

Legends dating back at least to ancient Greek times also tell of strange part-human creatures such as sirens or MERMAIDS. Sirens were described as being half-woman and half-bird, and as singing seductive songs to lure sailors to shipwreck on the rocks. Mermaids were said to have the upper body of a woman, with the lower body being that of a fish, and were also said to lure sailors to their deaths – in this case, with their beauty.

Throughout the centuries there have been innumerable unexplained disappearances at sea. Whole areas, such as the BERMUDA TRIANGLE, have become associated with such mysterious happenings; and the stories of individual disappearances, such as that of the crew of the MARY CELESTE, or tales of ghost ships, such as the Flying Dutchman, have captured the public imagination.

The sea continues to tantalize the world of modern science. While humankind has ventured into space, much of the area beneath the world's oceans remains relatively unexplored. Creatures of strange shapes and colours, many of them bioluminescent, are known to exist at great depths. Scientists are also still searching for explanations of the behaviour of many sea animals, such as the annual migrations of whales or the fact that great masses of fish always assemble to spawn at the same places, year after year. Research and exploration regularly yield new wonders and will, perhaps, continue to offer further solutions to many long-standing mysteries of the deep.

Martian face

The apparent image of a face on the surface of Mars.

In 1976, among the photographs taken of the surface of Mars by the Viking orbiter was one that appeared to show a giant three-dimensional human face rising up out of the ground. It was calculated that this feature was approximately 2.5 kilometres (1.6 miles) long and 2 kilometres (1.2 miles) wide. Estimates of its height ranged from 245 metres (803 feet) to 940 metres (3,083 feet).

NASA scientists soon dismissed this as an optical illusion like the Man in the Moon, produced by the play of shadows on a natural rock formation. However, some people believed it to be an artefact constructed by an unknown people, perhaps but not necessarily of Martian origin, and left on the planet for the human race to discover on venturing into space, as were the monoliths in *2001: A Space Odyssey*, filmed in 1968 by US director Stanley Kubrick (1928–99). It was further claimed that other structures, notably a pyramid, were also identifiable in these photographs and this was taken as proof of a (perhaps extinct) Martian civilization. Sceptics questioned the utility to its creators of constructing an image of a human face. Would it not have been easier to build a linear

The 'Martian face', captured on film by the Viking orbiter in 1976. (© Corbis)

feature that would be immediately recognized as artificial?

Higher-definition photographs of the same area taken by later orbiters, however, revealed nothing out of the ordinary, only natural geological formations. Even so, those who prefer to believe in the reality of the face maintain that in the intervening years the image had been destroyed by some kind of natural disaster.

Mary, Virgin *see* MARIAN APPARITIONS

Mary Celeste

The crew of the Mary Celeste *famously vanished without trace.*

The story of the brigantine *Mary Celeste* (or the *Marie Celeste*, under which name it was portrayed in a fictional work by Sir Arthur Conan Doyle) is perhaps one of the most widely known and enduring mysteries of the sea.

The legend surrounding the discovery of the *Mary Celeste* has been retold in a variety of forms. However, the common thread is that of the ship being found adrift with no sign of the crew and with every indication that they had vanished suddenly while going about their normal routine. The accounts include some intriguing 'facts' which give an eerie feel to the circumstances in which the vessel was found, such as the half-eaten breakfast on the table, the lack of damage to the structure of the ship and the fact that none of the crew's belongings had been taken. The theories propounded over the years as to the reason for the disappearance of the crew have included alien abduction, pirates, sea monsters, mutiny, the involvement of the captain in an insurance scam and, more recently, that the ship was the victim of a sea spout or seaquake.

The story of the discovery of the abandoned *Mary Celeste* owes much of its legendary status (and many of the more colourful elements) to the Arthur Conan Doyle story 'J Habakuk Jephson's Statement', first published in 1884, without which it may well have disappeared among the countless similar, lesser-known tales of disappearances at sea. Conan Doyle's story is a work of fiction built around some of the known facts of the case. It was written in such a way as to obscure its fictional status, and the confusion and controversy that followed its publication were said to have given its author some pleasure.

The records of the court proceedings and inquiries that followed the discovery of the *Mary Celeste* indicate that she had sailed from New York on 7 November 1872 bound for Genoa,

carrying a cargo of barrels of alcohol. On the afternoon of 5 December the crew of the *Dei Gratia* came upon her drifting between the Azores and the coast of Portugal and, after watching for some time and receiving no response to their hails, they boarded her. Contrary to some of the popular versions of the legend, the boarding party did not find a half-eaten meal, or that the boat was intact. In fact, the galley was in a mess and the stove had been knocked out of place. There were open hatches and water had found its way in, only one of the two pumps was working and there were no lifeboats (although it was not known for certain if there had been any on board when she set sail). Some of the instruments were damaged and, among other things, the ship's chronometer, sextant and register were missing. The captain and crew of the *Dei Gratia* brought both boats back to Gibraltar. Although it was originally believed that the cargo was intact, on unloading in Genoa it was found that nine barrels were empty.

No trace of the captain of the *Mary Celeste*, his wife and daughter (who were known to be on board) or the crew of seven was ever found, and despite the many rational and plausible explanations put forward, their fate remains a mystery. The ship itself, considered unlucky by many sailors, changed hands several times over the following years and was eventually wrecked off the coast of Haiti in 1885.

Masons *see* FREEMASONRY

mass hysteria

A term originating in the field of psychology that is popularly offered as an 'explanation' for a wide range of spontaneous mass panics or irrational group reactions (sometimes involving physical symptoms) based on an erroneous belief.

'Mass hysteria' (or 'collective hysteria') is used by psychologists to describe incidents involving groups of people suddenly appearing to display the physical symptoms of illness, without there being any apparent physical cause (for example, the MAD GASSER OF MATTOON) – the implication being that in such cases the symptoms are wholly psychological in origin. 'Hysteria' is something of an old-fashioned idea, having unfortunate associations with Sigmund Freud's discredited notion of 'female hysteria', and so alternative phrases such as 'mass sociogenic illness' are now often used in its place.

Other cases to which the label 'mass hysteria' has been applied include a wide range of incidents involving irrational beliefs or panic behaviour spreading rapidly and spontaneously through a group. These are often referred to in the fields of sociology or social psychology as 'collective delusions' and are further subdivided into categories which relate to the specific type of behaviour and nature of its spread. Classic examples would be the LONDON MONSTER, the MONKEY MAN SCARE and the reaction to Orson Welles' famous *War of the Worlds* radio broadcast. The concept of collective delusion might also be understood to include moral panics such as those surrounding claims of satanic ritual abuse and the European witch trials of the Middle Ages. Sceptics often suggest that it is also at the heart of such things as waves of UFO sightings, MARIAN APPARITIONS and many other claims to group witnessings of a 'paranormal' event.

In practice, an outbreak of a mass sociogenic illness will sometimes result in a collective delusion, and vice versa, and mass hysteria remains in widespread popular use as a catch-all term for incidents involving either or both of these phenomena.

medicine wheel

A circle of stones placed on the plains of North America by Native American tribes.

The term 'medicine wheel' was applied by white settlers in the 19th century to mysterious circular formations they found on the North American plains. The word 'medicine' refers to the supposed magical or mystical purposes for which they were thought to be used.

Medicine wheels are to be found at over 60 sites throughout the North American plains. Although many of them are of more recent origin than the STONE CIRCLES of Europe, the identity of their makers and the purposes they served still remain something of a mystery. The Plains Native Americans led a nomadic life, leaving behind them very little in the way of substantial

A modern medicine wheel at Sedona, Arizona, USA. (© 2004 Fortean/Aarsleff/TopFoto)

archaeological evidence. They did, however, leave behind a number of small rings of stones that have been identified as tepee rings (the stones being used to hold down the edges of the hide tepees) and larger rings known as medicine wheels. Although these wheels take many different forms, common elements are a large central stone or cairn, surrounded by one or two concentric circles of stones or smaller cairns, often tens of metres in diameter. Many wheels also have lines of stones radiating out from the central point or from the outside of the circle. The stones are generally placed on the ground rather than erected in the manner of a STANDING STONE.

As with the stone circles of Europe, there are a number of different hypotheses relating to the exact purpose of medicine wheels, although it seems likely that different types of wheel may have been used for different ends. It is also possible that they had different meanings to different tribes, and there is evidence that they were altered and reused over the centuries.

Archaeological excavations have revealed evidence of burials, within tepee rings, at the centre of some medicine wheels, including the Ellis medicine wheel near Medicine Hat in Alberta, Canada – an area associated with the Blackfoot people. This suggests that they may have been used among the Blackfoot as some form of honoured burial for important individuals.

Other theories include the ritual use

of medicine wheels for ceremonies such as the Sun Dance or (in common with those put forward for the stone circles of Stone Age cultures elsewhere) their use for purposes related to the seasonal movements of the sun, moon and stars. For example, the Bighorn medicine wheel at the top of Medicine Mountain in Wyoming has 28 radial spokes, which may represent the days in a lunar month. There are six cairns around the circle, two of which are positioned to be in alignment with sunrise and sunset on the summer solstice. Other cairns line up with the rise of the three bright stars Aldebaran, Sirius and Rigel. Similar alignments are also found elsewhere.

It seems likely that medicine wheels were used for a diverse range of purposes and that they may have been used for some or all of the above at any given time. Their exact cultural significance remains beyond the reach of modern investigators. This is, unfortunately, due partly to the fact that at the very time that archaeologists and anthropologists· were beginning to become interested in medicine wheels, the traditional culture that might have shed light on their secrets was being destroyed.

megaliths

Large stones associated with prehistoric monuments.

The term 'megalith' is derived from the Greek words *mega*, large, and *lith*, stone, and is usually applied to prehistoric monuments, whether in the form of STANDING STONES in groups (such as STONE CIRCLES or STONE ROWS), solitary pillars (monoliths or MENHIRS), or more complex structures built from large rocks. These constructions are of various types, ranging from simple, box-like burial features (known as cists) made from stone slabs, or tombs made of upright stones topped by a large capstone (DOLMENs), to veritable Stone Age temples consisting of earth or rock mounds containing stone-lined passages and internal chambers. The general purpose of megaliths was usually of a funerary and ritual nature (they were much more than merely graves), but other functions also seem to have existed in some cases. Some megaliths have also been interpreted as acting as signposts, boundary markers or representations of ancestral figures or tribal and religious symbols, and sometimes a mix of these functions can be seen at one site. There are literally hundreds of thousands of surviving megalithic monuments worldwide, built by diverse cultures throughout the ages – some stones were used rough and ready, others were dressed (that is, shaped and smoothed).

It is western and northern Europe where probably the greatest concentration of megaliths is to be found – it is said over 5,000 survive in the Brittany area of France alone, primarily in extensive stone row complexes (see, for example, CARNAC). In Scandinavia, stone settings in the shape of boats, and monoliths sporting runic engravings, date from the Viking era. A swathe of older megaliths (mainly dolmens) stretches from southern Denmark and northern Holland across northern Germany and into Poland. Lands around the Black Sea possess prehistoric stone monuments – such as the chambered burial mounds of Bulgaria and the rectangular slab-tombs of the Caucasus region – many with 'spirit holes' cut through their frontal stones. Some European megalithic sites are among the oldest known; material from megalithic tombs in southern Portugal yields radiocarbon dates of the 5th millennium BC, and some of the chambered mounds in Brittany have provided similarly ancient dates – two small chambered sites have been dated to c.5800 BC.

Ireland and the British Isles possess an exceptional megalithic heritage, with sites of world renown like England's STONEHENGE and AVEBURY, Scotland's CALLANISH and MAESHOWE, and Ireland's NEWGRANGE – older than Egypt's GREAT PYRAMID and possessing a stone-lined entrance passage over 18 metres (60 feet) long leading to a central chamber 6 metres (20 feet) high built of overlapping ('corbelled') stone slabs. But literally thousands of other megalithic sites grace these islands, including mysterious moorland stone rows, notably on Dartmoor.

Recent archaeological discoveries indicate that timber circles (see WOODHENGE) preceded the era of European megalith building, or at least overlapped with it, and there is evidence that stones were initially handled like timber. At Stonehenge, for

instance, there are mortise and tenon joints fixing horizontal stone lintels on upright megaliths, and some of the bluestones in the monument, the first stones to be erected there, display tongue-and-groove work.

The first sacred sites were probably venerated natural locations (usually distinctive landmarks), and many megalithic monuments are built in sight of such topographical features – in some cases aligning with them. On Bodmin Moor in south-west England, for example, stone circles were so precisely placed that a shift of 90 metres (100 yards) would have put them out of sight of a prominent distant peak. There also seems to have been a Stone Age tradition of circulating 'pieces of places', similar to the way medieval monks circulated relics of saints; this may have been because the very rock of certain venerated spots was viewed as possessing magical power or *mana*. This might explain why quartz from the Wicklow Hills is found built into Newgrange 96.5 kilometres (60 miles) distant, and why the bluestones of Stonehenge came from the Welsh Preseli hills some 400 kilometres (250 miles) away. The stone circle of Gors Fawr is situated so that Carn Menyn, the rocky outcrop where most of the bluestones originated, is prominent on the local skyline.

Sometimes such topographical associations have astronomical dimensions. For example, on the island of Jura, off the west coast of Scotland, there is a range of mountains called the Paps ('breasts') of Jura, on account of two rounded peaks in their midst. The midsummer sun appears to set into the Paps when viewed from a major standing stone group at Ballochroy on the Kintyre peninsula on the mainland. A site near Loch Finlaggan on the island of Islay, immediately to the south of Jura, further confirms the symbolic importance of these breast-like mountains in prehistory. A standing stone there is the survivor of a stone row; looking along the axis of the former row the eye is directed to Jura's two rounded peaks, visible in dramatic isolation on the skyline. A slightly different example is offered by Callanish, an important group of stone circles on the island of Lewis (also off Scotland's west coast). From this group of standing stones the eastern skyline is formed by the Pairc Hills, which resemble the shape of a reclining woman. Sometimes called the 'Sleeping Beauty', her Gaelic name is *Cailleach na Mointeach*, 'the Old Woman of the Moors'. Every 18.61 years, the time in the complex lunar cycle known as the 'Major Standstill', the moon rises out of the hills as if the Earth Mother is giving birth to it. It skims the horizon to seemingly set among the standing stones of Callanish.

menhirs
Individual megaliths.

A menhir is a single prehistoric MEGALITH or STANDING STONE. The word comes from Breton, meaning 'long stone', and was first used in the 19th century by French archaeologists studying such stones in Brittany. It is not known why early man conceived the idea of planting massive stones in the earth. Some suggest that they were used to mark routes, holy places or tribal boundaries, others that they commemorate dead heroes or significant events. Still others connect them with observation of the sun, moon and stars.

Whether standing individually or in alignments, as part of DOLMENS or STONE CIRCLES, menhirs were usually simple dressed stones, but some have been found in central Mediterranean regions that were decorated by carvings of human features. Whether this means they are connected with a god, a particular tribe or a dead chieftain remains impossible to say.

Merlin
Legendary magician associated with King Arthur.

In the legends and medieval romances about KING ARTHUR, he is advised and aided by the famous magician Merlin.

According to the traditional tales, as well as being a wizard Merlin had the gift of prophecy and foretold the eventual defeat of the Britons by the Saxons. As he was the son of a mortal woman impregnated by an incubus, tradition holds that he could not be killed. However, in different versions of the story, he met his end at the hands of his former pupil, the enchantress Nimue, imprisoned by her magic beneath a great rock, or through the spells of Vivien, the Lady of the Lake, who entangled him in a thornbush.

Among the magical feats associated with Merlin in Arthurian legend is the fixing of the sword into the stone, from which only the true king could withdraw it. His name was also connected with the construction of STONEHENGE, in which he was said to have used his magic to move and erect the great monoliths.

As to the possibility of there being a historical Merlin, there are references to him in the same chronicles that mention KING ARTHUR, most notably in the accounts of Nennius (fl.769), who describes his boyhood and youth under the name Ambrosius. The *Historia Regum Britanniae* (c.1136) of Geoffrey of Monmouth (c.1100–c.1154) contains a life of Merlin in which he is described as having been born in Carmarthen in Wales. One theory is that, rather than being King Arthur's wizard, Merlin was actually his bard, and several traditional poems have been attributed to him under the name Myrddin. In this version, Merlin is said to have died in battle beside his king. However, like King Arthur, it is most probable that the Merlin of legend is a composite figure, in this case partaking of elements of a traditional Welsh bard, a pre-Christian necromancer and a priest of the Druids.

mermaid

A mythical sea-creature with the upper body of a woman and the tail of a fish.

Stories of mermaids, sea-dwelling creatures of human size with the upper body of a beautiful woman and the tail of a fish, are common in ancient mythology; they persisted in European folklore from medieval times up till the 18th century, with many reported sightings. Mermaids, from Old English *mere*, meaning 'sea', and *maegden*, meaning 'maiden', are usually portrayed as having long flowing hair, silvery blonde to light red in colour, either blue or green eyes and pearly white skin with a silver sheen. They live much longer than humans, and dwell in magnificent undersea palaces decorated with gold and jewels salvaged from wrecked ships, but they frequently come to the surface and sit on rocks, with a mirror in one hand and a comb in the other, grooming their long hair and singing with unbearable sweetness. Their beauty and their bewitching voices often lure sailors to their deaths. In some traditions they are more actively malevolent, dragging humans, especially young men, under the sea and keeping their souls in cages, or else drowning their victims and eating them. When angered, they can call up powerful winds and storms by dancing through the waves.

Mermaids have the ability to change their fish-tails into human legs so that they can come ashore and mix with people whenever they want, and although they have no souls, it is said that they can gain one if they marry a human and are baptized. Stories of mermaids marrying human husbands are common in British folklore, but sooner or later the mermaid will long to return to the sea again. She cannot do so as long as her husband keeps some magical possession of hers hidden, such as a sealskin, comb, belt, necklace or cap, but as soon as she finds the object, she will escape back to the sea. Mermaids are often credited with the ability to grant three wishes and to see into the future, and sometimes they are caught and held to ransom for these gifts. However, if pressed to grant wishes they will do their best to twist the words of the wish to the person's disadvantage.

In Ireland, mermaids are said to be female pagans banished from the island by St Patrick along with snakes. The legend of the mermaid probably developed from ancient mythological figures such as Aphrodite, the Greek goddess who was born from the sea, or the Syrian fish-tailed moon goddess Atargatis. It has been suggested that many of the recorded sightings of mermaids were in fact brief glimpses of marine mammals such as manatees.

meteorites

Stones which 'fall from the sky', the very possibility of which made a dramatic transition from superstition, folklore and fragmentary scientific theories to accepted scientific fact at the end of the 18th century.

Meteors (from the Greek *meteōra*, meaning 'things on high'), also known as 'aerolites', 'fireballs' or 'shooting stars', are small bodies of rock from space that are observed as they burn up on entering the earth's atmosphere. Any part of it that reaches the earth's surface (in the form of a lump of stone or metal) is described as a 'meteorite'.

Shooting stars have long been the subject of superstitious beliefs all over the world – wishing on a shooting star is one such superstition of which most of us are probably still aware. They have also been incorporated into many religious belief systems, in which, ironically, it was usually accepted that they fell from the sky, a fact that could be explained in terms of the actions of gods.

However, by the 18th century, scientific orthodoxy held that the idea that rocks could fall from the sky was nonsense. Although, with the benefit of hindsight, the connection between shooting stars and the lumps of rock and craters found on the ground seems obvious, it must be remembered that to actually witness both the fall and the discovery on the ground of the still-hot rock is extremely rare. Even now, meteors remain unpredictable. Shooting stars were the subject of various competing theories along the lines that they were atmospheric or earthly in origin. Likewise meteorites, or 'thunderstones', were thought by many to be fossils, Stone Age tools or rocks that had been struck by lightning. Those who began to suggest the idea that the two were linked met with an entrenched mainstream scientific community, whose scepticism was bolstered by the fact that the eye-witness accounts offered in support of the theory were seen as just a small part of a wider collection of claims relating to FALLS from the sky.

A series of papers published in the final years of the 18th century and the first years of the 19th century established that there were rocks

The Ahnighito Meteorite at the American Museum of Natural History. It is the largest meteorite on display in a museum anywhere in the world. (Jonathan Blair/Corbis)

drifting through space and that the composition of most meteorites found on the ground was similar. This was followed by the testimony of the French scientist Jean-Baptiste Biot, who witnessed a fall in Normandy in 1803. Although the exact origin of meteors and meteorites remained the subject of debate for many years to come, the idea that they fell from the sky had been firmly established.

Meteorite falls still attract much attention and are of great interest to scientists for the clues that they can give as to the nature and history of our solar system. However, human-interest stories of meteorites hitting cars or houses, and especially the occasional claims that they have struck people, are the firm favourites in the media. Likewise, observations that extremely large meteorites have collided with the earth in the past, causing enormous craters and dramatic climate change, regularly lead to the publication of predictions that such an event is likely to occur again in the near future.

Minnesota Iceman

An 'apeman', frozen in a block of ice and displayed in American fairgrounds in the 1960s; the mysterious creature has since disappeared.

In 1968, leading cryptozoologists Ivan T Sanderson and Bernard Heuvelmans examined a controversial creature that has since become known as the Minnesota Iceman. The creature was being kept in a large freezer cabinet on the farm of Frank Hansen at Rollingstone, near Winona, Minnesota. Hansen had been exhibiting the Iceman in a travelling sideshow, advertising it as the 'missing link'. Sanderson and Heuvelmans examined the creature as best they could, encased as it was in ice. They took measurements and photographs, and described the Iceman as being around 1.8 metres (5 feet 10 inches) tall, and covered, with the exception of its face and groin, with long gorilla-like hair. One of the Iceman's arms was flung up above its head and appeared to be broken, and it seemed evident that the creature had been shot through the eye – one eye was dislodged and there was damage to the back of the skull – suggesting that this arm had been brought up in self-defence. Heuvelmans also described the smell of putrefaction, indicating that parts of the creature's body were starting to rot.

When Sanderson and Heuvelmans asked Hansen where the Iceman had come from, Hansen's answers were vague and contradictory; one of his explanations was that it had been found floating in the sea in an ice block, off the coast of Siberia, and he was exhibiting it for its wealthy anonymous owner. Nevertheless, Sanderson and Heuvelmans were convinced that the Iceman was genuine, concluding that it was a recently killed specimen of a Neanderthal-like human, which they thought might have been killed in Vietnam (where mysterious creatures of this type have been reported), and smuggled out in a body bag during the Vietnam War. They christened the species *Homo pongoides*. The publicity that followed the announcement that the scientists had discovered a real 'man-beast' caused concern to Hansen. As a body that showed evidence of having been shot, the FBI became interested in examining it, and Hansen withdrew it from display. When the Minnesota Iceman reappeared, Hansen said that it was a model, and not the original body. People began to suspect that the first Iceman had been a model too, and that Hansen had perpetrated a clever hoax.

Hansen continued to successfully exhibit the model for many years. The 'original' disappeared, and Hansen has since claimed that it is back with its owner, still frozen. Heuvelmans, who died in 2001, continued to believe that he had seen a real creature before it was replaced by a model, and while most now believe the Minnesota Iceman was nothing but a hoax, others still claim that one of Hansen's versions of its discovery was true, and that it was a genuine creature shot by Hansen in the Minnesota woods.

mirrors

Many superstitions have been attached to mirrors over the centuries.

One of the most common current superstitions in Britain holds that to break a mirror brings seven years' bad luck. This superstition has been reported since the late 18th century, although the fate of the person who does the damage has changed over the years. In his *A Provincial Glossary* (1787), Francis Grose notes:

> To break a looking-glass is extremely unlucky; the party to whom it belongs will lose his best friend ... Breaking a looking-glass betokens a mortality in the family.

The belief that a broken mirror brings seven years' bad luck has been popular since the mid 19th century.

Another mirror-related superstition is connected with babies. Documented since the mid 18th century, this belief is based on the idea that it is unlucky for a baby to look at its reflection in a mirror. An instance of this superstition was described in *Folklore*, the journal of the Folklore Society, in 1909. The young woman referred to resided in Lincolnshire:

> A young woman here has been troubled because her baby might see itself in the looking-glass at the back of her sideboard before it was a year old. Her mother, a native of Nottinghamshire, said by way of comfort – 'Just seeing it by itself by chance does not count. It is showing the baby its own reflection which is unlucky.'

The custom of covering a mirror after a death was common in the 19th and early 20th centuries, and mirrors have also been used for divination (often to see a future spouse), and have been covered in sick rooms, it being considered unlucky for someone who is ill to see their reflection.

Monkey Man scare

In April and May 2001 residents of New Delhi, India, claimed they were plagued by attacks by a creature which became known as the Monkey Man; many believe this was a case of mass delusion or mass hysteria.

The first known attacks by the Monkey Man were reported in April 2001. Residents of a village on the outskirts of New Delhi claimed that they had been bitten as they slept on their roofs at night, a practice that is common at that time of year in order to escape the heat. Some of the injuries that were reported were consistent with monkey bites, and at first it was believed that one of the many monkeys that live in the area was to blame, but victims also described a man with a monkey face or a masked man as the assailant. Panic spread, as did the reported incidents of attacks by the creature. By mid-May, stories of a creature that scratched with long metal claws and that could leap across the rooftops before mysteriously vanishing were rife in the poorer areas of the Indian capital. Despite police orders, vigilante groups scoured the streets in search of the creature. On 17 May the police offered a reward of 50,000 rupees (£769) for information leading to the arrest of the Monkey Man (believing that it was indeed a man or several men rather than a supernatural creature) and it was reported that on 19 May they received 328 calls relating to the Monkey Man from different parts of New Delhi. It was at this time that the police also arrested a number of people they described as 'mischief-mongers' and reports of the Monkey Man dwindled.

The majority of commentators have since concluded that the Monkey Man scare was a case of mass delusion or MASS HYSTERIA rather than something arising from an actual attacker. Although a small number of deaths were claimed to be directly linked to the 'monster', there was no evidence of this, and the other fatalities (and the majority of serious injuries caused) came about when people fell from their roofs as they tried to flee what they perceived to be the threat of attack. Often the police were summoned simply because a shadow or sound was thought to be suspicious or there was a rumour that the attacker was in the area. It has been suggested that a number of the injuries presented to doctors were self-inflicted, or caused by dogs, cats or rats, and that as panic spread a number of copycat attacks may have been perpetrated (see OSTENTION). Some have noted that New Delhi was suffering from power shortages at the time, and that not only might the darkness have contributed to the fear, but some of the people who reported incidents may have believed that by doing so the police would ensure that the power was switched on in order that they could investigate. However, none of these observations prevented a number of theories as to the cause

circulating among believers at the time, including a visiting alien and a remote-controlled robot.

Mother Shipton (1488–c.1560)

An English witch and seer who made a series of famous prophecies.

The English witch and seer known as Mother Shipton (originally Ursula Southeil) was reputedly born near Knaresborough, Yorkshire, in 1488. She is generally held to have married a builder called Tony Shipton at the age of 24, and to have lived for more than 70 years. Said either to be a child of the Devil, or to have inherited powers of clairvoyance from her mother, Shipton made a series of prophecies that rival those of NOSTRADAMUS, both in popularity and in alleged accuracy.

In a series of incredible prophecies written in crude rhyme, Mother Shipton is said to have foreseen the development of many scientific inventions, including the telegraph, the automobile, aeroplanes, submarines, ironclad boats and Crystal Palace, as well as making predictions of wars and political upheavals:

Chariots without horses shall go,

And accidents fill the world with woe.

Around the world thoughts shall fly

In the twinkling of an eye ...

Under water men shall walk,

Shall ride, shall sleep, shall talk;

In the air men shall be seen,

In white, in black, and in green …

Iron in water shall float,

As easy as a wooden boat;

A house of glass shall come to pass,

In England, but alas!

Sadly, however, it is thought likely that Mother Shipton never actually existed. The first book of Shipton's 'works' was published in 1641, but it contained no biographical information and omitted the most famous of the prophecies. In 1684, Richard Head published *The Life and Death of Mother Shipton … strangely preserved amongst other writings belonging to an old Monastery in York-shire, and now published for the information of posterity, etc*. This did contain biographical information, and although written many years after Shipton's supposed death, it contained a detailed description of her appearance:

> … with very great goggling, but sharp and fiery eyes; her nose of incredible and unproportionable length, having in it many crooks and turnings, adorned with many strange pimples of divers colours, as red and blue mixed …

In 1862, Charles Hindley published a collection of Shipton prophecies which he claimed he had copied from a manuscript in the British Museum. It is in this version that the famous rhyming prophecies such as those quoted above can be found. Hindley later admitted that he had concocted these predictions himself, and by

Mother Shipton, the English witch and seer, portrayed with a familiar.
(© Mary Evans Picture Library)

the time he wrote them, many of the 'prophecies' had already been fulfilled – for example, Crystal Palace was built for the Great Exhibition of 1851, and a practical telegraph system had been invented by the 1830s. However, some of Hindley's prophecies related to future events, including the famously inaccurate:

> The world to an end shall come
>
> In eighteen hundred and eighty one.

Mothman

A mysterious bat-like humanoid, alleged sightings of which are particularly associated with the US town of Point Pleasant, West Virginia. Reported sightings were famously seen to be connected with other strange occurrences in the area, and later taken to be an omen of the Silver Bridge disaster.

In the 1960s in West Virginia, USA, numerous reports were made of sightings of UFOs and of a winged humanoid creature which came to be known as Mothman. Witnesses who claimed to have seen Mothman generally described a large dark shape with glowing red eyes and bat-like wings. Mothman came to prominence with a number of widely reported sightings in November 1966, such as a sighting on 15 November, reported in the local newspaper, *The Athens Messenger*, under the headline 'Winged, Red-Eyed "Thing" Chases Point Couples Across Countryside':

> Point Pleasant – What stands six feet tall, has wings, two big red eyes six inches apart and glides along behind an auto at 100 miles an hour? Don't know? Well, neither do four Point Pleasant residents who were chased by a weird 'man-like' thing Tuesday night.

When the journalist and fortean John Keel (1930–) travelled to the area to investigate the claims, particularly in the town of Point Pleasant, he found that many of the witnesses said that since they had reported their sightings they had been visited by mysterious 'men in black', and told not to discuss their experiences with anyone. Keel also claimed that he was tormented over the phone by an entity called Indrid Cold, and he noted numerous other phenomena that are usually associated with poltergeist activity. The investigation was apparently characterized by intense fear on the part of the witnesses and the strange way that Keel, the investigator, was drawn further and further into the goings-on.

On 15 December 1967, the Silver Bridge at Point Pleasant, linking West Virginia and Ohio across the Ohio River, became backed up with traffic when traffic lights were stuck on red. The bridge collapsed, killing 46 people. Back in New York, John Keel heard about the bridge and put the UFO sightings, Mothman, disembodied voices and all the other mysterious occurrences he had heard about together and developed the theory that these had been omens of the disaster. He published *The Mothman Prophecies* in 1975. The story was later adapted and released as a film, *The Mothman Prophecies*, in 2002. In the same year that the film was released, the town of Point Pleasant (which now boasts a statue of Mothman) held the first annual Mothman Festival.

There have been many suggestions as to what occurred in the area of Point Pleasant during 1966 and 1967 – including alien visitations, giant mutant birds or mind control experiments. Some have also suggested that the bridge collapse and the Mothman visitations were the result of a Native American curse (known as 'the Cornstalk Curse') which was placed

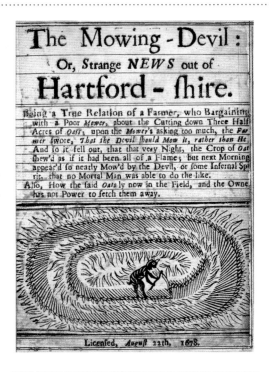

The pamphlet which told the tale of the 17th-century crop circle created by 'the Mowing Devil'. (© TopFoto/Fortean)

on the town by a chief of the Shawnee. Sceptics argue that the collapse of the bridge was due only to a terrible coincidental combination of events and an inherent weakness in its structure. It has also been suggested that the Mothman reports might have been generated by misidentifications of one of the larger species of owl, among other things – with artificial connection, misinterpretation, distortion and exaggeration being encouraged by the media.

Mowing Devil, the

The case of a legendary 17th-century crop circle, said to have been created by the Devil.

In 1678, a woodcut pamphlet was published in England which purported to tell a story of devilish intervention in human affairs. The pamphlet's title was *The Mowing-Devil: or, Strange News out of Hartford-shire*, and the tale it told was of a farmer of that county who refused to pay the fee asked by a labourer to mow his field of oats.

Somewhat rashly, the farmer swore that he would rather the Devil mowed it instead. That night, mysterious flames appeared among the crop and in the morning the farmer found it:

> ... so neatly mow'd by the Devil or some Infernal Spirit, that no Mortal Man was able to do the like.

The woodcut illustration on the front page of the pamphlet shows a devilish figure, complete with horns and tail, working away with scythe in hand. What is arresting to those with an interest in CROP CIRCLES is that the cut cereal has been mown in concentric circles rather than, say, in parallel rows. The case of the Mowing Devil (even if one allows for exaggeration and embellishment on the part of the pamphleteer) indicates that crop circles may not be an entirely modern phenomenon. It also offers an interesting example of the way that explanations for unusual occurrences often reflect the cultural context in which they occur.

Mu

Legendary lost land beneath the Pacific Ocean.

When the Jersey-born anthropologist Augustus Le Plongeon (1826–1908) studied the ruins and ancient writings of the Maya civilization in Yucatan he claimed to have discovered that the Maya had originally come to America from a land that had sunk beneath the Pacific Ocean. He stated that this lost continent was called Mu.

This idea was further developed by the English soldier and writer James Churchward (1852–1936) in a number of books, beginning with *The Lost Continent of Mu* (1931). Churchward believed that the civilization of Mu was the same as that of Atlantis. Others have identified Mu with the equally legendary LEMURIA.

However, theories about the existence of Mu, as about the existence of any lost continent, are not generally accepted by current science.

mysterious falls *see* FALLS

mythology

The word 'mythology' comes from the Greek words mythos, *a story or legend, and* logos, *a discourse. It is used to describe bodies of traditional stories about gods and superhuman beings, although many also include human heroes.*

It is very hard to give a firm definition; the lines between mythology, LEGEND and FOLKLORE are blurred, and in many instances the words are used interchangeably – as can be seen in the body of modern folk tales that are known (among other things) as both 'URBAN LEGENDS' and 'urban myths'.

Humankind has always demonstrated a need to create such stories, whether as the basis of religion or simply to try to explain in human terms phenomena or events that seemed mysterious. In preliterate societies these myths would be communicated orally and passed down from generation to generation, often being elaborated on and expanded as the need for more comprehensive accounts and explanations developed. Perhaps the earliest known examples of myths come from the worship of the moon and the sun by early cultures. The sun and moon were seen as possessing power, for good or evil, over human lives, while being changeable and largely unpredictable. Creation myths explain how life began and how the world and its inhabitants came to be – this is usually attributed to a deliberate act by a supreme being (or beings). Such myths often include an account of the first human beings, the progenitors of a whole race.

Often, what is called mythology by one culture, or a subsequent generation within a culture, should more properly be described as the elements of religious belief that have been superseded, have been discredited or are just considered not to describe the 'true' faith. This is the case, for example, with Classical mythology, perhaps the most familiar body of such stories within Western societies and passed down through centuries of literature and scholarship.

The ancient Greeks believed in immortal gods that emerged from the primeval chaos to control aspects of their daily lives, characterizing them as human-like beings whose capriciousness went a long way towards explaining seemingly random incidents. They inhabited a different world or 'heaven' (Olympus), from which they could look down on human affairs and interfere at will.

Below the rank of these Olympian gods was ranged a cast of thousands of lesser, but still superhuman, usually immortal, creatures such as nymphs, oreads and dryads, spirits such as the genius loci (literally, 'spirit of the place'), or monsters such as sirens. The existence of human beings who seemed to be possessed of extraordinary powers, such as strength, wisdom or musical ability, was often explained in terms of their being the offspring of an immortal and a mortal. This was the case with great heroes, often known as demigods, such as Heracles (or Hercules as the Romans knew him). Heroes in myths were often obliged to undertake dangerous quests, such as Jason's epic voyage in search of the Golden Fleece, or to carry out seemingly impossible tasks, such as the Twelve Labours of Hercules.

Often, cities or societies would seek to establish their legitimacy or ancient lineage by attributing their origin to some mythical figure. Examples of this include the story of the founding of Rome by the wolf-suckled twin brothers Romulus and Remus. Similarly, in the mythology of Japan, Japanese emperors were said to have had a common ancestor who was the offspring of the sun goddess Amaterasu.

The 'national myth' by which a nation or state sought to affirm its particular identity or right to independent existence typically featured heroes fighting to win freedom from tyrants or monsters and victoriously founding their own societies. Examples of this are to be found all over the world, not all of them being essentially ancient. A relatively recent national myth is that of the Swiss hero William Tell. Stories are told of his struggle for Swiss freedom from the Austrian oppressors, locating the events in the 14th century. Everyone knows the tale of Tell being forced to shoot an arrow through an apple placed on his son's head, even if they are unsure of the specific circumstances surrounding this feat of skill and courage. However, there is no evidence that William Tell ever existed in real life. His supposed deeds are echoed in myths found in other European countries, and it seems that he was actually a 15th-century product of a need to create a legitimizing mythical hero around whom a glorious tradition of fighting for freedom could be constructed. Such stories may not have any religious content and could, perhaps, be considered to be better categorized as legend.

In Britain the various peoples who invaded the country after the decline of the Romans brought their own brands of mythology. In particular, Norse mythology had many echoes of its Classical counterpart, with a pantheon of gods installed in a kind of heaven (Asgard) under a father figure (Odin). Heroes who died bravely in battle would be carried off by the Valkyries to the great hall in heaven (Valhalla), where they could continue to feast and brawl to their hearts' content. The Norse peoples, however, did not believe that this arrangement would last forever. The world would come to an end in a great,

mutually destructive conflict between good and evil gods (known as Ragnarok) – a better world would then emerge.

Enduring traces of many mythologies remain in modern society. We still talk of an uncertain outcome as being 'in the lap of the gods'. We continue to divide our week into days named after ancient gods: Sunday (from Sun), Monday (from Moon), Tuesday (from Tiw, Norse god of war), Wednesday (from Woden, a form of Odin), Thursday (from Thor, Norse thunder god), Friday (from Freyja, Norse goddess of married love) and Saturday (from Saturn, Roman god of agriculture). Similarly, in an increasingly secular age, many strands of mythology which are unconnected with mainstream modern religion continue to exercise a hold on believers.

Some myths go further than simply involving supernatural beings and human heroes; as well as numerous mythical beasts, mythical places also feature in many cultures. These often take the form of LOST LANDS or LOST CONTINENTS. Such stories show extraordinary persistence, the story of ATLANTIS, for example, having been current since the Classical period. To this day explorers make new claims to have discovered its submerged ruins.

Why does humankind still feel the need for mythology? Perhaps it fulfils a desire for larger-than-life heroes and feats, or helps satisfy a yearning towards the magical or mysterious that forms a fundamental, albeit unconscious, characteristic of the human psyche – or maybe we all just enjoy a good story.

Nazca lines

A series of straight lines and animal drawings on the ground in Peru.

The Nazca lines is the name given to a series of ground markings discovered in the Nazca Desert, a high, arid plain in coastal Peru. They were first detected in the 1920s by aircraft pilots beginning to make commercial flights over the area. Over 300 patterns have been identified, including many straight lines, drawings of animals such as spiders, birds and monkeys, and more abstract shapes. The markings were made by clearing away the stones on the arid surface, exposing the sand beneath, which is a much lighter colour. It is believed that they were created by the Nazca people, whose culture flourished in the region between c.200 BC and c.600 AD. The Nazca are known to have decorated pottery with stylized drawings of people and animals, but the marking out of such gigantic shapes must have taken many years and much communal labour. The lines' survival through the centuries testifies to the lack of rainfall or any other form of erosion in the region.

Why, then, was this done? One theory was that they formed some kind of astronomical chart and that the animal shapes represented constellations, but the drawings do not tally with the appearance of the stars in the night sky over the area. Another idea was that they were tracks used for ceremonial running races. While this might explain some of the markings, others would have made for rather tortuous races, some involving climbing from the plain into the surrounding hills.

The idea that the Nazca lines represented landing strips for extraterrestrial craft was popularized by the Swiss writer ERICH VON DÄNIKEN in his book *Chariots of the Gods?* (1968). However, while this theory might be used to explain the straight lines, it does not account for the animal figures and abstract shapes, which must have been somewhat distracting for the alien pilots. Also, it might be expected that any such take-offs and landings would have disturbed the markings as well as the surrounding ground and no such traces have been found.

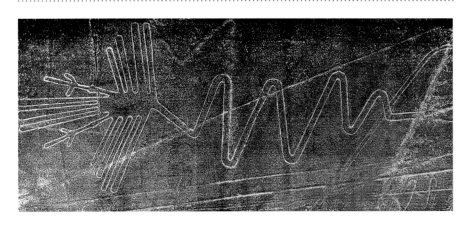

An aerial view of an image of a bird, one of the many animals represented in the Nazca lines in Peru. (© TopFoto)

Some theorists connect the lines with shamanic religion, interpreting them as images and guiding lines to be seen by those undertaking 'spirit flight', an out-of-body experience created by the ingestion of hallucinogens. The most likely explanation is indeed a religious one: that the markings are meant to be seen by gods or ancestral spirits, whether depicting these beings themselves or presenting images as symbolic offerings. The Nazca were a settled agricultural people and would have been likely to associate weather with deities who would have to be propitiated. However, all theories are essentially speculation, and the true origins and purposes of the Nazca lines remain mysterious.

Nessie *see* LOCH NESS MONSTER

Newgrange

A Neolithic passage tomb in County Meath, Ireland.

The vast burial mound at Newgrange predates Egypt's GREAT PYRAMID, having been built around 3200 BC. It is located near the town of Drogheda, north-west of Dublin, in an area which also includes two other great tombs at Knowth and Dowth. The passage tomb itself lay hidden for many years, until it was 'rediscovered' in 1699, when it was uncovered by the removal of stone for building work. What had been thought of as a solid mound was found to contain a large 'cave'. However, the tomb was not fully examined until the 20th century: the site was excavated, and restoration work undertaken, by archaeologist Professor Michael J O'Kelly of University College, Cork, from 1962 to 1975.

The mound itself, now with

reconstructed exposed stone walls and a turf top, is 76 metres (250 feet) across and 12 metres (40 feet) high. At its base are 97 kerb stones, including the beautifully carved entrance stone. Inside is a stone-lined passage entrance which is over 18 metres (60 feet) long. This leads to the central burial chamber which is 6 metres (20 feet) high and built of corbelled (overlapping) stone slabs. While most of the stones used in its construction have been found to be of local origin, the structure also includes quartz from the Wicklow Hills some 96.5 kilometres (60 miles) distant. The tomb is surrounded by an incomplete circle of STANDING STONES.

Many of the stones at Newgrange, such as the entrance stone already mentioned, are decorated with PETROGLYPHS – they have been carved predominantly with intricate spiral patterns. While the meaning of these patterns remains unclear, experiments in ARCHAEOACOUSTICS within the burial chamber have led some to go so far as to suggest that the patterns were made in an attempt to represent the patterns made in smoke by the reflected sound waves when chanting was taking place there.

Perhaps the most intriguing feature of Newgrange becomes apparent around the time of the winter solstice. Each dawn on the few days around the shortest day of the year, the sun shines directly through a slit above the passage entrance, known as the roof-box, and illuminates the floor of the burial chamber for around 17 minutes. It is generally agreed that the precision of the alignment cannot be an accident, and that the chamber and passage were built with this in mind. The solar alignment is certainly more precise than that at other tombs, such as MAESHOWE in Orkney, and while the exact reason for the alignment remains a mystery, it does display a considerable understanding of astronomy.

In Irish mythology, Newgrange is a fairy mound, or *sídhe*, and the home of Oenghus, the god of love.

Nixon, Robert, 'the Chesire prophet' (?15th century)

Also known as 'the ploughboy prophet', Robert Nixon was supposedly a 15th-century English prophet, who correctly predicted the outcome of the Battle of Bosworth.

According to some accounts, Robert Nixon was born in Over in Cheshire in the late 15th century. He was apparently a simpleton, who made his living working in the fields. He is said to have been unable to speak coherently, except for when he fell into a trance and made a prophecy, at which time his speech would become clear. He has been described as having a very large head and goggle eyes. He is most famously associated with his alleged prediction of the outcome of the Battle of Bosworth. Legend has it that during the battle, on 22 August 1485, Nixon was working in the fields when he stopped ploughing, fell into a trance and said 'Now Richard! Now Henry!' several times before crying 'Now Harry, get over that ditch and you gain the day!' News later reached the village that Henry Tudor had been victorious, Richard III having died during the conflict.

Many of Nixon's alleged predictions were political, and vague. They include:

A boy shall be born with three thumbs on one hand who shall hold three kings' horses whilst England is three times won and lost in one day.

and:

When a raven shall build in a stone lion's mouth
On a church top beside the Grey Forest,
Then shall a king of England be drove from his crown,
And return no more.

Nixon, and his predictions, became well known in the 18th century, when descriptions of both appeared in chapbooks. Unfortunately, there is no evidence of his existence, and while he remained popular until the late 19th century – as popular as that other famous English prophet, MOTHER SHIPTON – his popularity then waned, and he became almost forgotten.

Nostradamus (1503–66)

French physician and astrologer, also known as Michel de Notredame. His enigmatic predictions, written in rhymed quatrains, have established him as one of the most famous prophets in history.

Michel de Notredame, better known as Nostradamus, was born in Provence, France. He was Jewish by birth, but his family had converted to the Roman Catholic faith. From his youth, he showed an aptitude for mathematics, astronomy and astrology, and studied medicine at the University of Montpellier, becoming a doctor of medicine in 1529. A skilled apothecary, he travelled around France helping to treat victims of the plague, and during these travels he is said to have met and exchanged information with a number of underground alchemists, kabbalists and mystics. In 1537, after the death of his first wife and children, he resumed his travels all over France and Italy, exploring more mystical teachings and moving away from medicine to the occult. He remarried and settled down again in 1547, and rumours about his powers as a prophet began to circulate.

He then began on the body of work for which he would become famous – *Les Propheties*. This was a set of almost a thousand four-line rhymed poems, called quatrains, grouped into sets called 'centuries' because each group contained around a hundred poems. Nostradamus used a form of scrying in order to achieve the meditative state in which he composed these prophetic verses; this usually involved his gazing into a brass bowl filled with water. The first edition of his *Propheties* was published in 1555, and contained over 300 poems; the second edition, published in 1557, contained an additional 300 or so quatrains, and the third edition, published in 1568,

A portrait of Nostradamus seated at his desk; he is surrounded by symbols representing the twelve signs of the zodiac. The illustration is from the title page of Nostradamus's *Les Significations de l'Eclipse* (1559). (© Charles Walker/TopFoto)

two years after his death, included another 300 new poems. Each of the ten centuries is usually referred to by a Roman numeral from I to X. Most of these poems deal with the prediction of some sort of disaster, such as plagues, earthquakes, wars, fires, floods and droughts, although the prophecies do not appear to have been written sequentially by date. The quatrains are in general written in a very obscure and ambiguous style, using cryptic language and a mixture of Provençal, Greek, Latin, Italian and even Hebrew and Arabic. It is generally held that he wrote in such an enigmatic way in order to avoid persecution by the Inquisition. When the first edition was published, it had a mixed reception; some people believed him to be an agent of evil, some a fraud, some a madman, and others a divinely inspired prophet. Soon he was being sought by the nobility for his horoscopes and predictions, and Catherine de Medici, queen consort of King Henry II of France, had him made the Royal Counsellor and Physician-in-Ordinary.

Nostradamus has been credited with predicting many world events, such as the French Revolution, the rise of Hitler and the assassination of John F Kennedy. However, sceptics say that his reputation as a prophet is largely the result of modern-day supporters 'shoehorning' his highly obscure and metaphorical words to make them fit an event which has already happened – known as 'retroactive clairvoyance' – or of selective thinking. His writings have been frequently misquoted or altered by his believers to link them retrospectively to an event, and a number of quatrains have even been completely fabricated. But since his death in 1566, over 400 books and essays have been published about his writings, and today, more than four centuries later, people everywhere still puzzle over and debate the meanings of his quatrains.

omens

*Phenomena or occurrences seen as a
sign of some future event, either good
or bad.*

Since ancient times people of all
cultures have believed that future
events, both good and bad, cast a
shadow before them, which can be
read by those who have the wisdom
to recognize it. The interpretation
of omens is a form of divination,
and in most ancient and shamanic
cultures this function was performed
professionally by the recognized holy
man. Ornithomancy, the interpretation
of the flight and behaviour of birds, is
a form of omen-reading found all over
the world, the most famous example
being the augury practised by the
priests of ancient Rome. Omens were
also read by Roman priests from the
entrails of sacrificed animals.

Almost any natural phenomenon
can be interpreted as an omen. Of
particular significance in all cultures
are astronomical occurrences such
as solar and lunar ECLIPSES and COMETS.
An eclipse is almost always regarded

as an evil omen, and many cultures
developed elaborate rituals such as
sacrifices, drumming and incantations
to preserve the sun or moon during this
disruption of the natural order. Even
today, when the scientific cause for
eclipses is known, some people regard
them as omens of significant births and
deaths. Throughout history, comets
have been interpreted as omens of
social unrest, collapses in government
and other calamities, and the ancient
Greeks and Romans regarded them
as sure signs of warfare and disaster;
they were also believed to herald
the births and deaths of kings, and to
carry their souls to heaven, and seven
days after the death of Julius Caesar a
comet which appeared in the sky was
taken as a sign that he had become
immortal.

Many omens have survived in
modern times as SUPERSTITIONS,
with a large number of people still
believing that to break a MIRROR brings
seven years of bad luck, that a white
Christmas is an omen of a good year
ahead while an overcast or stormy
Christmas day warns of sickness in

The title page of a pamphlet from 1680. At that time sightings of comets were still often considered to be ill omens, presaging disaster. (© TopFoto/HIP)

the coming year, and that a ladybird landing on a person's clothes or hand is a lucky sign. The folklore of almost every country in the world also tells of certain supernatural creatures whose appearance is believed to be an omen of death, such as the BLACK DOG and the BANSHEE. Many people who would not consider themselves superstitious continue to regard certain events as warnings or signs caused by synchronicity, a term coined by psychologist and researcher Carl Jung

to describe a 'meaningful coincidence' of two or more events where something other than the probability of chance is taken to be involved. See also PORTENTS.

Order of the Knights Templar

see KNIGHTS TEMPLAR

ostention

The occurrence in real life of incidents or behaviour that has been guided by the content of fictional folk tales or urban legends.

The word 'ostention' was originally (and still is) used to describe the use of gestures to replace words in conversation, a coinage that is attributed to the Italian novelist and semiotician Umberto Eco. However, ostention developed an additional meaning when it was first used in connection with actions driven by fictitious folk tales and URBAN LEGENDS by the US folklorists Professor Linda Degh and Andrew Vazsonyi in a 1983 paper entitled 'Does the Word "Dog" Bite? Ostensive Action as a Means of Legend-Telling'.

The concept of ostention when used in this context is fairly wide in its scope. It can cover situations where people actually carry out actions which mirror those that are reported in fictional stories, or cases where the authorities follow a course of action through the mistaken belief that modern legends are based on truth (tales of devil worship and satanic ritual abuse have produced examples of both). It can also include the mistaken acceptance of unrelated occurrences as proof of the reality of an urban legend – such as the disappearance of a cat reinforcing the belief in claims that gangs are roaming the area stealing cats for use in the fur trade, or where sightings in Central Park in New York appeared to confirm the ALLIGATORS IN SEWERS story. Some people also include instances where individuals claim, for whatever reason, that an incident that forms the basis of a fictional modern folk tale has actually happened to them.

P

Patterson, Roger *see* BIGFOOT

petrifaction
The process of organic tissue turning to stone.

Petrifaction is the process by which organic tissue is turned into stone, with the original molecules being replaced over time by molecules of such chemicals as calcium carbonate or silica. It is this process that produces fossils of once-living animals and plants, immortalizing their remains in rock.

The Petrified Forest in Calistoga, California, is a famous example of a forest that has undergone petrifaction. The redwoods there have been dated back to the Pliocene epoch, over two million years ago, when they are believed to have been covered in volcanic ash. They were gradually exposed as the softer rocks around them eroded.

The discovery of petrified plants and animals may have given rise to the accounts in mythology of creatures with the power of magical petrifaction.

In ancient Greek legend, anyone who looked on the face of the Gorgon Medusa was instantly turned to stone. The hero Perseus was able to avoid this fate and kill her by only looking at her reflection in a polished shield.

Myths connected with many STONE CIRCLES in the British Isles and elsewhere often claim that the monoliths represent giants or legendary warriors that have been turned to stone, usually by a curse or through having earned the displeasure of a deity. On Dartmoor, for example, the Nine Maidens stone circle is said to represent maidens who were turned to stone for dancing on a Sunday, and in Cornwall the Blind Fiddler and the Two Sisters are also said to be people turned to stone for acting in an unchristian manner on the Sabbath – the Blind Fiddler played his instrument and the Two Sisters did not attend church.

petroglyphs
Pictures carved on stone by prehistoric peoples.

A petroglyph is an image either carved

or otherwise marked into the surface of a stone. The word comes from the Greek *petra*, meaning 'stone', and *glyphein*, 'to carve'. Petroglyphs have been found in various parts of the world, from Europe to the Americas, Asia and Australia, and most of them date from 10000 BC to 5000 BC. After this period they tended to be replaced by more sophisticated methods of art or communication such as cave painting, although some more isolated cultures such as the Australian Aborigines and Native Americans continued to make them for longer periods.

Various methods were used, including scoring, hammering and chipping away the surface levels of stone, depending on the hardness or sophistication of the tools available. The images tend to be stylized forms of human beings or animals, such as deer or other creatures that were the usual prey of hunter-gatherer societies, but in many cases it remains unknown what is represented. Some may have been a primitive form of pictorial writing, and markings found in Russia have been compared to runes, although it has not been possible to establish any firm connection.

It is thought that most petroglyphs had religious or cult significance, or show tribal or personal markings which established the ownership of territories or particularly significant sites.

Some analysts have claimed that they have detected similarities between petroglyphs in different parts of the world, and have used these to postulate cultural contacts in the prehistoric world. However, given that the images tend to represent the lives of the primitive peoples that created them, including the animals they hunted, it is hardly surprising that petroglyphs from different parts of the world should display common themes.

Particularly impressive petroglyphs are found, for example, at the megalithic passage tomb at NEWGRANGE in Ireland, where stones have been decorated with intricate spiral patterns whose meaning is unclear. At Dampier in Western Australia, the ancestors of the Aboriginal people created perhaps the world's largest number of petroglyphs in a single site. The Ica Stones of Peru constitute one of the more controversial collections of petroglyphs.

In the British Isles, one of the commoner types of petroglyph is the cup-and-ring mark. This is the name given to the characteristic pattern of a round hollow made in the surface of a rock and usually surrounded by concentric circles. The method for creating these seems to have been one of 'pecking' (chipping stone away using a sharp-pointed instrument) followed by grinding. Examples have been found marked on both megaliths and natural rock outcrops. There are fine examples of cup and ring marks on Ilkley Moor in Yorkshire, at Lordenshaw in Northumberland and at various sites in Argyll, Scotland. These designs are not unique to Britain, however, and examples have also been found in Brittany. It is not known

The Phaistos Disc, believed by some to be engraved with writing in an alien language. (© Gianni Dagli/Corbis)

what these patterns represent, but the fact that they are fairly widespread would suggest that they had some kind of cultural significance. They seem to have become less popular during the Bronze Age.

Phaistos Disc

A stone disc found in Crete that is inscribed with an as-yet-undeciphered set of symbols, said by some to represent an alien language.

Phaistos, near the Kashi Hills of Crete, was an important city during the Minoan civilization – a highly educated society that thrived for many centuries, more than 4,000 years ago. The region is considered by some to be a strong contender for the origin of the ATLANTIS legend – the Minoans possessed artistic and scientific skills before suffering a major earthquake that caused massive destruction.

In 1903 the Phaistos Disc was unearthed from a small room at the site of the palace in this ancient city. It was alongside pottery that was dated to c.1700 BC. The plate-sized disc carries glyphs or symbols in a spiral. They have not been decoded but are thought by many archaeologists to represent something mundane, such as a military record.

However, some supporters of the theory of ANCIENT ASTRONAUTS propose that the inscriptions on the disc may be written in an alien language, placed there by highly advanced extraterrestrial visitors that they argue lived on earth thousands of years ago. These beings are said to have inspired or guided both scientific discovery and enigmatic artwork across the world. Possibly owing to the similarity in shape to a modern computer disc, some theorists have suggested that the Phaistos Disc might be a technological device, perhaps used to measure distances through space.

philosopher's stone

An imaginary stone or compound sought by alchemists as a universal remedy and a means of transforming other metals into gold.

The magnum opus or 'great work' often referred to by alchemists was their quest for the philosopher's stone, a mythical substance which could transmute inexpensive metals into gold and create an elixir that could prolong life indefinitely.

> Our Stone is nothing but gold digested to the highest degree of purity and subtle fixation ... Our gold, no longer vulgar, is the ultimate goal of Nature.

The making of the philosopher's stone, also called by various other names, such as azoth, the Grand Catholicon, quintessence, philosophical powder

and philosopher's mercury, was thought to confer upon the alchemist a type of initiation, which was held by many to be the proper culmination of the great work – not the mere turning of lead into gold, or the production of an elixir to gain immortality, but the purification and perfection of the self. It was often said that in order to be able to create the philosopher's stone, the alchemist had to have already succeeded in the 'inner work' of attaining spiritual purity. Alchemists, it should be remembered, often used highly symbolic language, and it may be that the stone was in fact used as a symbol of man himself, and that the transformation of lead into gold was an analogy for spiritual progress; many modern writers believe that the goals of alchemy as symbolized by the philosopher's stone were really a metaphor for the transformation of the alchemist himself – his attainment of spiritual perfection, from a base state to one of purity, refinement and incorruptibility.

Pied Piper of Hameln

The German legend of a rat-catcher who made all the children in the town of Hameln disappear.

The legend of the Pied Piper of Hameln (or Hamelin) relates the story of a rat-catcher who rid the German town of Hameln of rats by luring them into the river by playing his pipe. In the best-known version, the townspeople then refused to pay the piper, who had his revenge by playing his music again, thus

An illustration from a children's book published in the 19th century, depicting the Pied Piper leading the children of Hameln away from the town. (© World History Archive/TopFoto)

luring all the children of the town away too. He led them to a hill or mountain, where a door opened and a cavern was revealed. The piper led the children into this cavern, the door shut, and the children disappeared. In some versions, including Robert Browning's poem *The Pied Piper of Hamelin* (1842), one lame child was left behind, who limped back to tell the townsfolk the news:

When, lo, as they reached the mountain-side,

A wondrous portal opened wide,

As if a cavern was suddenly hollowed;

And the Piper advanced and the children followed,

And when all were in to the very last,

The door in the mountain-side shut fast.

Did I say, all? No! One was lame,

And could not dance the whole of the way;

And in after years, if you would blame

His sadness, he was used to say, –

'It's dull in our town since my playmates left!

I can't forget that I'm bereft

Of all the pleasant sights they see,

Which the Piper also promised me.'

The first English version of the legend of the Pied Piper of Hameln appeared in 1605, apparently translated by Richard Verstegan, although he does not reveal his source. Robert Browning based his poem on this version, doing much to popularize the legend in Britain. Other popular versions include that of the brothers Grimm, but where did this tragic legend come from?

Some believe that a stained glass window depicting the story was placed in the church at Hameln in the 14th century, but this has since been lost. Written accounts seem to date from the 15th century. The date for the tragedy is variously given as 22 July 1376 and 26 June 1284, and over 100 children are said to have disappeared. Many believe that for this legend to have arisen, something must have happened to the children of the town. Various suggestions have been made to explain the genuine disappearance of the children, including a flood, an epidemic that made the children ill (the children perhaps then being led out of the town to protect the health of the adults) or a children's crusade. One of the more favoured explanations is that the children left voluntarily, with a figure later identified as the Pied Piper, to colonize Eastern Europe. It is said that one Bishop Bruno did recruit colonists for Olmütz in Bohemia, and that town records show that surnames there were similar to those in Hameln. Whichever is the real answer, modern Hameln still boasts a Rattenfängerhaus ('Rat-catcher's House').

Point Pleasant see MOTHMAN

portents
Signs foretelling future events, especially calamitous ones.

In every culture in the world, since primitive times, man has interpreted certain events as being portents, or signs of things to come. Anything which seemed to run contrary to the natural order was likely to be taken as a portent of disaster; ECLIPSES, particularly total solar eclipses, were almost always believed to be an evil OMEN, and in certain parts of Africa they are still thought to be a sign of a future drought. COMETS were also generally interpreted as a portent of doom, and the appearance in 1066 of the comet which later became known as Halley's Comet was thought to have foreshadowed the defeat of the Saxons at the Battle of Hastings. So significant was this heavenly sign that it is thought that it was incorporated into the Bayeux Tapestry. In more superstitious times, the birth of a deformed child or animal was also taken as a sure sign of coming disaster.

There are many smaller-scale portents which foretell death or misfortune to an individual, and which have been retained in modern culture as SUPERSTITIONS. If a bird, especially a robin, flies into a house, it is taken to be a sign of a death in the family. Some other signs of impending death are seeing a butterfly at night; a bat flying round a house three times; hearing an owl hooting in the daytime; a jackdaw settling on a house, or a single MAGPIE circling it; the sudden chiming of a clock which has not been working; and the sound of a deathwatch beetle. There are a number of supernatural creatures that are also portents of death. Apart from the many local ghosts which every area or castle lays claim to as its own particular harbinger of death, the sighting of a spectral BLACK DOG such as the Barghest of Yorkshire or the Trash or Skriker of Lancashire, even from a distance, is a sign of doom for the one who sees it. To meet your own double, or doppelgänger, is sometimes taken as a portent of your death. A mysterious human-like creature with moth wings called MOTHMAN is a more recent portent of doom; sightings of this creature in Point Pleasant, West Virginia, were later taken to be a portent of the Silver Bridge disaster, when 46 people were killed.

Another relatively modern death portent is the dead man's hand in poker. This hand, consisting of two aces and two eights, was the hand which Wild Bill Hickok is said to have been holding when he was shot in the back and killed in 1876, and it is mentioned as a sign of doom to the player holding it in a number of popular songs and books.

Presley, Elvis Aaron (1935–77)

Famous entertainer believed to have been sighted alive after his reported death.

According to the official record, Elvis Presley, the celebrated US popular entertainer, was born in Tupelo, Mississippi, in 1935 and died in 1977 in his Graceland mansion in Memphis, Tennessee.

In his heyday Presley, known as 'the King', was the world's most popular singer, its biggest-selling recording artist and an object of devotion to his millions of fans. His relatively early death produced widespread and intense mourning and his home became a shrine. However, not long after his official demise rumours began to circulate that he had never really died at all and that his 'death' was simply a stunt that would allow him to escape the pressures of being continually in the public eye.

Reported sightings of Elvis began to appear in the media and have not ceased to this day. In various places around the world, from all over the USA to Germany and Japan, people claim not only to have seen the King but to have spoken to him. He is said to have been spotted doing the most mundane things, including driving along suburban streets in unremarkable cars, fishing in remote rivers, going to the cinema or, unsurprisingly, given his notorious junk-food habits, eating in small-town fast-food restaurants.

The obvious explanation for many of these reports is that the world is full of Elvis impersonators and that those who prefer not to accept that he ever died will not go short of opportunities to shore up their belief.

In some ways, the Elvis sightings phenomenon is an echo of traditional myths of the dead king who will one day return to save his people, such as the idea of King Arthur as the 'Once and Future King'. It taps into a desire, even a need, for devotees to feel that their hero has not disappeared for good.

It may be that some of this is fuelled by the fact that Presley famously turned his back on live performances for seven years, only to return in triumph with a live television special in 1968, which, to his fans, showed the world that he still had the old magic. To followers of the Presley cult it is perhaps not such a great leap of faith to imagine fondly another miraculous comeback.

pyramids

Huge constructions built in ancient Egypt as monuments.

The pyramids of Egypt were built around 2000 BC as royal tombs on a gigantic scale – it has been calculated that the largest of them, the GREAT PYRAMID, was originally 147 metres (481 feet) high.

Earlier Egyptian kings were buried under stone mastabas, which had sloping sides but a flat roof, and the first pyramid was that of King Zoser, built at Saqqara in c.2700 BC, which had stepped sides. The classic, smooth-sided pyramid evolved later, when a stepped pyramid at Meydum had its steps filled in to give a uniform slope (c.2600 BC). The name 'pyramid' comes from the Greek, and some have claimed it derives, humorously, from 'wheat cake', but this has not been established. Over a hundred pyramids have been identified in Egypt, but it is the three great pyramids at Giza, those of Cheops, his son Chephren, and Menkaure, that are most famous.

It has been estimated that a workforce of at least 20,000 would have been necessary to build any of the three largest pyramids at Giza. This represents an enormous communal effort, and given the technology available at the time, it is an amazing feat. No one knows for certain how the pyramids were built, but the most likely method would involve the use of ropes and pulleys and great lubricated ramps of earth and bricks to allow the massive blocks of stone to be hauled or pushed into position. It has sometimes been assumed that those who laboured on these monuments must have been slaves, but graffiti and other inscriptions discovered more recently seem to indicate that at least some of the work was done by ordinary people, perhaps carrying out a period of obligatory service to their overlords. Despite the claims of the Jewish historian Josephus (37– c.100 AD) that the enslaved Jews were

The pyramids at Giza. (© Charles Walker/TopFoto)

made to work at pyramid-building, the pyramids were built long before the Jews arrived in Egypt.

The pyramid shape itself is believed to symbolize the ancient Egyptian belief in the emergence of new life from the ground. In this way the deceased monarch entombed inside would be given new life in the next world, where he would make use of the many artefacts buried with him.

In several excavated pyramids inscriptions known as pyramid texts have been found, written in an old form of hieroglyphics. These appear to be religious incantations, perhaps uttered by priests when the dead Pharaoh was

being entombed, intended to secure him power and protection in the afterlife.

Down through the ages, the pyramids have always inspired awe and wonder, with many people being unwilling to accept that ordinary human beings could have built them. The word 'pyramidology' is used to describe the body of theories that have been suggested as to their origins. Such ideas include those of occultists who believed that the pyramids must embody great secrets of magic power, and those who saw in them the remnants of a greater civilization, now lost, perhaps linked to the legendary lost continent of ATLANTIS. The space age spawned its own myths, with ERICH VON DÄNIKEN leading the ranks of those who contended that the pyramids must have been created by extraterrestrial beings.

However, the more that is discovered about the pyramids, the more they must be seen as the remarkable achievements of a gifted and resourceful human society with no need for divine or alien assistance.

R

rains, mystery *see* FALLS

Rasputin, Grigori Efimovich (1871–1916)

Russian peasant and religious mystic.

Although Grigori Efimovich Rasputin was sometimes nicknamed 'the Mad Monk', he spent only a matter of months in a monastery at the age of 18. Apparently born to a Siberian peasant family, it is known that he married and fathered children before joining a sect of flagellants known as *Khlysty*. He travelled widely as a pilgrim before ending up in St Petersburg in 1903, calling himself a *starets* or holy man.

Taking advantage of the fashionability of mystic religion at that time, he brought himself to the attention of the royal household of Tsar Nicholas II (1868–1918) and the Empress Alexandra (1872–1918), suggesting that he could use prayer and hypnotism to treat the haemophilia that afflicted their son, the Tsarevich Alexei. Whether or not he had any real healing ability, the Empress in particular was convinced that Rasputin had helped her son, and placed great trust in him.

He soon became notorious for his alcoholic excesses and sexual debauchery, apparently convincing women that intercourse with him was spiritually purifying. The more scurrilous rumours even hinted at a sexual relationship between Rasputin and the Empress. Whatever its nature, his hold over the royal family was deeply resented, especially his alleged ability to influence government appointments.

Rasputin's unpopularity grew when Russia entered World War I against Germany. He was closely identified with the Empress, who had been born a German princess, and it was even rumoured that he was a German spy. To many at the Imperial Court, Rasputin was seen not only as a source of scandal but also as dangerously undermining the standing of the monarchy at a time of great political unrest. His enemies were not only powerful but ruthless, and a group of aristocrats led by Prince Felix Yusupov (1887–1967) determined to do away with him.

A photograph of Grigori Rasputin from 1908. (© Mary Evans Picture Library)

Rasputin's murder became a focus of legend in modern folklore, as it was claimed that it showed Rasputin as miraculously immune to a series of attempts that would surely have killed any normal man. According to Yusupov's account, Rasputin was first poisoned, being given food and drink laced with large amounts of cyanide. When this failed to kill him, Yusupov took out a revolver and shot him. Again Rasputin refused to die. He attacked Yusupov and staggered out into the snow to make his escape. Here he was shot again, beaten and stabbed by Yusupov and several accomplices until, apparently unconscious, he was thrown into the partly frozen River Neva. When his body was recovered a few days later, it was decided that he had died by drowning.

While Yusupov may have been interested in creating a legend and glorifying his own part in the story, the truth seems to have been more prosaic. The actual report of the autopsy carried out on Rasputin apparently recorded no trace of poison. The mystic had indeed been beaten but the cause of death was identified as a bullet in the head.

In 2004 a BBC investigative documentary suggested that the fatal shot had not been fired by Yusupov but by a British intelligence agent attached to the Imperial Court. It was, of course, vital to British interests that

Russia continued to wage war against Germany, and Rasputin's activities were seen as a threat to this.

Rennes-le-Château

A medieval castle village in southern France. A 19th-century priest, Bérenger Saunière, was rumoured to have found a mysterious treasure in the church, and from the 1950s onwards, the location became the focus of various conspiracy theories linking Saunière's discovery to the Knights Templar, the Priory of Sion, the Holy Grail and the alleged bloodline of Christ and Mary Magdalene.

The medieval castle village of Rennes-le-Château is situated in the Aude department of the Languedoc area in southern France. In the late 19th century, rumours began to surround the local priest, Bérenger Saunière, who was said to have mysteriously acquired a great deal of sudden wealth; although poor when he took up his position there, he began to spend lavishly, renovating the church, decorating it elaborately with statues, and building a villa with a formal garden, a belvedere and a neo-Gothic tower dedicated to Mary Magdalene. It is thought that most of the money he spent came from the practice of trafficking masses, which eventually led to his suspension and prosecution by the ecclesiastical courts, and by the time of his death at the age of 65 in 1917, he was apparently penniless again.

In the 1950s, a local businessman,

Noel Corbu, opened a restaurant on Saunière's estate, and to attract business he suggested that Saunière had in fact amassed his wealth after uncovering something mysterious in the church; according to one version, he had discovered certain parchments in an ancient pillar, and, following the clues in these documents, had been led to a great treasure hidden there by Saint Blanche of Castille in the 13th century. This idea was taken up by a man called Pierre Plantard, who was at that time propagating the story of a mysterious organization he called the Priory of Sion. According to Plantard, Jesus had not died on the cross, but had founded a bloodline with Mary Magdalene – the Merovingian dynasty of France – whose descendants the Priory of Sion were charged with protecting. Plantard sought to prove that he was not only the current Grand Master of the Priory of Sion, but also the last descendant of the Merovingians, and therefore the legitimate heir to the throne of France, and he claimed that Saunière's 'treasure' included parchments that substantiated his story. To this end, in the 1960s either he or an accomplice anonymously deposited a collection of documents in the Bibliothèque Nationale in Paris which allegedly linked Saunière's secrets to the Priory and its sacred charge.

Although the documents were quickly dismissed as forgeries, they sparked off a national interest in the village of Rennes-le-Château, which became inundated by treasure-hunters, and fuelled a number of increasingly sensationalist conspiracy theories which suggested that whatever Saunière had found threatened the very foundations of Catholicism: some artefact or document of spiritual significance hidden by the KNIGHTS TEMPLAR, or by the Cathars in that region in the 13th century before their final defeat; proof that Jesus and Mary Magdalene had descendants; maps showing the location of Jesus's burial place, or documents proving that he was not resurrected; or scriptures challenging the legitimacy of the Church. These theories greatly influenced the authors of the popular 1982 book *Holy Blood, Holy Grail*, Umberto Eco's novel *Foucault's Pendulum* (1989), and Dan Brown's 2003 bestselling novel THE DA VINCI CODE. As a result, the village still attracts visitors from all over the world looking for evidence of conspiracy or for hidden treasure.

Robin Hood

Legendary English folk hero.

Robin Hood is perhaps the best-known English legendary figure. Numerous television and film adaptations of the Robin Hood story exist, and almost everyone knows of him as an outlaw and a master of archery, battling against the Sheriff of Nottingham and robbing from the rich to give to the poor. Fewer know the history of this legend.

Robin Hood has been popular since the 14th century, and where early sources place him at all, it is in Barnsdale (in either Yorkshire or Rutland) rather than in Sherwood Forest, which appears in later sources and is the location with which we are familiar today. Thirty-eight extant ballads from the 15th century onwards relate to Robin Hood. These ballads do not explain Robin's background, nor the reason for his being an outlaw. They do show him robbing from the rich, but only one has him then giving to the poor. Only in later literary sources is Robin a dispossessed member of the gentry. Maid Marian and Friar Tuck are also later inventions, but Robin has companions from the outset, and is supported by the amazing strength of Little John. Sir Walter Scott's *Ivanhoe* (1820) was the first work to popularize the political nature of Robin. Scott has Robin living during the absence of Richard I at the Crusades and battling against wicked Norman barons, but other traditions place him in the 13th or 14th centuries, rather than during the reign of Richard I (1189–99).

Sadly, it seems likely that Robin Hood is an entirely fictitious character, and attempts to identify him with a historical figure have not been convincing. Tales of Robin were initially widespread among the peasantry, and were not popular among the wealthy classes, so it has been suggested that he was an embodiment of rebellious disquiet among the poor in the time prior to the Peasants' Revolt. The chivalrous and noble nature of his character was added later, and that and his romance with Maid Marian are emphasized in modern retellings.

The main stone circle of the Rollright Stones in Oxfordshire, known as the King's Men. (© TopFoto/Fortean)

Rollright Stones

A stone circle formation in Oxfordshire connected with witchcraft.

The Rollright Stones are a megalithic STONE CIRCLE formation near the Oxfordshire villages of Little and Great Rollright. There are upwards of 70 standing stones in the main circle, known as the King's Men, which has a diameter of around 30 metres (100 feet). Nearby stands a smaller group, now thought to be the remains of a DOLMEN, called the Whispering Knights (so called because they appear to be leaning their heads together in confabulation), as well as a solitary stone known as the King Stone.

The stones are all made of a local limestone, but it has been shown that the three separate groupings were not erected at the same time.

The stones are on a much smaller scale than those of STONEHENGE or AVEBURY and many have weathered into grotesque and pitted forms. Most of them had fallen over by the 18th century, and as many were re-erected in the late 19th century it may be that the original arrangement was quite different.

According to legend, the Rollright Stones are the petrified bodies of a king and his invading army, turned to stone by the spells of MOTHER SHIPTON, a famous local witch, who is said to have accosted the invaders with the following words:

Seven long strides shalt thou take,

If Long Compton thou canst see

King of England thou shalt be.

To this the king is said to have replied:

Stick, stock, stone,

As King of England I shall be known.

The King thereupon paced out his seven strides but found that an ancient mound called the Archdruid's Barrow blocked his view of Long Compton (a nearby village). Mother Shipton then completed the spell with the following:

As Long Compton thou canst not see,

King of England thou shalt not be,

Rise up stick and stand still stone,

For King of England thou shalt be none.

Thou and thy men hoar stones shall be

And myself an eldern tree.

Quite why the triumphant witch felt obliged to turn herself into an elder tree remains unclear.

The area has long been associated with the occult and for centuries witches have been said to hold gatherings there. The stones have been associated with FAIRIES and fertility rituals and are said, at times, to move about, whether to dance or to go

for a drink at a spring at midnight on New Year's Eve. On Midsummer Eve, if a nearby elder tree is cut, its sap is said to run like blood. It is said to be impossible to count all of the stones with any accuracy, and that a local baker who tried to do this by placing a loaf on top of each stone simply ran out of loaves.

Rosicrucians

An occult secret society which was alleged to have been founded in the 15th century by Christian Rosenkreutz and then rediscovered in the 17th century; any of various modern societies based on this tradition.

The history of Rosicrucianism is a much-debated one. In the 17th century, the existence of a secret brotherhood of alchemists and sages called the 'Order of the Rosy Cross' was proclaimed with the publication of three German texts known as the *Fama Fraternitatis Rosae Crucis* (1614), the *Confessio Fraternitatis* (1615) and *The Chemical Marriage of Christian Rosenkreutz* (1616) – also collectively known as the Rosicrucian Manifestos. The first two works describe the foundation and aims of the order, and tell the story of a poor but noble 15th-century German who went on a pilgrimage to the Holy Land, and while there learned Arabic and studied with several Arabic alchemists. His occult studies led him to conceive of a form of Christianity united with theosophy as being an ideal religion, and he devised a plan for a universal and simultaneous reform of religion, philosophy, science, politics and art; to this end, on his return to Germany, he took the mystical name Christian Rosenkreutz (Christian Rose-Cross) and in 1407 he founded an order called the European Fraternity of the Rosy Cross, whose aim was 'to study Nature in her hidden forces' and to make its discoveries and inventions available for the benefit of mankind. Its eight members travelled incognito, healing the sick, and each had to find himself a successor so that the order could continue its secret work. After Rosenkreutz's death, so the story went, the order carried on, but nothing was known of its existence for nearly 200 years, until its founder's perfectly preserved body was discovered in a crypt, one hand clasping a parchment scroll in which the fraternity offered its secrets to the world. The publication of these three texts caused great excitement and sparked off many literary works, some arguing for Rosicrucianism, others against; some people eagerly sought admission to the order, while others claimed to actually be Rosicrucians, and everyone wanted to know who its members were. But all attempts to find out anything more about the order were unsuccessful.

Research seems to point to a Lutheran theologian called Johann Valentin Andrea as being the author of all three works (although some have argued that he based them on the writings and philosophy of John Dee). He was believed to have chosen the Rosy Cross as the symbol of his fictitious order because it was an ancient symbol of occultism. Some commentators think he wrote the documents as a hoax to show how eager the people of the age were to believe in the notion of such a secret organization, but most are of the opinion that he had a vision of an enlightened and reformed society, and had created the legend of the 15th-century order and its 17th-century 'rediscovery' and published his works in order to catalyse others into initiating Rosicrucianism as a reality. And it did in fact spread throughout Europe during the 17th century, with the formation of a number of Rosicrucian groups that combined a vision of social transformation with the study of alchemy, mysticism and Christian theology. Little was heard of Rosicrucian activity in Europe again until the end of the 18th century, when some of its teachings were revived by Alessandro di Cagliostro (founder of EGYPTIAN RITE FREEMASONRY) and Saint Germain, and there was a considerable diffusion of ideas between Rosicrucianism and Free-masonry in England. During the late 19th century and the early 20th century, various modern groups were formed which styled themselves as Rosicrucian and claimed to be the authentic heirs to a historical tradition; among these were the Ancient Mystical Order Rosae Crucis, the Fraternitas Rosae Crucis, the Rosicrucian Fellowship and the Societas Rosicruciana. See also SECRET SOCIETIES.

Roslyn Chapel

Fifteenth-century chapel south of Edinburgh in Scotland; it is noted for its ornate interior carvings, which display links with the Knights Templar and elements of Freemasonry. There is much speculation as to the contents of its vault, which has been unopened since the 17th century, and one popular theory is that the Holy Grail is hidden somewhere in the chapel.

Roslyn Chapel (also sometimes spelled Rosslyn or Roslin) is a 15th-century building situated a few miles south of Edinburgh in Scotland. It was founded in 1446 by Sir William St Clair, who had originally planned a much larger structure in a cruciform shape with a tower at its centre. However, he died in 1484 and was buried in the unfinished chapel. Even in its incomplete state, it is a remarkable and unique construction, but during the Reformation its many statues were smashed and the original altar was destroyed, and the chapel fell into ruin. It remained abandoned until 1736, when Sir William's descendants began to repair and restore it, and it was rededicated in 1862. Restoration work continues on it to this day.

The building is most remarkable for its exquisite interior stone carvings, which fortunately have survived relatively undamaged; these are among the finest in Europe, and display imagery not found in any other 15th-century chapel. They show both Christian and pagan themes, with the Green Man motif appearing many times, and much of their symbolism, along with the geometry and architecture of the building itself, links the chapel unmistakably with

the KNIGHTS TEMPLAR and FREEMASONRY. It is said that after their order was suppressed in 1314, some Knights Templar went to Scotland. Sir William St Clair is believed to have befriended some Templars, or perhaps even to have become one himself, and to have built the chapel as a lasting tribute to the order and its mysteries; it has been suggested that his intention was to construct it as a representation of the Temple of Solomon, and that this can be seen from its original foundations. Such is the richness of symbolism in its carvings that the chapel has been described as a 'tapestry in stone', a repository of arcane knowledge with its secrets hidden in plain sight – recorded on its very walls, ceilings and pillars, and only to be understood by those with the knowledge to decode it.

Outstanding among the chapel's carvings are the two pillars at its East end – the Mason's Pillar and the Apprentice Pillar. The latter is entwined by stone coils snaking up its length from the bottom to the top, thought to symbolize the Tree of Life, and a legend tells of how a stonemason began work on it and went to Rome to seek inspiration. While he was gone, his ambitious apprentice completed it, and when his master returned, he was so consumed by jealousy at the beauty of his work that he killed the apprentice with a blow to the head. A stone head halfway up a wall in the south-west of the chapel is thought to represent the murdered apprentice, while two carved heads elsewhere in

The Apprentice Pillar, Roslyn Chapel.
(© EE Images/HIP/TopFoto)

the chapel are said to depict his killer and his grieving mother.

The building has always attracted visitors from all over the world, but it has been the focus of increased interest since the publication of Dan Brown's 2003 novel *THE DA VINCI CODE*, in which the Holy Grail is said to be hidden in Roslyn Chapel. Brown's book is not the first to have made this suggestion; the contents of the chapel's vaults, which have been sealed up since the last burial there in the 17th century, have been the subject of much speculation over the years, and a number of books have been published suggesting that along with the remains of the St Clair family's ancestors the vaults house the Holy Grail, the Ark of the Covenant, the mummified head of Christ, a piece of the true cross of Christ, or scrolls bearing the lost gospels of Jesus. These various sacred relics are supposed to have been discovered by the Knights Templar while they were excavating in the Holy Land, and after their order was disbanded, they are said to have brought them to Scotland and hidden them in the chapel. One theory claims that the Holy Grail is built into the Apprentice Pillar.

S

salt

While most people know of the superstitious belief that it is unlucky to spill salt, numerous other less well-known superstitions also involve this commodity.

Many people know of the belief that if you spill salt you will receive bad luck, unless you avert the misfortune by taking a pinch of the spilt salt in your right hand and throwing it over your left shoulder. A superstitious belief regarding the spilling of salt has existed for over 400 years. At times, it was only the person towards whom the salt fell that received the bad luck, rather than the person who spilled it, as described in the *Gentleman's Magazine* (1833):

> If salt be accidentally overturned, it is unlucky for the person towards whom it falls. But if that person, without hesitation or remark, take up a single pinch of salt between the finger and thumb of his right hand, and cast it over his left shoulder, the threatened misfortune will be averted.

The explanation generally given for the action of throwing spilled salt over your left shoulder is that the Devil sits there, and the salt will blind him, but this is a relatively recent addition to an old superstition. Some say that the belief that spilling salt is unlucky dates back to the Last Supper, claiming that on that occasion Judas Iscariot spilled the salt, but there is no evidence to support this theory.

Salt has also been used as a protective talisman – as a protection against evil spirits, or burned to counteract witchcraft. At one time, salt was sprinkled in a new house to protect and cleanse it, as described in *Folklore*, the journal of the Folklore Society, in 1909:

> When anyone moved into a new house, or changed houses, a child was sent into every room with a bag of salt, which he was told to sprinkle on the hearths and in every corner. I have myself been told off for the job.

Salt was also used in the ritual of laying out a body at home, when a shallow dish of salt was placed on the corpse. It was said that this would prevent the body from swelling before burial, although some suggest that this was a more mystical rite. This practice was common into the early part of the 20th century.

sasquatch *see* BIGFOOT

Seahenge
An ancient circle of wooden stumps found on a beach in Norfolk, England.

In 1998 high tides washed away a layer of peat near the shore on the north coast of Norfolk, exposing an obviously man-made circle of more than 50 oak stumps. A similar formation had been uncovered in the 1970s but it had been washed away, leaving no traces. It was discovered that the stumps revealed in 1998 were actually upturned tree trunks and that a larger object in the centre of the circle was a large upside-down oak tree. Carbon dating has shown the trees to be over 4,000 years old.

Who put them there and why? It is important to bear in mind that the 'sea henge' was not originally so close to the sea; rather, the sea encroached on the land, which was salt marsh, to 'claim' it. Nothing can be known for certain about the site's purpose, but it has been conjectured that it had religious significance to the Bronze Age culture that constructed it. It may have had a funerary role, with a dead body being placed on the central upturned tree to decompose, or it may have simply been a shrine. Trees, particularly the oak, were certainly sacred to the

much later Celtic inhabitants; perhaps Seahenge is an earlier manifestation of this.

The timbers were removed for preservation and further study, the fear being that without their peat covering they would quickly decompose, and it was discovered that many of them bore the impressions of the tools that had been used to cut and shape them.

secret societies
Exclusive groups whose existence and purpose are often shrouded in mystery.

Secret societies can be divided into three broad categories – spiritual, criminal and political – though these may overlap. It is the spiritually based secret societies that are discussed here. Whichever type they might be, secret societies tend to share some of the same characteristics. They are exclusive rather than inclusive (they are often difficult to join and, therefore, elitist) and are generally concerned with the acquisition of knowledge and/ or power (the first often leading to the second). Some, like the Freemasons (see FREEMASONRY), are secret in full view – their existence is open and public, with identifiable buildings, but what goes on in their ceremonies and rituals is secret; indeed, they have described themselves as 'not a secret society but a society with secrets'. Others are known about but don't advertise their presence (the Mafia, for example). Others might have a public face but a very different private purpose; conspiracy theorists would point to various international political bodies such as the Bilderberg Group. With some, their existence and purpose are suspected but unproven, and we can assume that there are others so secret that even their existence is not guessed at.

Of the spiritually based secret societies the best known are the ROSICRUCIANS and the Freemasons – and whatever protestations there might be, they are indisputably close relatives in ideas and ideals, even if the latter might not be directly descended from the former. However, this is the story with most esoteric societies, secret or not.

In the days of classical Greece and Rome there were numerous mystery cults dedicated to various gods and goddesses, including Mithraism (men only) and the Eleusinian mysteries (men and women). These were initiatory societies to which people of different ranks in the outside world could belong equally; in Mithraism, for example, a grizzled common soldier might be at a higher initiatory level than a young noble officer. The same principle holds true in Freemasonry today. There is a bond in their normal lives between members who go through the same secret rituals together; Freemasonry is sometimes called 'the Brotherhood'.

Although today Freemasonry might be considered by many to be akin to a charitable social club (albeit with some unusual rituals), it has at its symbolic heart a deep mystical spirituality which can be seen in the writings of A E Waite, W L Wilmshurst and others. This was inherited from the Rosicrucians and Hermetic philosophers of the 17th century.

Rosicrucianism almost certainly did not exist, at least not under that name, before the publication in Germany in 1614, 1615 and 1616 of the three Rosicrucian Manifestos. These told of a secret brotherhood dedicated to spiritual self-improvement for the betterment of the whole of mankind. Such people did exist, dedicated to the same ideal of a search for spiritual knowledge and power, and engaged in the same practices: alchemy, astrology, astronomy, mathematics, medicine, scientific enquiry and so on. Because many of their activities (from raising demons to scientific experimentation) would get them into serious trouble with the Church, secrecy was essential – the esotericist Giordano Bruno was burned at the stake in 1600 for teaching his beliefs. Alchemical treatises, for example, were written in symbolic language sometimes several layers deep.

The Rosicrucian Manifestos did not include an address or a membership form. For years radical thinkers, both spiritual and scientific, searched Europe for a Rosicrucian society they could join – in the end some of them founded their own. Early Rosicrucians spoke, perhaps as a joke, of an Invisible College, but there were meetings of 'natural philosophers' at Gresham College in London during the Protectorate, which transmuted into the Royal Society when Charles II came to the throne. The Invisible College had been reified, and was to become one of the most important scientific institutions in the world (while demonstrating that secret societies do not always have to remain secret). But the links between spiritual and scientific exploration were not completely severed; many of the early Fellows of the Royal Society were Freemasons, and some of them (including Isaac Newton, their president from 1703 to 1727) were engaged in alchemical research and other spiritual quests. Science and spirituality did separate during the 18th century, 'the Age of Reason', but not in a single move.

In the 18th and 19th centuries numerous Rosicrucian-related societies were formed in Europe, and later in the USA – many of them laying dubious claim to be direct descendants of an original secret order. The HERMETIC ORDER OF THE GOLDEN DAWN, founded by three members of the Masonic order *Societas Rosicruciana in Anglia*, even had forged letters from a non-existent German order granting it 'legitimacy'. It is paradoxical that organizations pledged to the improvement of self and society often have deception in their origins. The *Prieuré de Sion*, first brought to prominence by Baigent, Leigh and Lincoln in *The Holy Blood and the Holy Grail* (1982), was not founded in the Middle Ages to protect the bloodline of Jesus, or for any other esoteric purpose; it was the creation of a few eccentric Frenchmen in the mid-1950s, and everything about it,

including its much-vaunted list of Grand Masters, is a fake.

Although most of today's many esoteric or occult societies are open about their existence (some, such as the Ancient Mystical Order Rosae Crucis, even advertise themselves in magazines), the majority can still be called secret societies because they have graded levels of knowledge which are only revealed as members rise up the initiatory ladder.

Prostitution and the priesthood (along with espionage) vie for the title of 'the world's oldest profession'. Unlikely as it may seem, they are linked by an ancient symbol of secrecy and a Latin phrase. Traditionally, a prostitute would have a rose carved into her bed head; it signified that anything said to her in pillow talk would go no further. The grill between priest and penitent in a Catholic confessional often shows a rose; 'the seal of the confessional' is inviolable. Freemasons use the phrase 'under the rose' or *sub rosa*; a rose on or above the dining table guarantees that anything said incautiously after too much wine will not be repeated outside. The rose is a symbol of the HOLY GRAIL and it lies at the heart of Rosicrucianism. The perfection of the rose symbolizes purity and virginity, and hence the Virgin Mary; but the opening rosebud, surrounded by thorns, symbolizes female sexuality. The rose, beauty surrounded by suffering (its thorns), also symbolizes a very different passion, the passion of Christ. With all these hidden meanings, some of them contradictory, there is perhaps no more suitable symbol for secret societies.

Serpent Mound

A huge effigy mound depicting a snake in Adams County, Ohio.

The Serpent Mound is a large earthwork, of a type known as an effigy mound, depicting what is believed to be an uncoiling serpent. The mound is 400 metres (over 1,300 feet) long, 6 metres (over 19 feet) wide, and up to 1.5 metres (nearly 5 feet) high, and stands on a plateau overlooking Brush Creek Valley. Many interpret the shape as that of a serpent with its mouth open ready to swallow an egg, again represented by a mound, although it has also been argued that the 'egg' is simply a platform that either served a ritual purpose or supported a structure. Others have suggested that the Serpent Mound represents the Horned Serpent, a mythological motif present in many Native American cultures.

The mound was excavated in the late 19th century by Harvard archaeologist Frederic Ward Putnam, who attributed its creation to the Adena culture between c.1000 BC and c.100 AD. More recent excavations indicate that it was constructed much later, around the 12th century AD. Other

An aerial view of the Serpent Mound, Ohio. (© 2004 TopFoto)

artificial mounds exist in the USA, depicting both humans and animals, and many conclude that they were created by a succession of cultures. Like many pictorial earthworks and the ground markings of Peru known as the NAZCA LINES, the Serpent Mound is best appreciated from the air.

Exactly who constructed the Serpent Mound, and why, remains a mystery. Some suggest that it was built to honour a god, or to ward off evil. Others believe it was created to invoke the Horned Serpent of mythology, which brought rain and therefore fertility. It has also been suggested that the Serpent Mound had an astronomical significance – its head points to the summer solstice sunset, and it has been said that its coils align with the winter solstice sunrise.

SHC *see* SPONTANEOUS HUMAN COMBUSTION

Shipton, Mother *see* MOTHER SHIPTON

Shroud of Turin *see* TURIN SHROUD

Siberian Hell Hole

In the 1990s, a story began to circulate in the media that a team of Russian geologists conducting an extremely deep drilling operation in Siberia had actually opened a hole into Hell.

According to the story the drill had penetrated over 14 kilometres (8.5 miles) into the earth when it broke through into empty space. The geologists were said to have measured the temperature in this cavity as greater than 1,100°C, leading them to believe that they had reached the hollow centre of the planet. Not content with such an astonishing reading, the intrepid Russians felt moved to lower a microphone into the hole. When this picked up sounds identified as the agonized cries of a multitude of human beings in intolerable pain, the only conclusion to be reached was that a window had been opened into Hell itself. According to some versions of the story, this diabolical outcome was further emphasized by the brief emergence from the hole of a luminous gaseous bat-like being that could only be the Devil.

Whether one believes it or not, how did such a story originate? According to *Scientific American*, it seems that in 1984 a Russian geological expedition in the Kola Peninsula (in north-west Russia, not Siberia) did carry out drilling to the extreme depth of 12 kilometres (7.5 miles), encountering temperatures of around 180°C as well as discovering gas. Some have suggested that this inspired various accounts, published in Christian fundamentalist publications, in which Hell began to feature – seen as a blow against atheism and proof of the existence of eternal punishment for sin. Perhaps sensing the mileage in this story, a Norwegian citizen claimed to have been inspired to perpetrate it as a deliberate hoax on such publications and radio shows after having been exposed to some of their more extravagant excesses on a visit to the USA.

The story acquired the status of an URBAN LEGEND, spreading rapidly via the Internet, where recordings of the alleged cries of damned souls in agony could be downloaded by the curious. Sceptics would point out that drilling equipment or microphones would have to be made of stern stuff indeed to function undamaged at such extraordinary temperatures. Questions could also be asked as to why no further exploration of this fortuitously discovered underworld has ever taken place. Conspiracy theorists might reply that this would have been covered up by those involved, but they must have had the devil of a time keeping it quiet.

Silbury Hill

A Neolithic earthwork near Avebury in Wiltshire, England.

Silbury Hill, near AVEBURY in Wiltshire, is one of the greatest prehistoric earthworks in Europe. It is around 40 metres (130 feet) high at its flat summit and is ringed by a ditch that is 6 metres (20 feet) deep in places. Its base is round, and has a diameter of 168 metres (550 feet). This great mound, made from the earth and chalk dug out of the ditch, is believed to have been created in c.2600 BC and would probably have been much higher at that time It was built in terraces that were filled in to give a smooth conical shape when it was completed, although visible

remnants of these remain. It has been estimated that it would have taken ten years for 700 men to construct it.

The reason for building Silbury Hill is not known. The obvious purpose would be as a burial mound, and local folklore has it that it marks the grave of the legendary King Sil, who was said to have been interred astride a golden horse. While the antiquary William Stukeley (1687–1765) claimed to have unearthed bones and artefacts on the site, subsequent excavations, most recently in the 1960s, have failed to uncover any important finds. In another folk tale, the Devil was preparing to drop an apronful of earth on the nearby town of Marlborough (just for devilment?) when priests from Avebury forced him to dump it elsewhere.

One theory links Silbury Hill with LEYS, maintaining that it is a kind of way-marker connecting, among other places, Avebury and STONEHENGE. Certainly, the area has so many Neo-lithic sites that the obvious inference is that it was of particular religious significance.

simulacra

Spontaneously occurring forms, faces and figures.

The word 'simulacra' comes from the Latin, usually meaning devotional objects in the likeness of sacred objects. In earlier times, the term would have applied to a cult statue of a deity, with the sense of being a vessel for the spirit or essence of that deity; something more than a mere

The simulacrum of a giant's profile at a rocky outcrop on Dartmoor known as Bowerman's Nose. (© TopFoto/Fortean)

lifeless effigy. While most simulacra of this type would have been crafted by artisans for ritual purposes, some images were believed to have been created by divine power as expressions of that divinity – for example, the TURIN SHROUD and the Veil of Veronica. In the Catholic Church, historians called these magical images 'acheropites', from the old Greek meaning an image not made by human hands. Other religions also have their acheropites and simulacra; Buddhists venerate designs in the shape of the idealized footprint of Buddha, especially if they have occurred naturally; and animists the world over hold sacred rock formations that resemble gods and heroes.

By Victorian times, the meaning of simulacra had shifted towards implying a relatively valueless copy or imitation. In modern usage – especially in forteana – simulacra are a genre of spontaneous images (see IMAGES, SPONTANEOUS), especially natural formations of figures or faces.

Typical types of modern simulacra would include the shapes of animals perceived in clouds, faces in the bark of trees or rock formations, and marks in vegetables that resemble the Arabic script for 'Allah'. More specific examples would include the Japanese crab 'Heikegani' (*Dorippe japonica*), whose carapace bears the distinct form of a samurai warrior mask, found mainly at the location where, legend tells, the remnant of the Heike clan committed suicide by jumping into the sea; the image of the Virgin of the Hermits found imprinted on hailstones that fell in Remiremont, France, on 26 May 1907; and the complete sequence of numerals and alphabet found in the scale patterns of butterfly wings.

skulls

Skulls are associated with various superstitious beliefs and legends; skulls were once used in traditional cures, and some ancient skulls are said to scream if removed from their dwelling-place.

Skulls were once used in cures for toothache and epilepsy, among other ailments – either the skull was used as a drinking vessel, or parts of the skull were grated into medicines or food. Apparently, the skulls of hanged criminals were used as the source materials, as mentioned in Reginald Scot's *The Discoverie of Witchcraft* (1584):

> Against the biting of a mad dog. Take pilles made of the skull of one that has hanged.

Moss that had grown on a human skull was also said to beneficial, as described by Francis Grose in *A Provincial Glossary* (1787):

> Moss growing on a human skull, if dried, powdered, and taken as snuff, will cure the headache.

Such cures are less frequently mentioned after the 18th century, and it is not known how often they were used before that time.

Screaming skull superstitions are associated with at least 20 different buildings in England, including Burton Agnes Hall, Yorkshire; Calgarth Hall, Cumbria; and Wardley Hall near Manchester. In each case the skull has been preserved in the dwelling for hundreds of years and its origin is often uncertain. The skull must not under any circumstances be removed – otherwise psychic disturbances including screams, poltergeist phenomena and bad luck are said to follow.

Most famous of all screaming skulls is the specimen still preserved at Bettiscombe Manor in Dorset, said to be that of a male black servant of the Pinney family. Legend tells that this servant had come to England from the West Indies in the 17th or 18th century, and that on his deathbed he asked that his body be returned there for interment. This wish was disregarded, and the servant was buried in the local churchyard. It is said that almost immediately screams and moans were heard coming from the grave. Pinney was forced to have the body disinterred and (for reasons that are unclear) the skull was preserved in the house. Traditionally, attempts to bury or otherwise dispose of the skull have led to psychic disturbances and ill-fortune.

Apparently, an examination of the Bettiscombe skull carried out in 1963 indicated that it was, in fact, that of a European female, possibly 2,000 or more years old. This has led some to believe that the skull was originally venerated at a Celtic shrine. In a number of ancient traditions skulls had a protective function, they were said to preserve the fertility and prosperity of farmland.

spontaneous combustion

The ignition of something without flame being applied.

Spontaneous combustion is not an unfamiliar phenomenon in science. Its causes include a slow process of oxidation in a substance or material. Rags soaked in flammable liquids such as petrol can also spontaneously combust when the surrounding temperature reaches a particular level (the spontaneous ignition point of the liquid).

However, some cases of apparently spontaneous combustion are not so easily explained. In 2004, in the village of Canneto di Caronia, Sicily, a series of spontaneous fires erupted in several houses. Local police were quick to ascertain that arson or pyromania were not involved, and demonic activity was soon ruled out by representatives of the Catholic Church.

As the fires seemed to be associated with electrical appliances, some mysterious electrical phenomenon was suspected, but even when the power was disconnected the fires continued. Sicily is home to an active volcano, Mount Etna, and vulcanologists were called in to determine if volcanic effects were playing a part in the phenomenon. No obvious connection was found, but one theory is that methane gas emanating from volcanic channels in the ground beneath the village was being ignited by electrical discharges.

No definitive explanation, however, has been universally accepted. See also SPONTANEOUS HUMAN COMBUSTION.

spontaneous human combustion

The apparent sudden incineration of a human body.

Accounts of spontaneous human combustion (SHC) have been known for centuries, one of the most famous being that of the Countess Bandi of Cesena, a case that inspired Charles Dickens to include a fictional example in his novel *Bleak House* (1853).

Typically, the victim's body, or most of it (often legs or other extremities remain unburnt), is completely consumed, while furniture or other fittings around the body are not damaged at all – merely coated with a glutinous ashy deposit. Reported incidents tend to have taken place in a closed room in which the victim was alone. For this reason, it is thought that there has

The remains of Dr John Irving Bentley of Coudersport, Pennsylvania. Many believe that he was a victim of spontaneous human combustion. (© Mary Evans Picture Library)

never been a case of the phenomenon that was witnessed while it was actually in progress. Instead, SHC is usually suggested as an explanation for a death by fire that has mysterious aspects to it.

Another celebrated instance of SHC is the death of a Frenchwoman, Nicole Millet, who in 1725 was found burnt to death in a room at her inn in Rheims. Her husband was accused of her murder but was acquitted when the court was convinced that she had died from SHC. Apparently, the court's verdict was that she had died 'by a visitation of God'.

In 1763 the French writer Jonas Dupont published *De Incendiis Corporis Humani Spontaneis*, a collection of accounts of alleged SHC. This was far from scientific and included cases purportedly brought about by excessive drinking of alcohol, no longer considered to be a possible cause.

The modern scientific consensus on the idea of a human being bursting into flames without the presence of an external fire source is that it is impossible, and that in well-documented cases there is always a logical explanation. The human body contains too much water to burn readily, and extremely high temperatures are needed in crematoria to reduce a corpse to ashes. However, there are scientists who believe that the phenomenon does exist, suggesting such theories as the action of localized static electrical discharges or an unexplained molecular effect within body tissue.

One of the most commonly suggested theories to explain SHC is known as the wick effect. According to this idea, victims are unconscious at the start of the fire, whether through intoxication or illness – such as through the effects of a stroke or heart attack. In some cases, the victim is thought to have been already dead before being burnt. This means that the person will not have been aware of, or able to move away from, the source of the flame, which may be a lit cigarette, an open fire or an oil-burning lamp. As the flame begins to ignite the victim's clothes, the flesh also begins to burn. The natural water content of the body tissue is gradually evaporated by the heat. As subcutaneous fat is then exposed and liquefied this too burns with a slow but intense heat until the tissue is completely burned, leaving only ashes.

Attempts have been made to reproduce the wick effect in a controlled environment using the remains of animals such as pigs, but the results have been inconclusive. In the absence of a reliably witnessed instance of SHC, the phenomenon, if it truly exists, has yet to be satisfactorily explained.

spontaneous images *see* IMAGES, SPONTANEOUS

Spring-Heeled Jack
The name given to a mysterious male phantom who supposedly haunted many parts of England between 1837 and 1904.

Numerous crimes and assaults (particularly against young women) were reputedly perpetrated by Spring-Heeled Jack, although most of his victims seem to have suffered shock rather than serious injury. That Spring-Heeled Jack was no ordinary mortal was shown by his reputed ability to jump great distances, breathe blue flames and appear and disappear seemingly without trace.

The first reported sightings of Spring-Heeled Jack were noted in the London press in 1837, with witnesses describing a mysterious figure who could jump over high railings and who had bulging, glowing eyes. A report of a physical assault by this strange creature soon followed, and news of the phantom spread, but some of the best-known accounts date from the following year. In February 1838, Jane Alsop (the teenage daughter of an East End family) apparently opened the door in response to a policeman's cries of 'For God's sake, bring me a light, for we have caught Spring-Heeled Jack here in the lane.' When she ventured outside, the 'policeman' attacked her, and after her screams roused help from within the house, Spring-Heeled Jack leapt high into the air and disappeared. Alsop described her attacker as having long metallic talons and eyes like fire, and said that he wore some sort of helmet and a tight garment of white oilskin. She also said that he vomited blue and white flames.

During the winter of 1838–9 rumours of his attacks in central London were taken so seriously that special patrols led by the Duke of Wellington were organized to calm public fears. Incidents such as the widely reported alleged attack on Jane Alsop had done much to fuel such fears, and Spring-Heeled Jack's fame spread. Although reports of him were less frequent in the subsequent decades, they did become widespread – he was apparently seen in many different parts of England, and a number of crimes were attributed to him, including murders. In 1888, the name 'Jack' lent itself easily to the far more real and deadly Jack the Ripper, the unidentified murderer of six prostitutes in the East End of London.

The last reported manifestation of Spring-Heeled Jack was in Liverpool in 1904, and after this he was seen no more. Various explanations postulated for Spring-Heeled Jack include a ghost, a bear, a human prankster (particularly the Marquess of Waterford, a well-known practical joker) or even an alien humanoid originating from a high-gravity planet and capable of performing great leaps in the lower gravity of earth. However, for modern folklorists Spring-Heeled Jack provides an example of a powerful URBAN LEGEND.

standing stones

Large stones set erect in the ground by prehistoric people.

Standing stones, or large stones set on end in the ground, have been found in various places all over the world, but the most famous examples occur in Western Europe, particularly in France (for example at CARNAC, in Brittany) and the British Isles. However, little can be known for certain about the purposes of these monuments. Standing stones occur in four main forms: individual stones (known as MENHIRS), DOLMENS, STONE ROWS or alignments and STONE CIRCLES.

The most basic of these forms is, of course, the single standing stone. There are various theories as to why, in different cultures around the world, prehistoric humans were impelled to erect these monuments. Some say that they are simply markers of some kind, perhaps to indicate the boundary of the territory under the control of a particular tribe or chief, or to guide travellers from place to place in a hazardous landscape in much the same way as later Christian crosses were set up to guide pilgrims on the route to a shrine.

Others believe that the significance of these stones must have been religious, that their erection was a form of religious duty or demonstration of faith. The fact that their very form gives them phallic overtones leads some to interpret them as belonging to the worship of a fertility deity or as offerings to ensure the continuing fertility of the tribe itself. Or perhaps they were intended as commemorations of important events or colossal gravestones to mark forever the last resting place of some hero or great leader.

Another idea is that they played an astrological or astronomical role. Study of some of the more complex megalithic structures has led to the conjecture that the early peoples who erected them had fairly sophisticated knowledge of the movements of the stars and planets. It may be, then, that standing stones were used to mark the position of the moon, the sun or some other conspicuous heavenly body at times of the year that were particularly vital, such as the solstices or equinoxes, times when the seasons were changing and primitive peoples would have to know which elements of their agricultural year should be in progress.

That they were considered of great importance is beyond doubt. We can only theorize about the physical methods used, but the immense labour needed to carve, transport and erect these massive stones would have been no small sacrifice in an age when life was relatively short and spent, by the majority at least, in daily work just to ensure that everyone had enough to eat. Also, having been made of the most durable material available,

they can only have been meant to last, long beyond a human lifetime or even the collective memory of the people to whom they were obviously so significant.

At least in this way, their creators have achieved a kind of immortality, even though their motives and beliefs must remain mysterious. See also MEGALITHS.

stone circles
Great circular patterns of megaliths erected by prehistoric cultures.

When people think about the stone monuments erected by prehistoric cultures, most tend to visualize the great stone circles such as at STONEHENGE or AVEBURY. Perhaps this is because it is evident to all that they are the product of great feats of engineering, or that they show the artistic impulse present in humankind even in primitive times, much more so than individual STANDING STONES or DOLMENS can do.

The earliest known stone circles appeared in the British Isles in the Neolithic period and their construction seems to have died out during the Bronze Age. Some are more extensive than others; some use greater individual megaliths; some have stones with lintels, while others are composed of rough undressed stones; some are more complex, with concentric circles, 'avenues' and deep ditches, but in every case the reasons for their construction remain in the province of conjecture.

Do they show evidence of astronomical sophistication in the cultures responsible? Some of those who have studied stone circles believe that they are colossal calendars or observatories, erected by agricultural peoples as a guide to the changing seasons of the year. At Stonehenge, for example, it has been shown that the axis of the circle is aligned with the position in which the sun rises on the longest day (21 June) and that in which it sets on the shortest (21 December).

It is also argued that this kind of astronomical alignment was not an end in itself but more probably an aspect of their true purpose, which was as centres of worship of the sun or moon. In other words, the positioning of the stones was a symbolic homage to these heavenly bodies rather than an attempt to track or mark their progress with any degree of accuracy.

Graves have been excavated within some stone circles, but the very size of the circles tends to argue against the idea that their sole purpose was as elaborate funerary monuments. Some argue that it seems inconceivable that any one individual (or even family) could have been so important as to justify such elaborate commemoration.

Different circles show different standards of preservation. Depending on the actual stone used, long centuries of weathering have played their part in eroding stones, and toppling or burying others. Human interaction has also played a part, with generations of inhabitants removing stones, whether to clear fields for cultivation or to supply materials for buildings of their own. Sometimes, antiquarians have caused fallen stones to be re-erected. This means that many circles are far from complete and others may not reflect the original design, which means that their intended purposes are even more obscured.

Whatever the aims of the builders, it cannot be denied that astonishing amounts of cooperative work were necessary to carry them out: in hewing the stones, transporting them from their quarries (often at some distance) and erecting them in position. There must have been a purpose of overriding concern to the whole tribe for these great labours, sometimes carried on over many generations. This might indicate that religion must have played a major part in the motivation of those who built these enigmatic structures. See also MEGALITHS.

Stonehenge

A colossal stone circle on Salisbury Plain in Wiltshire, England.

On Salisbury Plain, an upland chalk moor in Wiltshire, stands Stonehenge, probably the most famous STONE CIRCLE in the British Isles, if not the world. The name itself essentially means 'stone gallows', deriving from the comparison made by Old English speakers between a gallows and a trilithon (a pair of MEGALITHS topped by a lintel stone). The site is a complex one, with a surrounding ditch and at least three concentric circles, and work seems to

Stonehenge is one of the most famous prehistoric sites in the world.
(© TopFoto/Robert Piwko)

have gone on there over a period of almost 1,500 years, beginning before 3000 BC, that is, before the building of the PYRAMIDS. However, the instantly recognizable element is that of the main inner circle of trilithons.

This circle is built of dolerite, the source having been identified as the Preseli Mountains in Wales. Exactly how these massive stones were transported to the site remains unexplained, but the circle seems to have been built in c.2500 BC. The outer circle consists of sarsen stones, quarried from Marlborough Downs. The English antiquarian John Aubrey (1626–97) noted the existence of over 50 shallow pits within the surrounding ditch, and these are known as the 'Aubrey Holes'. The construction of the site undoubtedly called for an

enormous communal effort over many years, a fact which alone points to its importance to those who built it.

The purpose of Stonehenge is open to conjecture. It has been shown that the axis of the circle is aligned with the position in which the sun rises on the longest day (21 June) and that in which it sets on the shortest (21 December), when sighted against the free-standing Heel Stone outside the entrance. Some have deduced from this that the site is some kind of giant astronomical calendar perpetualized in stone so that its builders could track the movements of sun and moon and mark the changing of the seasons. Others, however, maintain that this is to ascribe too great a sophistication to the builders and that the alignment is simply a reflection of the site's true purpose: as a centre of worship of the sun. To support this theory, it has been pointed out that the shadow of the Heel Stone casts a phallic shadow into the circle, perhaps symbolizing the mating of the sun and the earth.

Nothing is known for certain about the eventual abandonment of Stonehenge. Changes in religious belief probably played a part, and it has been suggested that climate change turned what had been a lush and fertile area into a bleak and unwelcoming one, with cloudy skies tending to obscure the heavens, making consistent observation impossible.

The site was not lost to history, however, and the medieval chronicler Geoffrey of Monmouth (c.1100–c.1154) identified it as the burial place of the Dark Age King Constantine. Early antiquarians connected the site with the rituals of the Druids, and modern-day druidic devotees took their cue to mark the summer solstice there. While it can be shown that Stonehenge had fallen into disuse long before the cult of the Druids arose, this does not discourage periodic revivals of interest in it, from the hippies of the 1960s and 1970s to the New Age travellers of the 1980s and 1990s.

stone rows

Linear arrangements of standing stones.

When a number of STANDING STONES can be seen to have been arranged in a particular straight line, this is known as a stone row, or alignment.

The great prehistoric site at CARNAC in Brittany has some of the most extensive surviving stone rows, comprising well over two thousand individual standing stones. These are grouped into the Alignments of Kerlescan, with 555 stones in thirteen rows, the Alignments of Kermario, with 1,029 stones in ten rows and, largest of all, the Alignments of Menec, with 1,169 stones in eleven rows.

There are different theories as to why such alignments were constructed. Many believe that they have some kind of astronomical significance, whether as a form of grid on which to plot the movements of heavenly bodies, or as elaborate pointers indicating the place at which the sun or moon is seen to rise or set on particular important days of the year. Others argue that it is more likely that alignments had a more symbolic role for the people who erected them, perhaps as tribal or territorial markers or as monuments to the power and importance of those who ordered them to be built.

It may be that these massive constructions will never be satisfactorily explained, as many of them are so incomplete (stones having been quarried over the centuries for other uses) or partially and not always accurately restored that their current appearance may be greatly different from their original arrangement. See also MEGALITHS.

stones, standing *see* STANDING STONES

superstition

A deep-rooted but irrational belief in the supernatural, and especially in omens and luck; a rite or practice based on such a belief.

Since ancient times, people of every culture all over the world have subscribed to superstitions and have indulged in rites or practices based on these. A superstition is generally defined as an irrational and erroneous belief in a supernatural agency or in a connection between two unrelated events; a superstitious person may see OMENS and PORTENTS everywhere, and believes that a future event or outcome can be caused or influenced by some unrelated occurrence or act – for example, that putting new shoes on a table will bring bad luck or even death. Superstitions are not based on reason, and may be a result of unenlightened fears or the misinterpretation of some correlation as cause and effect, or they may have a basis in some fact which has long since been forgotten, leaving only the superstition. Most superstitions involve omens or causes of good or bad luck, many of them regarding the most important phases of human life – birth, marriage and death – and some professions, such as the theatre and sailing, are particularly given to superstitions. Certain times of year, such as Christmas, May Day and Hallowe'en, have many superstitions connected with them. Sometimes there is a way to increase one's chances of good luck in an undertaking, or to counteract the bad luck which an omen indicates – for example, crossing one's fingers or knocking on wood.

Many people have their own individual superstitions: for example, they might insist on always keeping a particular talisman or charm with them to ensure no bad luck befalls them. However, other superstitions are so widespread and deep-rooted in popular culture that even the most cynical individual may still feel uneasy about disregarding them: that breaking a MIRROR brings seven years' bad luck, that misfortunes come in threes, that FRIDAY THE 13TH and the number 13 in general are unlucky, and that it is bad luck to walk under a LADDER, open an umbrella indoors or spill SALT, unless, after doing the last, you immediately throw a pinch over your left shoulder. And many people still consider it lucky to find a four-leaf clover, have a black cat cross their path, find a pin on the ground or see a shooting star (which entitles them to make a wish). Brides today still try to wear 'something old, something new, something borrowed, something blue' on their wedding day, and are given representations of horseshoes for good luck, while May is still traditionally considered an unlucky month for a wedding. A baby born on Hallowe'en is believed to have second sight, while one born with a caul will enjoy good fortune and will never die of drowning. There are countless superstitions involving omens of death, such as a bird flying into the house or an owl hooting in daytime, and a funeral on a Friday is thought to portend another death in the family during the year.

Even those who are not involved in

the theatre know that Shakespeare's *Macbeth* is considered to be an unlucky play, so much so that actors do not mention it by name, but refer to it indirectly as 'the Scottish play', and will not quote lines from it while in the theatre, except when on stage. It is thought unlucky to quote the last line of any play until its first-night performance, whistle in the theatre or have real flowers on stage, while no actor ever wishes another 'good luck' before a performance, but instead urges them to 'break a leg'. Sailors are equally given to superstitions, the best known of which is that it is disastrous to kill an albatross, as Coleridge's Ancient Mariner found to his cost. Whistling on board ship is also unlucky because it is thought to call up a wind, especially if it is done by a woman – although a woman on a ship is considered to be unlucky in any case, and a whistling woman is just as bad luck on dry land as she is at sea.

Surrey Puma *see* ALIEN BIG CATS

T

Templars *see* KNIGHTS TEMPLAR

Ten Lost Tribes of Israel

Tribes of Israel that never returned after deportation in 721 BC.

According to the Old Testament, the conquering king of Assyria took ten tribes of Israel away into Assyria as captives. History ascribes this act of mass deportation to Sargon II (died 705 BC) and dates it as happening in 721 BC. These ten tribes were those of Asher, Dan, Ephraim, Gad, Issachar, Manasseh, Naphtali, Reuben, Simeon and Zebulun, and they are traditionally believed never to have returned to their homes.

Throughout history, various theories have arisen to account for the fate of these tribes. The Spanish rabbi Benjamin of Tudela (died 1173) was the first European traveller to describe the Far East. In an account of his travels he claimed to have found the descendants of some of the lost tribes, still worshipping as Jews, in Persia and Arabia.

When the Americas were discovered by Europeans, it became a fairly popular theory that the Native American peoples must be descended from the lost tribes – some travellers claimed that they detected Jewish influences in the speech and religious observances of some Native American tribes.

The idea that the lost tribes were the progenitors of the English people took hold in Britain, especially in the 17th century. Part of the driving force behind this concept was the belief in the Old Testament prophecy that Israel would be restored and that this would mark the coming of the Millennium. Puritan extremists at the time of the English Civil War seized on this as proof that the second coming of Christ was at hand. While this did not happen, the idea of Anglo-Israelites persisted, and in 1793 the English religious fanatic Richard Brothers declared himself Prince of the Hebrews and Nephew of the Almighty. In fact, this theory still has its adherents in Britain and the USA today.

Descendants of the lost tribes were identified by others as living as far from Israel as Ireland, Africa, Australia, Siberia, China, Japan and Afghanistan, where the Pathan people were said to have customs similar to those of the Jews. Other candidates included the black Jewish people of Ethiopia, known as Falashas, many of whom were welcomed into Israel in the late 20th century.

Were the tribes really lost? Some maintain that when the Persian Emperor Cyrus the Great (c.600–529 BC) conquered the Babylonian captors of the Jews and allowed them to return to their homeland, the 'lost' tribes simply went back with them.

There is very little real evidence for the survival of the lost tribes of Israel as a separate ethnic group. It would take a superhuman will to maintain a collective identity over a period of thousands of years. Also, if they were able to travel, as some of the more outlandish theories suggest, to the very ends of the earth, why could they not have reversed their direction and returned to Israel? Much more likely is the idea that, assuming they did not in fact make their way back to their ancestral homeland, these people would simply have become assimilated over the generations into the communities in which they found themselves.

Titanic

Legends surrounding the sinking of the 'unsinkable' ship.

When the British passenger liner *Titanic* was launched in Belfast in 1912 she was considered to be unsinkable. However, on her maiden transatlantic voyage she struck an iceberg and sank on 14 April 1912. More than 1,500 of her passengers died through drowning or hypothermia.

The fact that an 'unsinkable' vessel so quickly ended up at the bottom of the sea led people to search for reasons beyond those commonly accepted for her demise. Among the most fantastic was that the sinking was a gigantic insurance scam by the ship's owners, the White Star Line, in order to rid themselves of the already damaged sister ship, the *Olympic*. Having switched the ships' identities, it was alleged, the conspiracy went catastrophically wrong, leading to the unintentional loss of many lives.

Another popular idea was that the ship was cursed. Many believed that a series of coincidences that took place before the disaster show that the ship was 'fated' to sink and that nothing could have saved her. These include the fact that the ship's 'unsinkability' was based on the series of watertight compartments beneath her decks. If the ship had struck the iceberg head-on, damage would have probably been limited to the first of these and the ship was designed to remain afloat even if more than one of these compartments was flooded. As it was, after the iceberg was spotted the ship was turned in an unsuccessful attempt to avoid a collision, resulting in the side of the vessel being gashed open, allowing too many of the compartments to fill with water.

Also, various other ships had sent radio messages to the *Titanic* warning

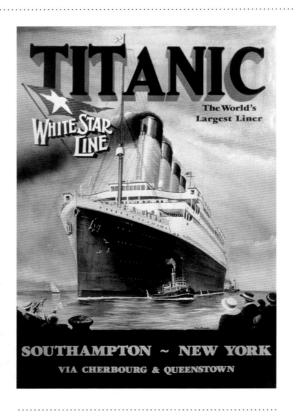

A poster advertising the maiden voyage of the *Titanic*. (© 2006 Charles Walker/TopFoto)

of icebergs in her path, but these seem to have been ignored or discounted by her captain, who did not allow her speed to be slackened.

Premonitions were also said to have forecast the fate of the *Titanic*. In particular, the US writer and avowed psychic Morgan Robertson (1861–1915) had in 1898 published a novel, *Futility*, in which a gigantic liner called the *Titan* collides with an iceberg and sinks in mid-Atlantic. Some say that the real

and fictional vessels shared so many features in common that surely the work predicted the *Titanic*'s demise, although others argue that Robertson was simply very knowledgeable about ships, and iceberg collisions did happen.

The English journalist and reformer William Thomas Stead (1849–1912), who was drowned in the sinking, was reputed to have secretly had the mummy of an Egyptian priestess of

Amon-Ra carried aboard, which was supposed to be cursed. He is said to have discussed the 'mummy's curse' over dinner on the night of the sinking. Some even said that the mummy appeared on deck after the iceberg was struck. However, the truth is that this mummy had never left the British Museum. Intriguingly, however, Stead had published a short story in 1892 entitled 'From the Old World to the New', in which an ocean liner picks up survivors from an iceberg collision in the Atlantic. The fictitious captain is named E J Smith, the same name as the captain on the *Titanic*, and neither the fictional nor the real vessel was carrying enough lifeboats.

Others claimed that they had premonitions of the sinking of the *Titanic*. The second engineer, Colin McDonald, refused on a number of occasions to sign on as crew, later claiming that he knew that something terrible would happen. Passengers who decided not to travel also claimed that they had hunches that something would go wrong, and some claim that a small English boy witnessed a vision of the sinking as it took place.

The *Titanic* disaster was very productive of legends, one of the most popular and enduring being that the ship's band continued to play as the vessel went down, famously ending with the well-known hymn 'Nearer, My God, to Thee'. It is undoubtedly true that the band members sacrificed their own lives in order to keep frightened passengers calm. However, some survivors remembered the last tune played, not as a fittingly solemn and spiritual piece, but as a chirpy ragtime dance.

Toft, Mary (c. 1701–1763)

A woman who claimed she gave birth to rabbits.

In September 1726, something of a medical sensation occurred in England when the surgeon John Howard was summoned to the bedside of Mary Toft, a 25-year-old married woman of Godalming in Surrey. She had had a miscarriage a few months before but had claimed to be still pregnant. However, more amazing than this, Howard apparently assisted her to give birth to several rabbits.

To be accurate, they were actually parts of rabbits, all dead. Howard was convinced that something unknown to science was happening and wrote to various eminent men about his experience. The story became a national sensation and the king sent his surgeon-anatomist, Nathanael St André, and Samuel Molyneux, secretary to the Prince of Wales, to look into the matter. Mary explained that before her miscarriage she had experienced cravings for rabbit meat, dreamt about rabbits and had tried to catch some. Meanwhile, in the presence of these illustrious witnesses, she continued to deliver stillborn and dismembered rabbits.

In November, Mary was taken to London for further investigation, to the intense curiosity of the public. In the house where she was lodged, she was to be observed round the clock, and, disappointingly, the phenomenon ceased. Stories began to circulate that, while they were still in Godalming, Mary's husband had been taking delivery of unusually large numbers of rabbits. When it was suggested that a surgical operation should be carried out to examine Mary's womb, she suddenly confessed that the whole thing had been a hoax.

Apparently, she had inserted the rabbit parts into her vagina in private to be 'delivered' later, for no more compelling reason than to achieve fame and make some money. She was accused of fraud, arrested and confined to the Bridewell prison. However, after a few months she was released without being put on trial. Some suggested that this was a cover-up and that something out of the ordinary really had been going on, but in reality it was probably done to save blushes all round. If that was indeed the motivation, the plan failed.

The main effect of the hoax was to attract ridicule to the medical profession in general and to John Howard and Nathanael St André in particular, whose careers never recovered. The famous English painter William Hogarth (1697–1764) created a satirical print 'The Wise Men of Godalming', showing the esteemed medicos reacting with astonishment as a line of rabbits is seen escaping from beneath Mary's skirts.

How could experienced medical practitioners have been so easily conned? In a way, they were merely reflecting contemporary misconceptions. Folk wisdom had long held to the belief that if something made a deep impression on a pregnant woman, this would be shown somehow in the child. For example, it was believed that an expectant mother frightened by a dog would give birth to an exceptionally hairy baby. The famous English 'Elephant Man', Joseph Carey Merrick (1862–90), was convinced that his deformity was caused when his pregnant mother was trampled by an elephant. The surgeons involved in Mary's case were perhaps the last men of science to give this idea any credence.

tumulus

A prehistoric burial mound.

A tumulus is a prehistoric burial mound, examples of which have been found in many countries around the world, particularly dating from the Neolithic and Bronze Ages but often belonging to more recent cultures. Some of these mounds are made of earth, others of mixed earth and stones, and some completely of stones (in which case they are usually known as CAIRNS). One of the largest known tumuli is that heaped above the tomb of Alyattes, king of Lydia, which was completed near Sardis in c.560 BC. It is around 61 metres (200 feet) in height and 360 metres (1,180 feet) in diameter.

In the British Isles, a type of tumulus known as the long barrow often covered a chambered tomb or DOLMEN built from huge megaliths, a fine example being that of MAESHOWE

The Maeshowe tumulus on the Orkney Islands. (© 2005 TopFoto/Houghton)

in Orkney. Burial mounds have also been excavated in central Asia (where they are known as kurgans) to reveal the rich tombs of Scythian royalty and nobility. The Vikings also often buried their rulers beneath mounds, sometimes large enough to contain a whole ship. Extensive mounds have also been identified in North America, particularly along the Mississippi, where at the site of the ancient Native American city of Cahokia some have been shown to contain richly furnished tombs.

Little is known about the methods of construction used but in each culture a tremendous co-operative effort must have been required. This, along with the sheer scale of these monuments, constitutes a testimony to the importance to their peoples of the great personages buried within.

Tunguska Event, the

Mysterious explosion, accompanied by a fireball, which occurred in Siberia in 1908.

On 30 June 1908, an enormous explosion occurred over the Tunguska region of Siberia. Locals reported a huge fireball in the sky, followed by a blinding flash and a shock wave that flattened trees and shattered windows. The resulting seismic wave was detected in various locations throughout Europe and Asia, where, in addition, abnormal light effects at twilight had been reported in the days before the event.

The explosion seems not to have been immediately investigated, probably through a combination of circumstances: the site was in a remote area, and the political and societal turmoil that preceded the Russian Revolution of 1917, and the subsequent civil war, might have hampered any attempts at investigation for some years. It was only in the late 1920s and 1930s that the Russians are recorded as mounting expeditions to the area. It was believed that they might find a large meteorite containing valuable minerals. However, no such meteorite was found and there was no crater on the ground to indicate the point of impact. The only apparent explanation was that the explosion had taken place in the air and not on the ground.

Subsequent Russian expeditions concluded that a meteorite had been involved, exploding before it hit the earth. As with other known meteorite strikes, they found minerals and glass particles in the soil. The post-war development of atomic bombs and observation of their effects during weapons tests influenced some lines of inquiry, but the fact that scientists on these expeditions detected no unnatural levels of radiation led them to conclude that it was certainly not a nuclear explosion. The most common scientific explanation remains that of a meteor exploding in the air several kilometres above the ground.

There are other theories, however. It has been suggested that an asteroid rather than a meteor was responsible, or perhaps rocky detritus from a comet trail. Most scientists, however, discount these ideas as unlikely. The area was once the site of an active volcano and some have suggested that the explosion was caused by the ignition of massive amounts of methane gas emerging from the earth. More imaginative ideas include the arrival from space of a body of antimatter, or even of a black hole, although current science does not recognize these explanations as physically possible.

Believers in extraterrestrial life claim that the explosion was caused by the firing, intentional or otherwise, of an alien weapon of unimaginably destructive power. Others say that an interstellar craft crash-landed on the site, even going so far as to suggest that the Russians (in an echo of the American Roswell stories) actually recovered wreckage and alien technology. This kind of theory has generated numerous science-fiction interpretations.

Whatever the origin of the explosion, it has been shown that the forest was extremely quick to regenerate afterwards, and some have claimed this as evidence of something not quite natural going on. However, while controversy continues as to the exact scientific explanation of the event, extraterrestrial interpretations remain on the outer fringes of the debate.

Turin Shroud

A shroud claimed to be that used for Christ.

In the Cathedral of St John the Baptist in Turin, a length of linen cloth is kept which many believe to be the shroud in which Jesus Christ was wrapped after the Crucifixion. Imprinted on the fibres is an image of the naked body (front and back) of a bearded man, hands crossed over the groin, who appears to bear the marks of a victim of beating and crucifixion. Dark brown stains, which some have identified as blood, are also present on the cloth.

The authenticity of the shroud is still a matter of debate. Some accept it as a genuine and divinely created image, known as an *acheiropoietos* (from the Greek, meaning 'made without hands'). Others claim it is a medieval fake (and an example of pious fraud).

While there were previous reports of items claimed to be the shroud of Jesus in various parts of the Christian world, it is only possible positively to trace the provenance of the Turin Shroud to the 14th century. In 1357, it was displayed in a church in France, and it was subsequently displayed on several other occasions throughout the century. Even at that time there were clerics who denied its authenticity, claiming that it had been painted by an artist.

During the 15th and 16th centuries it passed through various hands and was stored or displayed in several European cities, until it eventually arrived at its present location in 1578.

Leaving aside any supernatural explanation, scientific opinion is divided as to how the image was produced. Some claim that it was painted on with a pigment intended to suggest blood; others maintain that the image has three-dimensional characteristics and must have been formed by contact with a body (not necessarily that of the crucified Christ).

In 1988, with the agreement of the Vatican (its owner), a piece of one corner of the material, not containing any of the imprinted image, was detached and divided into three parts, each of which was subjected to radiocarbon dating by a different academic institution, including the Oxford Research Laboratory for Archaeology. The results of the analysis showed that the cloth must have been made between 1260 and 1390.

While some scientists have questioned these findings, arguing that the method is not infallible and the fibres analysed may have been contaminated by much later handling or repairs to the cloth, the general scientific consensus is that the dating is probably not far out. Further, and hopefully finally conclusive, radiocarbon dating tests on an area of the cloth impregnated with the image have been ruled out by the Vatican. It is argued that damaging the image, if it is authentic, would be sacrilegious. Sceptics, however, maintain that fear of its being definitively revealed as a fake is behind this.

The Roman Catholic Church has never made any pronouncement on whether or not it considers the shroud to be a genuine relic, declaring that it is a matter of faith.

Tutankhamen, curse of

The legend that the discoverers of the tomb of Tutankhamen were cursed.

The tomb of Tutankhamen (died c.1340 BC), an Eighteenth-Dynasty king of Egypt, was discovered and excavated in the Valley of the Kings in 1922 by the English Egyptologists Lord Carnarvon and Howard Carter. Unlike any previously discovered tombs it was virtually intact, having been hidden by the debris created when a later tomb was built nearby, and it contained many rich and informative artefacts.

It was perhaps the idea that the tomb had been largely undisturbed for so many years that led to the belief that those who desecrated it would call down punishment on themselves. It was rumoured that an inscription had been found inside the tomb warning that anyone entering it would be cursed, but this has never been produced. Those who believe in the curse maintain that Lord Carnarvon removed and hid it so as not to alarm the workers. In any case, Carnarvon died a few months later, as the tomb was still being excavated. It was said that at the moment of his death all of the electric lights in Cairo went out. At the same time, back in England, it is claimed that his faithful dog began to howl before dropping dead.

British newspapers were quick to pick up on these events and sen-sationalize them, probably influenced by popular horror stories featuring mummies that mysteriously became reanimated to terrorize the living. The story of the 'curse' was too appealing to be allowed to drop and it was duly trotted out every time a member of the expedition happened to die, especially over the following ten years. How much could this be substantiated by the facts?

Lord Carnarvon was already an elderly man by the time the tomb was discovered and not in the best of health. His cause of death was pneumonia, contracted after his system had been weakened by an infection arising from the bite of a humble mosquito. Such was the state of the contemporary electricity system of Cairo that sudden blackouts were by no means uncommon. As to the wider group of people involved in the expedition, those who died in the years immediately following the discovery tended to be the older members; the younger members mostly lived out their natural terms. Most significantly perhaps, Howard Carter, the man who actually opened the tomb and might have been supposed to have borne the full weight of its protective maleficence, survived Lord Carnarvon by 16 years, dying in England at the age of 65. As for Carnarvon's dog, perhaps it had a particularly empathetic connection with its master, or its death was simply a coincidence.

Scientists have looked at possible causes for any assumed fatal effects of opening a tomb that had been sealed

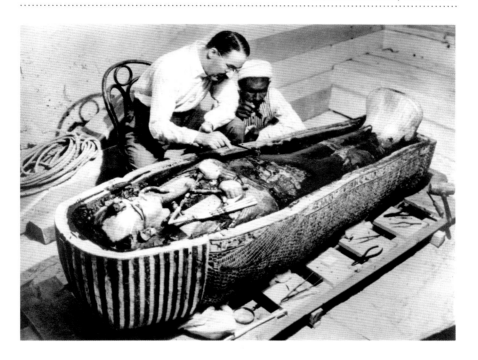

Howard Carter examining the sarcophagus of Tutankhamen in 1922. Although there were claims that a curse brought about the deaths of others involved in the expedition, Carter lived for a further 16 years. (© Topfoto)

for generations. The most common theory is that the inrush of fresh air into the previously confined spaces could have disturbed moulds whose spores could then have been breathed in by the excavators, possibly causing adverse medical reactions. Whether this actually caused any premature deaths cannot be established; it is certainly the case that modern Egyptologists tend to wear masks when working with mummies, but this is as much to prevent them introducing contamination as to protect them against it.

Uffington White Horse

The figure of a horse cut into the chalk of an escarpment near Uffington in Oxfordshire, the earliest and largest of the 'Wessex' white horses.

The Vale of White Horse in Oxfordshire is named after the great stylized figure of a horse that has been carved there on a north-facing chalk hill. The elongated figure measures more than 106 metres (350 feet) in length and is now believed to have been cut into the turf during the Bronze Age, contrary to the traditional theory that it was made to celebrate the defeat in battle of the Danes by Alfred the Great at nearby Edington in 878.

Stylized it may be, but does it actually represent a horse? Some, notably the English archaeologist Jacquetta Hawkes (1910–96), believe that the figure is actually meant to suggest the dragon killed by St George. According to local legend, the dragon's blood was spilt onto the nearby Dragon Hill, where it is said that no grass will grow. Most archaeologists, however, believe that it may be a symbol of a horse goddess of a local Celtic tribe or some kind of tribal symbol stamping ownership of territory on the land itself.

Whatever its provenance, the Uffington White Horse is an amazing feat of artistry as on the ground it would have been impossible for those actually cutting the turf to make out the overall design. The full form can only be appreciated from far across the vale or from the air, where in the days of its creation only the gods would have been looking down.

underwater ruins

Undersea stone structures that appear to be submerged buildings.

At various sites around the world, structures have been found beneath the sea which have been interpreted not as natural features but as the remains of buildings.

For example, in Japan in 1995 divers swimming at around 15 metres (50 feet) off the coast of the island of Okinawa discovered what appeared to be massive, coral-encrusted ruins. The 'buildings' were thought to resemble

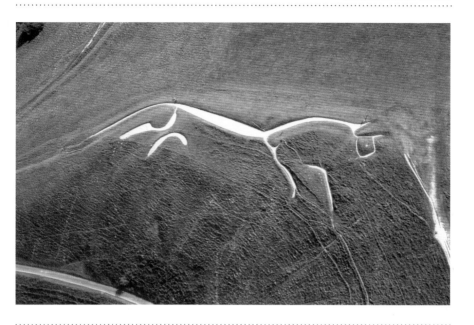

An aerial view of the Uffington White Horse. (© 2004 Charles Walker/TopFoto)

traditional Japanese temples but they appeared to be solid, composed of great monolithic blocks of stone, with no rooms or passageways within them. Some of those who later studied the formations detected similarities to stone temples found in Hawaii and other Pacific islands, leading to postulations of an ancient, extinct trans-Pacific culture. It is thought that the buildings were submerged when sea levels rose or land masses sank, but their age has not been established.

Further formations were found in 2004 off the coast of Atami on Honshu, the main island of Japan, including what appeared to be stone walls, paving stones, platforms and carved steps. It is speculated that these are

the remains of a city thought to have sunk into the sea in the 13th century, although some believe they may be much older than that.

One by-product of the highly destructive Asian tsunami in 2004 was the exposure of a submerged temple off the coast of Tamil Nadu in southern India. Local observers watched as the sea receded prior to the onslaught of the tidal wave, revealing hitherto undetected buildings offshore, including the ruins of both the temple and a house, as well as fragments of giant statues. This seemed to confirm legends of temples being engulfed by the sea as divine punishment.

Perhaps the best-known underwater structure is the 'Bimini Road', a row of parallel stones discovered in shallow water off the Bahamian island of Bimini by a low-flying pilot in 1968. The apparent regularity of the stones and the way in which they were closely fitted together led to claims that they were the remains of a submerged 'cyclopean megalith roadway', created by unknown hands. Speculation was fuelled by the fact that the American psychic Edgar Cayce had predicted that the lost civilization of ATLANTIS would be discovered near Bimini. However, sceptical archaeologists who have made detailed analyses of the composition of the stones claim that they represent a natural formation known as beach rock. This type of rock is formed by tidal action beneath the sand, precipitating calcium carbonate that accretes into large solid masses. The fact that this rock forms quickly is shown by the examples that have been found in which World War II artefacts have already become embedded. The formations become covered by any rise in the level of the sea. Another submerged site in the Bahamas, the so-called Andros Platform, was discovered in 2003 and has been similarly explained.

Any discovery of underwater ruins inevitably gives rise to speculation connecting them with the legendary Atlantis. Whether or not such a place ever existed has yet to be established, but, obviously, not every submerged site around the world belongs to the same civilization. Some have origins that remain unexplained, while others are simply ruins belonging to identifiable cultures that have become inundated by natural rises in sea level, landslips or earthquakes.

unicorn

A fabulous beast resembling a horse, but with one long spiral horn growing from its forehead; often used as a symbol of strength and purity and in heraldry.

Travellers throughout the centuries have made claims of sightings of the fabulous unicorn and have given conflicting descriptions of this beast. There have been accounts of unicorns in China, Mongolia, the Middle East, Egypt, North Africa, India, Japan, Europe and America. The Indian unicorn, it was said, was like a horse in form, but was a much swifter beast, and had a white body, a red or purple head, blue eyes and a long horn about 45 centimetres (18 inches) long growing in the centre of its forehead. This horn was white at the base, black in the middle and red at the tip. The European version of the unicorn is usually depicted as being pure white and having the head and body of a horse, the hind legs of an antelope or stag, the whiskers of a goat, the tail of a lion and a white or pearly spiral horn.

In folklore, unicorns are said to be very aggressive towards their own kind, except at mating season, when they become gentle. The colts are born without horns, and stay with their mothers until their horns are fully grown. All the medieval bestiaries which give accounts of unicorns agree

A detail from one of a series of medieval tapestries collectively known as 'The Hunt of the Unicorn'. (© Rob Crandall/ The Imageworks/TopFoto)

that they are attracted to virgins, and that the only sure way to capture a unicorn is to use a virgin as bait, when the unicorn will come and lay its head in her lap. It therefore became a symbol of purity, and came to be depicted with various female saints and the Virgin Mary, and, in its role as a willing sacrificial victim, it was also used as a symbol of Christ. The horn, called an alicorn, was highly prized in the Middle Ages for its properties; it was said that it could purify water and protect against poison and disease. For this reason, prudent monarchs drank from a supposed unicorn horn, which was said to sweat in the presence of poison and neutralize or reduce its effects, and the poor would beg to be given water into which a unicorn horn had been dipped, as this was believed to cure all maladies. The horns were much sought after in the 16th and 17th centuries and were a popular ingredient for sale in apothecaries' shops, where it may be assumed that many narwhal and rhinoceros horns were passed off as unicorn horns. In addition, a magical ruby or carbuncle was said to grow at the base of the horn, and this also had powerful healing properties, especially against the plague.

Because they are seen as a symbol of strength and nobility as well as purity, unicorns frequently appear as heraldic beasts, and when James VI of Scotland became James I of England in 1603, he chose one lion and one unicorn as the supporters of his royal shields.

urban legends

Modern popular stories of dubious veracity, often viewed as something distinct from historical folk tales but probably simply a continuation of the same cultural phenomenon.

Urban legends (sometimes also referred to as 'urban myths' or 'contemporary legends') are so called to distinguish them from older folk tales – 'urban' in this instance does not describe their setting. The term was popularized during the 1980s by the US professor of English Jan Harold Brunvand, who is perhaps the best-known researcher in this area. They are often passed on as true stories by those that tell them, and frequently begin with the assertion that they happened to a 'friend of a friend' (or FOAF), which has led to their other popular names – 'foaftales' and 'foaflore'.

Although describing a story as an urban legend is usually taken to imply that it is completely untrue, this does not have to be the case. However, they are generally at the very least exaggerated, sensationalized, misattributed or corrupted and are characterized by their repeated retelling by a narrator who implies that they are wholly true and happened to someone not too far removed from them. Many are believed by those who hear them and they are occasionally mistakenly reported as fact in newspapers or on news broadcasts. In recent years the growth of the Internet and widespread access to email have created something of a boom in such stories, allowing new ones (or, more frequently, recycled old ones) to be disseminated throughout the world in minutes. As with the older traditional forms of FOLKLORE, the stories vary and change with each telling, although the same basic forms reappear over and over again.

It is very difficult to produce a fixed definition of what constitutes an urban legend. In a similar way to many classic folk tales, urban legends often contain elements of horror, sensation, humour and a moral message. They are generally compelling and entertaining, which is perhaps why they remain popular and are retold. They can take a wide variety of forms – from the tales of ALLIGATORS IN SEWERS in New York to the story of the VANISHING HITCH-HIKER, which regularly reappears in a variety of forms throughout the world.

In an interesting twist, it has been observed that some urban legends can appear to generate occurrences that render them (at least partly) true – a phenomenon referred to as OSTENTION.

urban myths *see* URBAN LEGENDS

Valentich, Frederick (c.1958–)

An Australian pilot who apparently vanished in midair while being pursued by a UFO.

On the evening of 21 October 1978, trainee pilot Frederick Valentich was flying solo in a Cessna 182 across the Bass Strait, from Melbourne to King Island, to buy some crayfish for friends. The journey would add to his limited night-flight experience and increase his hours flying over water – both were necessary for him to obtain his full licence.

For some unknown reason he had changed his flight plans at the last minute, meaning that both legs of the 257-kilometre (160-mile) trip would have to be completed in the dark. He crossed the coast just after 7pm and began to descend towards the island. This placed him below radar cover – a normal state of affairs for the final 20 minutes of the journey. However, a few minutes later, at 7.06pm, he radioed air traffic control back in Melbourne, telling them that something was flying very near to him – he described a dark mass showing four landing lights. Melbourne assured him that there was no other traffic in the area, and even checked military sources to confirm this.

Six minutes into the close encounter, at 7.12pm, Valentich explained that the UFO was 'orbiting' directly overhead. He described it as metallic with a green light attached, adding that the engine of his aircraft was 'rough idling' and failing. He indicated that he was going to try to make it the last few miles to King Island before finally saying, 'It's not an aircraft it's …' before his voice tailed off and the transmission was interrupted by scraping noises, followed by a static hiss and then silence.

Despite an extensive aerial search, and a four-year aviation accident enquiry, no trace of the pilot or aircraft was ever found. The enquiry report, published in May 1982, included the consideration of a number of theories but concluded that the reason for the disappearance remained a mystery.

Many suggested that the plane had crashed as a result of its proximity to the reported UFO or because the pilot had been distracted by its presence. Valentich's father believed for many years that his son had been the victim of an alien abduction, and that he may be returned one day.

Other theories explored the idea that the pilot had fallen foul of smugglers (they were known to operate in the area, towing their loads in large nets attached to planes) or that a meteor had struck and destroyed the aircraft, although the protracted length of the sighting counted against this. It was even suggested that Valentich had faked his own disappearance by inventing the UFO story; at the time Australia was in the middle of a major wave of UFO sightings, and this was something of which Valentich was well aware – he had a scrapbook containing a number of press cuttings of the stories. However, no reasons for him wishing to 'disappear', or explanations as to what he would have done with the aeroplane, were ever offered. The case remains unsolved.

vampire *see* VAMPIRISM

vampirism

In folklore, the action of drinking the blood of the living, as thought to be practised by the returning dead, known as vampires; also a clinical condition in which the sufferer believes he or she is a vampire and must drink the blood of the living to survive.

The vampire legend is universal, and bloodsucking demons appear in the folklore of Haiti, Indonesia, the Native Americans, the Inuit and many Arab tribes. All cultures, however ancient or primitive, have long understood that blood is the essential fluid of life, so it is natural that legends of monsters who drain the living of blood would have become a prevalent feature of worldwide folklore. Most of the European myths of vampires are of Slavic or Romanian descent; the etymology of the actual word 'vampire', which first appeared in French and English literature and correspondence in the late 17th century, is still debated, but most contemporary scholars favour the theory that it is of Slavic origin. The European vampire is usually a dead person who has returned to feed on the blood of the living. According to Slavic lore, there are many ways in which a person can become a vampire: if they were born with a caul, teeth or a tail; if they were conceived on certain days; if they were excommunicated in life, or died a violent, sudden death or committed suicide; if they died before being baptized; if, after their death, an animal, especially a cat, walked over the corpse; and, the best-known method, if they were bitten by a vampire and the curse has been passed on to them. Werewolves also become vampires after their death. From the early 19th century, the word and the concept were firmly established in English literature, and the first real English vampire story, called *The Vampyre*, was published

Bela Lugosi plays a handsome vampire in the 1931 film version of *Dracula*. Prior to Bram Stoker's novel *Dracula* (1897), vampires were portrayed as repulsive monsters. (© TopFoto/Arenapal)

in 1819. Its success was partly due to the erroneous belief that it had been written by Lord Byron, although it was in fact written by Byron's one-time physician, John Polidori.

Until the 19th century, vampires were still depicted as repulsive monsters, but when Bram Stoker's 1897 novel *Dracula* was adapted into a highly successful stage play in 1924, and then into a classic film starring Bela Lugosi (1931), the Count was portrayed as a handsome, seductive figure, and since then popular culture has tended to represent the vampire as being evil but irresistibly attractive. The *Vampire Chronicles* series of novels written by Anne Rice have also done much to foster the image of the vampire as a romantic and enthralling character.

The vampire has hypnotic powers and the strength of many men. He can shapeshift into a cat, a dog, a bat and especially a wolf, and has the power to command various animals, such as rats. He can also turn into mist and enter a room through the keyhole or under the door. He has a pallid complexion and long, pointed incisors with which he bites his victims, and having no soul, he casts no shadow or reflection in a mirror. He is reluctant to enter or cross a body of running water, and cannot enter a house unless he is invited in the first time. Contemporary lore states that a vampire is destroyed by sunlight and has to return to his native soil to rest during daylight hours, although there is no basis in folklore for either of these beliefs. Vampires are repulsed by garlic and iron, although their aversion to crosses is a relatively recent imposition of Christian influences on a much older pagan folklore tradition. Old customs to prevent and destroy a vampire include filling the coffin with small seeds such as poppy or millet, which the vampire will spend all his waking hours counting obsessively; decapitating the body, pinning it to the coffin with a stake, or burning it to ashes; and exorcism. If a person is suspected of being a vampire, the body may be exhumed for the telltale signs – an undecomposed corpse with a healthy, lifelike bloom and fresh blood on its lips.

There exists a pathological condition known as clinical vampirism, also known as Renfield's syndrome after the character in *Dracula*, in which the sufferer believes he needs to drink the blood of the living to survive. Among the magical community there is also a strong belief in psychic vampirism, in which instead of blood the 'vampire' either deliberately or unknowingly drains others of energy and vitality.

vanishing hitch-hikers

Ghostly hitch-hikers, the subject of ubiquitous folk tales in which a hitch-hiker is picked up by a driver only to vanish during the journey.

The basic theme of the story involves a motorist picking up a hitch-hiker, usually a young woman, at night. The hitch-hiker travels some distance only to vanish inexplicably from the vehicle. On reporting the disappearance to the authorities (or going to an address mentioned by the hitch-hiker in the course of the journey), the motorist often learns that she was killed in a road accident in the recent past. Versions of the story have been recorded in every state of the USA and in many British counties. Examples are also known from other countries, including Italy, Pakistan and Colombia. Alternative versions of the story from the late 1960s have the hitch-hiker as a hippy who utters prophecies to the driver of disasters or the Second Coming. A study of over 100 different variants of the story, carried out in 1984 by the folklorist Michael Goss, concluded that such stories have been in circulation for many years and long predate the motor car: in a Swedish case from 1602 the vehicle was a sleigh.

Although tales of vanishing hitch-hikers are widespread, the stories invariably lack any hard facts capable of corroboration. Also, reliable first-hand accounts for any such phenomena are virtually non-existent, as most tales seem to relate to 'a friend of a friend who picked up a hitch-hiker', giving them the status of URBAN LEGENDS. One of the few British cases in which a named witness is cited is the story of Roy Fulton. Fulton claimed that he picked up a silent male hitch-hiker on 12 October 1979, along a road at Standbridge, near Dunstable, Bedfordshire. The passenger then vanished without explanation during the journey; subsequent investigation revealed that Fulton had reported the case to the police but no similar encounters were known in the area. Reviewing such stories, Goss concluded that the vanishing hitch-hiker is a 'classic fabrication', though some would argue that it is likely that occasional genuine apparitional encounters may have contributed to its propagation and survival as a story.

Wandering Jew

A Jew who according to Christian legend mocked Jesus on his way to Calvary, and as a punishment is condemned to wander the earth until the Second Coming.

The earliest written reference to the legend of the Wandering Jew is in the medieval English chronicler Roger of Wendover's *Flores Historiarum* (1228). In this version of the story, which was said to have come from an Armenian archbishop who claimed to have seen him in person, the Wandering Jew was a shoemaker called Cartaphilus, who taunted and struck Jesus on his way to the Crucifixion and urged him to keep moving when he stopped for a rest. Jesus cursed him, saying, 'I will stand and rest, but you will go on until the last day', thus condemning him to travel the earth without hope of rest until the Second Coming. In 1602, the legend was published in a German pamphlet, which brought it to the attention of the general public, and with its figure of a doomed sinner forced to wander without respite, it captured the popular imagination, spreading quickly through Germany and on to the rest of Europe. In this version the Jew is called Ahasuerus, the name by which he subsequently became best known, and the pamphlet quotes the line from Matthew 16.28 which some people believe is the origin of the story:

> Verily I say unto you, there be some standing here, which shall not taste of death, till they see the Son of Man coming in his kingdom.

The anti-Semitism prevalent in the Middle Ages helped to increase the popularity of the legend, and in most tellings of the story, the Wandering Jew is baptized as a Christian in the hope of receiving salvation. In the Italian version he is known as Giovanni Buttadeus ('strike God'), and to the Spanish he is Juan Espera en Dios ('John Hope-for-God'). He became a staple figure of the Christian oral and literary tradition, and sightings of him have been claimed throughout the centuries, most frequently during the Middle Ages, when he was said to have been seen in Armenia, Poland, Moscow and virtually every western European city including London. His legend has been the subject of many poems, short stories and books, including science fiction and graphic novels, as well as several films.

Watkins, Alfred *see* LEYS

werewolf *see* LYCANTHROPY

wheels of light
Patterns of light seen in the sea.

For centuries, sailors, particularly those travelling in the Persian Gulf and the Indian Ocean, have reported seeing anomalous 'wheels of light' below the surface of the water. It is believed that sightings are most common in these regions as the seawater there is particularly clear.

These light displays have been described as having dimensions ranging from several feet to several miles across. The wheels often appear in a group of three and are not stationary, but usually have rotating spokes, which are often compared to the shape of a flattened letter S, with the direction of rotation apparently changing at random. Overlapping between wheels has been reported, as well as some examples of their being concentric.

Sometimes the light displays are affected by the passage of the ship from which they are observed, changing in pattern or even following the vessel for distances of miles. Occasionally, a swishing or boiling sound is heard in the water. A few accounts even speak of the light wheels appearing to rise out of the water and be visible in the air.

In 1879, a report was published of such a sighting, attributed to the hydrographer of HMS *Vulture*, a Royal Navy gunboat cruising in the Persian Gulf:

> On looking towards the east, the appearance was that of a revolving wheel with centre on that bearing, and whose spokes were illuminated, and looking towards the west a similar wheel appeared to be revolving, but in the opposite direction.

Various explanations have been offered for this phenomenon. One theory is that the lights are produced by a kind of natural electromagnetic discharge, or 'earth energy' from LEYS, being transmitted through particles or microscopic life forms in the water.

Some have suggested that such a large and bright amount of light must be produced by mechanical means, and as no human activities are known to be involved the source must be extraterrestrial. Comparisons have been made between the wheel shapes and patterns and some of the formations and whorls seen in CROP CIRCLES, giving rise to speculation that similar unexplained forms of energy may be involved in creating them.

If there is alien activity under these waters, what is it that they are doing? One idea is that unidentified submarine craft are being used to generate the lights and that some kind of trawling for fish is going on. Observers have reported seeing large numbers of fish swimming away from the light wheels in alarm. Perhaps they are being herded to a place where they may be easily captured. It remains to be explained whether the purported alien interest in the planet's fish population is driven by a purely scientific quest for knowledge or by appetite.

Another theory is that the lights are caused by the natural phosphorescence of microscopic animals in the water, such as *Noctiluca*. Such phosphorescent effects have been known to science since the 19th century. However, this does not account for the peculiar wheel-shaped form that it takes in this particular instance, or for the fact that these displays are most common in a particular region of the earth's oceans.

white birds of death

In folklore, the appearance of a white bird has sometimes been taken as an omen of death; legends of white birds of death are particularly associated with the Oxenham family and the Bishop of Salisbury.

One of the earliest recorded legends of a white bird of death is that of the Oxenham family of Devon. The matter was discussed in the collected edition of *The Gentleman's Magazine* (1862).

> In Howell's 'Familiar Letters' I find a letter dated Westminster, July 3, 1632, in which he says:— 'I can tell you of a strange thing I saw lately here, and I believe 'tis true. As I pass'd by

St. Dunstan's in Fleet Street the last Saturday, I stepp'd into a lapidary or stone-cutter's shop to treat with the master for a stone to be put on my father's tomb: and casting my eyes up and down, I might spie a huge marble with a large inscription upon't, which was thus, to my best remembrance:— "here lies John Oxenham, a goodly young man, in whose chamber as he was struggling with the pangs of death, a bird with a white breast was seen fluttering about his bed and so vanished. Here lies also Mary Oxenham, the sister of said John, who died the next day, and the same apparition was seen in the room. Here lies hard by, James Oxenham, the son of the said John, who died a child in his cradle a little after, and such a bird was seen fluttering about his head a little before he expir'd, which vanish'd afterwards." At the bottom of the stone there is:— "Here lies Elizabeth Oxenham, the mother of the said John, who died sixteen years since, when such a bird with a white breast was seen about her bed before her death."'

As the John Oxenham mentioned died in 1635, three years after the date of the letter, and Howell is known to have included fictional accounts in *Familiar Letters*, written for the publication rather than for one intended recipient, we cannot know whether he actually saw the gravestone he described (which has never been seen since), but while the names sometimes differ, it generally agrees with standard versions of the legend of the white bird of the Oxenhams.

The origin of the legend is not known, but the white bird is said to have been seen in 1618, before the death of Grace Oxenham, and to have appeared as late as 1873, prior to the death of one Mr G N Oxenham. Different sources suggest different birds, but all agree that the white bird of the Oxenhams had a white breast, though none know why this family was singled out for this particular death omen.

The post of Bishop of Salisbury is also associated with a legend of a white bird of death. The first instance of this omen is said to have occurred in 1414, when the bishop of the time died when attending the Council of Constance. It is said that a flock of strange white birds perched on the roof of the building in which his body was lying in state. However, the legend did not become widely known until the 19th century, when it was popularized by Annie Moberley. Moberley was the daughter of a Bishop of Salisbury, and she claimed that in 1885 she saw white birds flying out of the gardens of the bishop's palace as he lay dying. A further instance of the omen was reported in 1911, when Edith Olivier, who apparently had no previous knowledge of the legend, saw strange white birds on the day another Bishop of Salisbury died.

white horses *see* CHALK FIGURES

Williams, Rhynwick *see* LONDON MONSTER

will-o'-the-wisp

An elusive moving light sometimes seen over marshes or bogs at night, thought in folklore to be a mischievous fairy or a restless spirit.

The will-o'-the-wisp is a natural phenomenon which occurs all over the world, and every region has its own name for this mysterious moving light which is sometimes seen hovering over marshes or bogs at night. Scientists generally agree that the light is caused by the spontaneous ignition, by traces of hydrogen phosphide, of the methane produced by the decaying organic matter found in marshes. It has also been suggested that the little-understood phenomenon of BALL LIGHTNING may be the cause. However, in folklore, the will-o'-the-wisp is feared as an ill OMEN which foretells the death of the person who sees it, or of someone close to them. When seen near a graveyard it may be called a corpse light or corpse candle, and is believed to light the way from the victim's house to the grave, and in Ireland it is often thought to lead a spectral funeral procession. It is also popularly believed to be a wandering soul rejected by both heaven and hell or, in some places, the spirit of an unbaptized child. In northern Europe it is sometimes seen hovering over burial mounds, when it is said to be the souls of the dead, guarding the treasure buried in their graves. In German and Swedish folklore it may also be the soul of a person who, in life, disregarded boundary markers and stole a neighbour's land.

An engraving showing one interpretation of the phenomenon of will-o'-the-wisp, or 'corpse candles'. (© 2006 TopFoto/Fortean)

When approached, the will-o'-the-wisp vanishes, often reappearing just out of reach, so that in many parts of the world it is seen as a mischievous spirit which delights in leading travellers astray, a fairy which either appears as a ball of light or carries a lantern to lure the unwary over cliff-tops or into a bog. However, these spirits have occasionally been known to help rather than hinder, showing travellers the way to safety.

The will-o'-the-wisp is known by many other names, such as ignis fatuus ('foolish light'), jack-o'-lantern, friar's light, fairy light and fox fire, and the word is also used figuratively to refer to any elusive or deceptive person or idea which leads people astray.

Willy Howe

A grave mound in Yorkshire associated with one of England's earliest fairy tales.

The grave mound, or TUMULUS, of Willy Howe, near the village of Wold Newton, East Yorkshire, is thought to be the location of one England's earliest fairy tales. The mound itself is around 36.5 metres (120 feet) across and 7.5 metres (24 feet) high, and it is now covered by trees. The earliest record of Willy Howe's association with a stolen 'fairy cup' comes from the writings of the 12th-century chronicler William of Newburgh (died c.1198), who claimed that he had known the tale since childhood, and relates it as though he was referring to real events:

> In the province of the Deiri, also, not far from the place of my nativity, an extraordinary event occurred, which I have known from my childhood. There is a village ... near which those famous waters, commonly called Gipse, spring from the ground at various sources ... A certain rustic belonging to the village, going to see his friend, who resided in the neighbouring hamlet, was returning, a little intoxicated, late at night; when, behold, he heard, as it were, the voice of singing and revelling on an adjacent hillock, which I have often seen, and which is distant from the village only a few furlongs. Wondering who could be thus disturbing the silence of midnight with noisy mirth, he was anxious to investigate the matter more closely; and perceiving in the side of the hill an open door, he approached, and, looking in, he beheld a house, spacious and lighted up, filled with men and women, who were seated, as it were, at a solemn banquet. One of the attendants, perceiving him standing at the door, offered

him a cup: accepting it, he wisely forbore to drink; but, pouring out the contents, and retaining the vessel, he quickly departed. A tumult arose among the company, on account of the stolen cup, and the guests pursued him; but he escaped by the fleetness of his steed, and reached the village with his extraordinary prize. It was a vessel of an unknown material, unusual colour, and strange form ...

William goes on to say that the cup was presented to Henry I (1100–35), who subsequently gave it to King David of Scotland, his brother-in-law. It remained in Scotland's royal treasury for some time, until 'a few years since, as we have heard from authentic relation, it was given up by William, king of the Scots, to Henry the Second, on his desiring to see it'. What happened to it next is not known.

A similar tale is told in relation to a mound in the Forest of Dean. In this story Gervase of Tilbury (c.1150–c.1220) describes a jewelled drinking horn stolen from a fairy mound and presented to Henry I, and it is possible that Gervase was adapting William's tale. However, Willy Howe's association with treasure does not end in the 12th century. Local lore also states that a man once found a chest of gold in the mound, which he had nearly succeeded in dragging out of it when it was lost to him through the use of blasphemous language. That it was believed that Willy Howe was inhabited by fairies, once a common belief relating to burial mounds, is shown in yet another tale. It is said that a fairy once told a man that he would find a guinea on top of Willy Howe each morning, but only if he mentioned this to no-one else. He did very well, collecting his guinea each day, until he boasted of it to someone else, and the presents stopped.

Wilmington, Long Man of

A chalk figure of a man on a hillside near Wilmington in East Sussex.

On Windover Hill, near Wilmington in East Sussex, the figure of a naked man, holding a staff or pole in each hand, is cut into the turf. The image is some 70 metres (229 feet) in height. Various theories have existed as to who created the figure and why. Some connect it with the same Bronze Age culture responsible for the UFFINGTON WHITE HORSE; some ascribe it to the Romans on the strength of similar figures found on coins; and some to the Anglo-Saxons, who are known to have carved helmeted figures as decorations. It has also been suggested that it could be the work of Phoenician traders, echoing a figure from their culture shown holding two pillars of a temple.

Whatever its age, the figure is known to have been changed over the centuries. A drawing made by the English surveyor John Rowley in 1710 shows facial features and a helmet that are no longer visible. Such details may have been removed when the figure was extensively restored in the Victorian era. The staffs or poles have not been satisfactorily explained, with some claiming that they once represented a scythe and a rake and others conjecturing that they were spears. In local legend the Long Man is the outline of a giant, traced around him where he fell dead on the hillside.

The true age of the Long Man may never be known, but research by environmental archaeologists in 2003 established that a great deal of chalk debris was produced on the site in the 16th century, leading them to the conclusion that the figure may only be 400 years old.

Woodhenge

Concentric circles of Neolithic wooden posts in Wiltshire.

Pilots flying over Wiltshire in the early 1920s identified strange circular markings on the ground near Amesbury. Aerial photographs were taken and archaeologists excavated the area later in the decade to discover a Neolithic site consisting of six concentric circles of wooden stumps. Like other HENGES, its central area was enclosed by an earthen bank and ditch, and as this was only 32 kilometres (20 miles) from STONEHENGE the find was quickly christened Woodhenge. The structure has been dated to c.2300 BC but its purpose has not been satisfactorily established.

Some have interpreted the wooden stumps as the remains of supporting pillars for the roof of an extensive wooden building. Others maintain that the posts are too numerous and too

An aerial view of Woodhenge in Wiltshire – the six concentric circles of wooden stumps are now marked with concrete posts. (© 2003 Charles Walker/TopFoto)

close together to serve this purpose, and that the wooden pillars would have been free-standing, as in a STONE CIRCLE. As at Stonehenge, there was an entrance at the north-east, and a general alignment in the direction of the midsummer sunrise. This led to theories that the original construction must have had religious purposes, and this interpretation was further supported by the discovery at the centre of the remains of a three-year-old child, whose split skull suggested ritual sacrifice. Another theory is that the structure may have been a tribal meeting-place, built of wood rather than stone precisely because it was *not* a religious site. However, the truth may never be known.

The wooden stumps have been replaced by concrete posts to mark out the site.

Y

yeti

The name given to the famous 'abominable snowman' said to inhabit the Himalayan mountain range, but which may describe more than one cryptid.

For well over a century, mountaineers scaling the Himalayan peaks that straddle the borders of southern Tibet and Nepal have reported seeing man-sized, shaggy-haired, ape-like creatures, sometimes walking on their hind legs and leaving footprints in the snow that are up to 33 centimetres (12 inches) long. Referred to as yetis by the Nepalese people, and also known as the 'meh-the' ('man-beast'), in the West they have become known as abominable snowmen, and their identity remains one of the greatest cryptozoological mysteries of modern times.

According to many eyewitnesses, the yeti appears to be some form of predominantly terrestrial, fruit-eating ape, standing about 2 metres (6.5 feet) tall when bipedal, with long reddish-brown fur, a very powerful well-muscled body, noticeably lengthy arms, a generally hairless face and a large head with a prominent crest running along the top of its dome-shaped skull. Some have suggested that it may be a type of ground-living orang-utan, spending much of its time in the rhododendron forests on the mountains' lower reaches, only ascending to the snow-covered higher regions when food is scarce. However, some sceptics would dismiss all the reports of yetis as misinterpreted sightings of bears, while others would say that it is a non-existent creature of traditional local folklore.

Even so, a number of alleged yeti relics have come to light over the years. Perhaps the most controversial are several reputed yeti scalps, displaying this cryptid's familiar crest of hair. When examined, however, these items were found not to be scalps at all, but pieces of pelt taken from the shoulders of a species of mountain-dwelling goat-antelope called the serow. However, the lamas whose monasteries loaned these relics for examination responded that they were never claimed to

This footprint in the snow, discovered by a climber on Mount Everest in 1980, is said to have been left by a yeti. (© Topham/PA)

be genuine yeti scalps, but merely costume items representing yeti scalps which are worn by participants taking the role of the yeti in ceremonies. More intriguing was the skeleton of an alleged yeti hand, formerly owned by the Pangboche monastery in Nepal. When examined by Western scientists, the consensus was that it had come from an unknown species of primate, but, tragically, this vital piece of evidence was mysteriously stolen from the monastery in May 1991, and its current whereabouts remain unknown, though photographs of it still exist. Possibly most significant of all was a sample of supposed yeti hair collected in 2001 by British zoologist Rob McCall from a

hollow cedar tree in Bhutan. When this hair sample's DNA was analysed at the Oxford Institute of Molecular Medicine, it could not be identified as that of any species of animal currently known to science.

The yeti is very commonly confused with a much bigger, flatter-headed mystery primate, usually reported from eastern Tibet, Sikkim, Bangladesh and other mountainous regions outside the Himalayas, and known locally as the dzu-teh ('hulking beast') or giant yeti. Unlike the true yeti, which often runs on all fours, the dzu-teh is habitually bipedal, and stands at least 2.7 metres (8.9 feet) tall. Its fur is said to be blackish-brown, and it apparently includes meat in its diet. Some zoologists have speculated that the dzu-teh may be a surviving descendant of *Gigantopithecus* – a huge ape that is now known to have lived in Asia until at least 100,000 years ago. Others believe it to be a very large, possibly still unknown species of bear. In 1953, a Tibetan lama called Chemed Rigdzin Dorje Lopu claimed to have examined two giant mummified dzu-tehs, which resembled enormous apes. One was housed in the monastery at Riwoche in Tibet's Kham Province, the other at Sakya monastery. Many Tibetan relics and monasteries were destroyed following China's annexation of Tibet a few years later, so whether these remarkable specimens still exist somewhere is unknown.

GLOSSARY

This glossary contains additional terms that may not directly relate to myths and mysteries, but that may nevertheless assist readers in their use of the book.

apport
The supposed transport or sudden appearance of material objects without the involvement of a material agency.

augury
The art or practice of interpreting signs and omens, such as the flight or cries of birds, to gain knowledge of secrets or to predict the future.

clairvoyance
Strictly, the claimed ability to see things which are not normally visible. However, the term is more generally used to include any form of discerning information that is beyond the normal range of sense or perception.

cryptid
A term, coined in 1983, that describes any creature classed as a cryptozoological animal. Previously, such creatures had been referred to by a plethora of loose, generalized terms, such as 'mystery animal', 'hidden animal', 'unknown animal', 'undiscovered animal' or 'unidentified animal'.

cryptozoology
A term derived from the Greek roots *kryptos* ('hidden'), *zoon* ('animal') and *logos* ('discourse' or 'study'), which translates literally as 'the study of hidden animals'. It is generally defined as the study of unexpected animals whose existence or identity is currently undetermined by science.

divination
The art or practice of seeking to learn the future, or unknown things, by **supernatural** means.

esoteric
A term originally used to mean knowledge that was 'inner'. When the word entered the English language in the early 18th century it loosely retained this meaning, and was applied to secret societies such as FREEMASONRY. However, its use has since developed to include any knowledge relating to the **occult**, or anything that is mysterious or difficult to understand.

forteana
A collective noun for a wide range of subjects dealing with reports and analysis of strange experiences and anomalous phenomena.

Goddess, the
One of the two primary deities (or aspects of the supreme deity) in neopagan witchcraft, the worship of whom is based on earlier pagan beliefs that possibly survived in some form in the witchcraft practice of the Middle Ages. Also referred to as the Great Goddess, the Mother Goddess, the Moon Goddess, Diana, Aradia, the Great Mother and many other names.

incubus
A demon said to assume a male body and have sexual intercourse with women as they sleep.

kaballah
A secret, **occult** or mystical doctrine, especially the Jewish mystical tradition based on an **esoteric** interpretation of the Old Testament and other texts.

mass sociogenic illness
An illness affecting members of a cohesive group, such as that found in a school or workplace, where the physical symptoms are believed to be the result of fear and anxiety rather than the effect of any pathogen. Also known as MASS HYSTERIA.

medium, physical
A medium who apparently manifests physical evidence of the existence of spirits. Physical mediums claim to be able to produce (with the assistance of spirits) materializations such as **apports** or ectoplasm, or physical effects such as table-turning or levitation.

men in black
The term used to describe visitors, of unknown origin, who are sometimes reported to have approached witnesses following a **UFO** sighting. They are often said to try to prevent the witnesses from revealing their stories.

mind-reading
The supposedly direct mental accessing of thoughts within the minds of other individuals.

occult
The doctrine or study of mysterious or hidden things. The term is commonly used to refer to knowledge meant only for certain people, or knowledge that must be kept hidden, but is often misused as being almost synonymous with 'evil' or 'satanic'.

Some people's use of the term encompasses all forms of magic, witchcraft and sorcery, while many would also include fields such as astrology, numerology and all forms of **divination**. Others consider all aspects of the **paranormal** to be occult.

ornithomancy
Divination by observing the flight and behaviour of birds.

out-of-body experience
An experience in which an individual allegedly has the sensation of the self leaving the body – usually claimed to involve being able to observe the physical body from elsewhere.

out-of-place-animals
Creatures of an already-known species that are sighted in an unexpected geographical location.

paranormal
Something that cannot be explained in terms of the laws of nature and reason as we currently understand them.

parapsychology
The study of **paranormal** experiences: interactions between individuals, or between an individual and the environment, that seem to be inexplicable in terms of current scientific understanding. Main areas of study are 'anomalous cognition' (normally referred to as extrasensory perception, or ESP), and 'anomalous influence' (**psychokinesis**, or PK).

pious fraud
A fraud motivated by misguided religious zeal rather than by a desire for profit.

plasma vortex
A suggested cause of crop circles. Plasma is the scientific term for a very hot, highly conductive form of ionized gas, which is formed in the earth's atmosphere by electrical discharge such as that found in lightning. One explanation for the apparently overnight formation of crop circles is that the patterns are created instantly by vortices of plasma forming and discharging in the air above the affected fields. The theory is that these strike the ground and heat the stalks of cereal to a point at which they wilt. The plasma vortices themselves are said to be created by mini-vortices in the magnetic field in the earth's ionosphere.

precognition
Prior knowledge of future events gained by **psychic** means.The term comes from the Latin *praecognitio*, which literally means 'prior knowledge'.

premonition
An intuition or foreboding of a future, and usually unpleasant or disastrous, event by means of a **psychic** experience. The term comes from the Latin *prae-*, meaning 'prior', and *monere*, meaning 'to warn'.

psychic
A term describing both **paranormal** powers and the possessor of such powers. When someone claims to be a psychic, they are now normally understood to be claiming that they possess certain powers above and beyond the normal physical abilities and senses of the human body – these would include such things as extrasensory perception, **psychokinesis** and **precognition**.

psychokinesis (PK)
The movement of material objects, or the influencing of mechanical systems, using only the power of the mind. Also known as 'mind over matter' or 'telekinesis', it is usually sub-divided into the two categories of macro-PK and micro-PK, depending upon the scale of the effect under consideration.

scrying
Divination by gazing into a reflective surface, such as a crystal ball, mirror or bowl of water.

second sight
The supposed ability to be able to 'see' into the future. Second sight is a form of **precognition** in which the future is apparently literally 'seen' in the form of a vision. As such, it might also be described as a type of **clairvoyance**.

seer
A person who has the **psychic** ability to see into the future.

supernatural
Something that is above or beyond nature and any naturalistic explanation or understanding. The word differs in use from **paranormal** in that it is often understood to mean that the phenomenon concerned is not amenable to a scientific approach.

telepathy
Direct mind-to-mind contact with another individual so that thoughts and images can be shared.

teleportation

The apparently instantaneous transportation of an object or living entity from one point directly to another, seemingly without going through the intervening space or around physical obstacles.

UFO

The acronym for 'unidentified flying object'. In simple terms it applies to any strange object seen in the sky that cannot immediately be identified by the witness.

ufology

The study of **UFO**s.

INDEX

CHAMBERS UNEXPLAINED

Chambers Dictionary of the Unexplained

Chambers Dictionary of the Unexplained is a fascinating and illuminating book, and an essential reference for anyone with an interest in unexplained phenomena. Written in consultation with experts in their field of study, its carefully researched, unbiased entries cover topics ranging from alien abductions to the zodiac. Special panels are devoted to subjects of particular interest, while numerous colour photographs and illustrations make the book a joy to browse.

ISBN: 978 0550 10215 7

Chambers Ghosts and Spirits

Delve into the mysterious world of the afterlife in this guide to ghostly phenomena, including hauntings, spiritualism, folklore and past lives. *Ghosts and Spirits* provides balanced and in-depth coverage of a broad range of topics, such as Britain's most haunted castle, the poltergeist that pelted journalists with marbles and the psychic sisters who sparked the modern spiritualism movement.

Drawing on *Chambers Dictionary of the Unexplained*, and including a wealth of new material, *Ghosts and Spirits* makes irresistible reading for anyone interested in the possibility of an existence beyond death.

ISBN: 978 0550 10393 2

Visit **www.chambers.co.uk** for further details, or call 0131 556 5929 for a Chambers catalogue.